Praise for
American Messiah

"Another insightful and important book by the leading Jefferson scholar of the world. Highly recommended for students of American history, the founding, and religion."
—**Garrett Ward Sheldon,** Professor Emeritus, University of Virginia

"A lucid and sophisticated analysis written in stimulating prose, Holowchak's book provides an excellent grasp of Jefferson's religious views. By excavating Jefferson's original documents and correspondence, this book provides readers with a well-researched and well-resourced path toward a copious understanding of Jefferson's views on a variety of topics, including God, the cosmos, natural religion, morality, the afterlife, and Jefferson's support for a separation of church and state in order to enhance religious liberty—a necessary outgrowth of Jefferson's support for free thinking. This work is especially refreshing given the attempts by some contemporary pseudohistorians who too often superimpose their own religious views onto the founders in order to pursue existing ideological goals."
—**Brian W. Dotts,** author of *The Political Education of Democritus* and professor, University of Georgia

"Holowchak has, again, written an important book on Thomas Jefferson. Holowchak's style of deciphering Jefferson's religious thought by consistently comparing other scholars' claims and errors with his own findings in the Jefferson archive is fascinating—and time and again, spot-on!"
—**Ari Helo,** author of *Thomas Jefferson's Ethics and the Politics of Human Progress* and senior university lecturer, University of Helsinki

"For over 250 years, Thomas Jefferson's religious beliefs have been enigmatic—denounced as an atheist and celebrated as a champion of religious freedom, both during his lifetime and afterward. Holowchak's book, more than any other source, clarifies Jefferson's thoughts about religion. A careful reading of this volume reveals what this fascinating man really believed."
—**John P. Kaminski,** director, Center for the American Constitution, University of Wisconsin-Madison

AMERICAN MESSIAH

AMERICAN MESSIAH

The Surprisingly Simple Religious Views of
THOMAS JEFFERSON

M. ANDREW HOLOWCHAK

Abilene Christian University Press

AMERICAN MESSIAH

The Surprisingly Simple Religious Views of Thomas Jefferson

ACU
PRESS

Copyright © 2020 by M. Andrew Holowchak

ISBN 978-1-68426-071-3

Printed in Canada

LIBRARY OF CONGRESS CATALOGING-IN-PUBLICATION DATA
Names: Holowchak, Mark, 1958- author.
Title: American Messiah : the surprisingly simple religious views of Thomas
    Jefferson / M. Andrew Holowchak.
Description: Abilene, Texas : ACU Press, [2020] | Includes bibliographical
    references.
Identifiers: LCCN 2020019701 (print) | LCCN 2020019702 (ebook) | ISBN
    9781684260713 | ISBN 9781684269556 (ebook)
Subjects: LCSH: Jefferson, Thomas, 1743-1826—Religion. | Jefferson,
    Thomas, 1743-1826—Political and social views.
Classification: LCC E332.2 .H658 2020 (print) | LCC E332.2 (ebook) | DDC
    973.46092 [B]—dc23
LC record available at https://lccn.loc.gov/2020019701
LC ebook record available at https://lccn.loc.gov/2020019702

Cover design by Bruce Gore | Gore Studio Inc.
Interior text design by Sandy Armstrong, Strong Design

For information contact:
Abilene Christian University Press
ACU Box 29138
Abilene, Texas 79699

1-877-816-4455
www.acupressbooks.com

20 21 22 23 24 25 / 7 6 5 4 3 2 1

Contents

PREFACE

I n the middle of his life, Thomas Jefferson had a "religious conversion," as it were. Much due to the influence of religious scholars like Unitarian ministers Richard Price and Joseph Priestley, Jefferson came to view Jesus not just as a greatly praised and admired religious figure but also as the world's greatest religious reformist and moralist. Jefferson became convinced that the person and preacher in the four Gospels—a being avowedly born of a virgin, and with superhuman capacities, the ability to conquer death, and a gift for sermonizing through parables—was the result of years of disfigurement by religious "schematizers" (or "Platonizers," as Jefferson called them) with politically ambitious intentions. He thus set out on two separate occasions (first in 1804 and again in 1819) to reconfigure the disfigured moralist by crafting his own version of the New Testament, devoid of all corruptions and mythologies. This new "bible" aimed to reveal to the world a personage and parabolist of superordinary wisdom and magnanimity, but a personage all too human, whose message was so simple and pure that even a child could assimilate it. That was Jefferson's take on the inordinate value of the teachings of Jesus. For Jefferson, religious truth, like moral truth, should be simple, unadulterated, and easy to ascertain.

Yet Jefferson vacillated about whether his bible adaption should be published, and if the project had fully come to fruition, he likely would have used a pseudonym, due to his strong stance throughout his life that his religious views should never be known, except by a few intimate friends. Religion, he was wont to say, was a private affair between a man and his deity.

Still, Jefferson did more than any other American figure to preserve the right of all individuals to believe and practice religion as they saw fit. He generated various political reforms—including repealing entail and primogeniture; updating the curriculum at William & Mary during his time as the governor of Virginia; and, in particular, creating his Bill for Religious Freedom—with the aim of promoting equality and liberty by removing the corruptive influence of religious empleomania via the prohibition of state sanction of any religious sect, thereby affording a person of any sect the same rights and access to public offices as all other sects. Religious freedom took root in Virginia in 1785 and soon became the standard for progressive, liberal nations across the globe. Thus Jefferson himself may be regarded as a "messiah" of sorts, whose message of religious freedom is perhaps only today being fully ascertained.

Jefferson's religious views continue to be a matter of prodigious confusion among scholars. Much of this is due to Jefferson's reticence to reveal his views to anyone. "Say nothing of my religion," says Jefferson to John Adams (11 Jan. 1817). "It is known to my God and myself alone. Its evidence before the world is to be sought in my life; if that has been honest and dutiful to society, the religion which has regulated it cannot be a bad one." When Jefferson does write of religion in letters, he tends to be laconic, not profuse.

Fortunately for scholars, there are some exceptions to this trend in the form of Jefferson's revelatory letters to John Adams, William Short, Peter Carr, Thomas Law, and James Fishback. Other noteworthy resources include passages from Lord Bolingbroke's thoughts on religion, commonplaced in Jefferson's *Literary Commonplace Book* as a youth; Query XVII of Jefferson's *Notes on the State of Virginia* (1787), titled "Religion"; his previously noted reconstruction of the Bible; and his copious notes on religion, recorded in 1776. Under meticulous scrutiny, these sources clarify much of the confusion—once thought to be ineliminable. This book aims to show that Jefferson's religious views, much like his views on morality, are astonishingly simple and appear radical only from the perspective of the complex sectarian religions of his time, which Jefferson thought had quixotic, nonsensical, and slippery metaphysical claims.

American Messiah: The Surprisingly Simple Religious Views of Thomas Jefferson is a fleshing out and critical investigation of Jefferson's view of religion, which up until this point has been greatly misunderstood. Chapter One begins with an elucidation of Jefferson's views on God and the cosmos. By dispelling any confusion on this topic and clarifying Jefferson's core beliefs (insofar as utmost clarity can be achieved), this initial chapter provides a strong foundation for the discussion of other less axial religious matters, which have been a source of debate and much befuddlement in scholarship to date. Chapter Two examines Jefferson's thoughts on natural and sectarian religion. Natural religion, we come to find, is right-intended behavior, merely in keeping with the sentiments of each person's moral sense. The third chapter details Jefferson's attempts to reconstruct the morality and life of Jesus by extracting what he considered to be the essential portions of the four Gospels and scrapping the rest of the text. Chapter Four explores Jefferson's view of the afterlife—an issue that lacks scholarly consensus—and aims to show that he did not believe in a hereafter. The unsettled issue of Jefferson's Unitarianism is covered in the fifth chapter, wherein it is shown that his embrace of Unitarianism was in the broadest moral, nonsectarian terms. The final chapter fittingly ends with Jefferson's true religious legacy: freedom of all persons to believe and practice religion as they wish to believe and practice it.

One may ask why I have chosen to don this scholarly exploration "*American Messiah*"—a moniker to which Jefferson himself likely would have objected. That can be answered largely by his gravestone. The fact that Jefferson admitted "Author . . . of the Statute of Virginia for Religious Freedom" among his three most noteworthy accomplishments on his stone—along with "Author of the Declaration of Independence" and "Father of the University of Virginia"—is telling. Each was, in some sense, a Herculean feat, accomplished with the aid of trusted friends and colleagues—such as James Madison, John Adams, Benjamin Franklin, and Joseph C. Cabell—and an enduring testament to their bold ideas.

In those achievements and in numerous others, Jefferson can be readily likened to a secular messiah, not unlike his own demystified Jesus. Jefferson's enduring vision of a nation of citizens—free and self-sufficient, yet engaged in activities for their mutual benefit—drove him to decades of public service at the expense of personal gain. For Jefferson, Jesus proposed sweeping "democratic" or equalitarian religious/moral reforms through certain simple and chaste moral precepts: love of God; love of others; and belief in an afterlife. Over time, Jefferson articulated an equalitarian and liberal political philosophy based on his own moral vision—which was essentially the same as Jesus's (love of God and love of others)—without attachment to an afterlife. For Jesus, all people, not just the Jews, were God's children and loved by God. For Jefferson, all people, not just Americans, were happiest when free and governed by the intellectual and moral elite, ever mindful of the rights of each citizen. Jesus preached kindness, based on benevolence, not personal gain, and Jefferson considered equanimity to be a sort of personal gain—thereby vastly exceeding the great ancient ethicians like Epicurus, Epictetus, and Plato. Jefferson's political reforms were focused on national and international benevolence, based on Jesus's actual words and life. While Unitarian minister Joseph Priestley, who believed in the second coming of Christ, wrote scholarly works on religion, preached fiery sermons, and waited for Christ to return, Jefferson worked tirelessly for political changes to enhance personal liberty and free citizens from the yoke of tyrannical government. Yet Jefferson's preoccupation was with this world. He aimed to make it better in his time and for those persons whose time had not yet come.

Jefferson appropriated most of Jesus's benevolence-grounded morality. A critical part of that appropriation was religious reform, and the first step of that reform was freedom of religious expression. With free expression of religion and the reform of laws regarding religion—essentially placing all religions on equal footing—the path was opened for rational debate between the various sects, with the possibility that the true religion, if any particular one should be true, would be found through rational discussion and a collision of opinions. Jefferson mused that through rational debate over time, there would be a slow recognition that all, or most, religions adhere to two core truths—love of God, who is one, not many, and love of one's fellow man—the essence of Jeffersonian Unitarianism, a naturalized religion of religions, serviceable for true republicans. That, for Jefferson, was Jesus's greatest moral contribution. He offered humans no sectarian religion to replace the religion of the Jews. He instead offered humans a religion of religions or a meta-religion, and thus went beyond the religionists of his day. For universalizing religion—that is, getting at its moral core, characteristically beautiful in its simplicity and purity—Jesus was misunderstood, betrayed, persecuted, and crucified.

Jefferson, "as a reformer who dared to challenge priestly power,"[1] could only have, in some sense, identified with Jesus. Like Jesus, he entertained "radical" religious views—radical because they were unconventional, simple, and did not fit neatly with any religious sect—and was calumniated for his religious radicalism, even though he was not forthcoming about his views, even with the most intimate members of his family. His moral/religious views were remarkably straightforward: they were Jesus's twin duties—"Thou shalt love the Lord thy God with all thy heart, and with all thy soul, and with all thy strength, and with all thy mind; and thy neighbour as thyself" (Luke 10:27 KJV)—minus a belief in the afterlife.

Overall, Jefferson did not seek a break between religion and politics, as his Bill for Religious Freedom suggests. Jeffersonian republicanism needed a religious grounding—a naturalized religious grounding or a

---

[1] Peter S. Onuf, *The Mind of Thomas Jefferson* (Charlottesville: University of Virginia Press, 2007), 148.

metareligion. For Jefferson, a naturalized religion or a religion of religions, based on love of God and love of others, would require a cynosure, a moral exemplar, or a model citizen. That model citizen, of course, was Jefferson's demystified Jesus, depicted best in his own 1820 reconstruction of the four Gospels. Through his biblical adaptations, Jefferson sought to lead his readers to the true Jesus, in an effort to morally ground his republicanism.

In closing, I have four procedural comments.

First, I have adopted the convention here, as in other publications, of labeling Jefferson's epistolary writings by reference only to his correspondent and to the date of the letter, if known, thereby granting readers the opportunity to refer to the edition of Jefferson's writings that is most readily available to them. There are several major compilations of Jefferson's writings. The most widely used are as follows: *The Writings of Thomas Jefferson: Being His Autobiography, Correspondence, Reports, Messages, Addresses, and Other Writings, Official and Private—Published by the Order of the Joint Committee of Congress on the Library, from the Original Manuscripts, Deposited in the Department of State*, ed. Henry Augustine Washington, 9 vols. (Washington, DC: Taylor & Maury, 1853–54); *The Works of Thomas Jefferson*, ed. Paul Leicester Ford, 12 vols. (New York: Putnam, 1902); *The Writings of Thomas Jefferson, Definitive Edition*, ed. Andrew Adgate Lipscomb and Albert Ellery Bergh, 20 vols. (Washington, DC: Thomas Jefferson Memorial Association, 1907); and *The Papers of Thomas Jefferson*, ed. Julian Boyd et al., 42 vols. to date (Princeton: Princeton University Press, 1950–). There are also several one-volume compilations of Jefferson's writings—notably, Merrill D. Peterson's *Thomas Jefferson: Writings* (New York: Library of America, 1984). Moreover, many of Jefferson's writings are readily available online through sources such as the Hathi Trust Digital Library, the Online Library of Liberty, and Founders Online. His nonepistolary writings, in contrast, are fully referenced throughout this book.

Second, in many cases, I have chosen not to append *sic* to misspellings (e.g., "Kaims" and "vertue"), grammatical errors (e.g., placing a period after a number that occurs in the middle of a sentence), linguistic conventions that differed in Jefferson's day (e.g., "it's," "tranquillity," and "traveller"), and peculiarities of Jefferson's writing (e.g., his tendency not to capitalize the first word of a sentence, unless it is a proper noun). I merely trust that these instances will be readily recognizable to readers, given this cautionary remark.

Third, as is the case with my other books on Jefferson, I often use direct quotes from Jefferson in place of paraphrasing. That is because many of the scholarly discrepancies that have arisen over time are the direct result of reading into, instead of simply *reading*, what Jefferson has written or said.

Last, I overpass discussion of Jefferson and slavery. This book is chiefly a look at Jefferson's religious views, not an assessment about whether he lived up to his religious and moral ideals. Moreover, Jefferson's views on race and slavery and an assessment of his authenticity or lack of it require much fuller discussions than I can here offer. I merely refer readers wanting fuller discussion to two of my recent publications.[2]

---

[2] M. Andrew Holowchak, *Rethinking Thomas Jefferson's Views on Race and Slavery* (Newcastle upon Tyne, UK: Cambridge Scholars, 2019), and *The Cavernous Mind of Thomas Jefferson, an American Savant* (Newcastle upon Tyne, UK: Cambridge Scholars, 2019).

CHAPTER ONE

"Fabricator of All Things from Matter and Motion"

Jefferson's God and Jefferson's Cosmos

"Anyone who concedes that the gods exist must grant them activity, an activity of the most exalted kind. Now nothing can be more exalted than the governance of the cosmos. Thus, the cosmos is governed by the wisdom of the gods."

—Cicero, *On the Nature of the Gods*

T he preface made note of the prodigious scholarly confusion that exists concerning Jefferson's religious views. Generally speaking, despite Jefferson's repeated claims to be a devoutly religious person and a true Christian, most scholars would consider him to be anything but religious—his views were and still are considered to be too heterodox.

Here, much hinges on a generally acceptable definition of "religious." The *Oxford Living Dictionary* gives the following general definition: "related to or believing in a religion." The following subdefinitions are also provided: "(of a belief or practice) forming part of someone's faith in a divine being," "belonging or relating to a monastic order or other group of people who are united by their practice of religion," and "treated or regarded with a devotion and scrupulousness appropriate to worship."[1] While Jefferson

---

[1] *Oxford Living Dictionary*, s.v. "religious (adj.)," accessed May 15, 2017, https://en.oxforddictionaries.com/definition/religious.

fails to be religious in that he never belonged to "a monastic order or other group of people who are united by their practice of religion"—we will return to the sticky topic of his "Unitarianism" in Chapter Five—he certainly did have "faith in a divine being." He claimed, as we shall read, to "see" God in the cosmos.

This initial chapter is an expiscation of Jefferson's Divine Being and the cosmos God created. Beginning in this way is fitting, for if we do not have a secure grasp of Jefferson's world and of the Supreme Being causally responsible for it—and the metaphysics and epistemology driving them—then we run the risk of retracing the footsteps of other scholarly works that, I believe, fall short on this foundational topic.

I begin this chapter, oddly enough, with some discussion of the absence of God at Jefferson's University of Virginia in the final years of his life. I then turn a discussion on Jefferson's concept of cosmological materialism—a materialism so complete that even God, as the cause of the cosmos, is a material being and mind is a property of matter, particularly disposed. I end by teasing out what we can ascertain about Jefferson's material God.

"In Conformity with the Principles of Our Constitution"
A Purely Secular Institution

Jefferson, in formulating his plan for the University of Virginia, aimed to provide a superior alternative to the Federalist-leaning education one might attain at Harvard or Yale in the north. He writes to Senator Joseph C. Cabell (28 Dec. 1822) about the need to entice top professors from Europe to join the university:

> the great object of our aim from the beginning has been to make this establishment the most eminent in the United States, in order to draw to it the youth of every state, but especially of the South and West. we have proposed therefore to call to it characters of the first order of science from Europe as well as our own country; and, not only by their salaries, and the comforts of their situation, but by the distinguished scale of it's structure and

preparation, and the promise of future eminence which these would hold up, to induce them to commit their reputations to it's future fortunes. had we built a barn for a College, and log-huts for accomodations, should we ever have had the assurance to propose to an European Professor of that character to come to it? why give up this important idea, when so near it's accomplishment that a single lift more effects it? it is not a half-project which is to fill up the enticement of character from abroad. to stop where we are is to abandon our high hopes, and become suitors to Yale and Harvard for their secondary characters, to become our first. have we been laboring then merely to get up another Hampden Sidney, or Lexington? yet to this it sinks if we abandon foreign aid.

The University of Virginia, in keeping with Jefferson's grand vision, was to be unique among American universities[2] in a number of ways (as described in more detail later)—hence his insistence on enlisting the best professors he could find, even if that meant searching in Europe. We now turn to focus on the university's architectural and religious uniqueness.

Jefferson's university was architecturally unique. It was Π-shaped, as seen from the south. There were five two-story pavilions to the west and five pavilions to the east, and those pavilions sandwiched single-story student dormitories, connected by walkways, to facilitate interaction between students and faculty. The pavilions, each to house a professor on the second floor and to allow space for lectures on the first, were a curious admixture of the best of modern and ancient architectural techniques, and each was architecturally unique. Architectural historian Richard Guy Wilson indicates the following about the differently configured pavilions: "One can interpret the different facades [of each professor's pavilion] as an attempt to teach architectural taste to the students by providing ten

---

[2] The notion of a state-sanctioned university was not unique to Jefferson. For more, see Eldon L. Johnson, "The 'Other Jeffersons' and the State University Idea," *Journal of Higher Education* 58, no. 2 (1987): 127–50.

different [architectural] models, but the meaning may go deeper, since a dialogue takes place on the lawn between the ancients and moderns."[3] What conjoined the east and west wings of pavilions and dormitories to the north was Jefferson's gem—the Rotunda, which was modeled after Rome's Pantheon, being "half that of the Pantheon [in diameter] and consequently one fourth in area, and one eighth in volume."[4] The Π-shaped design, likely modeled after modern hospitals Jefferson saw in France, and the architecturally unique pavilions were put in place to engender learning, to promote physical health through prophylaxis with the free flow of air between buildings, to encourage students' interaction with faculty, and to create a milieu of complete self-sufficiency. The emphasis on self-sufficiency is why Jefferson called his institution an "academical village,"[5] not a school. The design and functionality of the institution were crafted to engender self-sufficiency through maximum liberty for students in an academic setting, and the practicable knowledge gained in classrooms and outside of the classrooms through interaction with professors and fellow students would give them sufficient knowledge for the broadest actualization of their talents. In addition, the university's architectural beauty was designed to attract students and professors alike.

The university was also religiously unique. What made it religiously unique was not something it had but something it did *not* have: a church or chapel for religious worship. That religious building would, on Jefferson's singular design, naturally have occupied the focal place of what is today the Rotunda. Nevertheless, Jefferson's focal structure was to be a library, filled with books useful to human flourishing, not a church, presumably housing God or inspiring thoughts of God. Books were Jefferson's gods, or at least, as we shall see, windows into Jefferson's God.

---

[3] Richard Guy Wilson, "Thomas Jefferson's Classical Architecture: An American Agenda," in *Thomas Jefferson, the Classical World, and Early America*, ed. Peter Onuf and Nicholas P. Cole (Charlottesville: University of Virginia Press, 2011), 120.

[4] John S. Patton, *Jefferson, Cabell, and the University of Virginia* (New York: Neale Publishing, 1906), 186.

[5] TJ to Hugh L. White et al., 6 May 1810.

Once inside the Rotunda and looking upward, Jefferson had planned—though the plan never materialized—that one would not see the image of God, saints or angels, or Christ and his apostles painted on the dome (as is often the case with many Orthodox Christian churches), but instead the night sky with images of prominent celestial bodies to facilitate astronomical wonder and instruction.

The design of the Rotunda speaks volumes about Jefferson's religiosity and Jefferson's God. He wanted the University of Virginia to be a secular institution, and so there was to be no professorship of religion. "I agree with you," says Jefferson to Dr. Thomas Cooper (7 Oct. 1814), whose heterodox Unitarian views, made public, kept him from a professorship of law at the University of Virginia, "that a professorship of theology should have no place in our institution."[6] Concerning that omission, Jefferson writes the following in his 1818 Report of the Commissioners for the University of Virginia:

> In conformity with the principles of our Constitution, which places all sects of religion on an equal footing, with the jealousies of the different sects in guarding that equality from encroachment and surprise, and with the sentiments of the Legislature in favor of freedom of religion, manifested on former occasions, we have proposed no professor of divinity; and the rather [sic] as the proofs of the being of a God, the creator, preserver, and supreme ruler of the universe, the author of all the relations of morality, and of the laws and obligations these infer, will be within the province of the professor of ethics; to which adding the developments of these moral obligations, of those in which all sects agree. . . . Proceeding thus far without offence to the Constitution, we have thought it proper at this point to leave

---

[6] He goes on to express skepticism concerning a third-tier institution being able to open without one, for "those with whom we act, entertaining different views, have the power and the right of carrying them into practice."

> every sect to provide, as they think fittest, the means of further
> instruction in their own peculiar tenets.[7]

Here there is much that Jefferson does not say. Thus, this issue warrants some discussion.

There is a considerable amount of literature on the topic of Jefferson's reasons for omitting a professorship of religion, but no consensus has been reached, and this lack of consensus is partly a product of Jefferson's silence on this omission. On one hand, Jerry Newcombe and Mark Beliles maintain that Jefferson wished for no professorship of divinity because of his great respect for and full acceptance of all denominations—his so-called transdenominationalism.[8] For Jefferson, freedom of religion meant full expression of, full respect for, and full acceptance of all denominations. Such things are illustrated by stories of Jefferson befriending many religious clerics, his often generous donations to churches, and his attendance at religious masses.[9] On the other hand, Arthur Scherr argues that Jefferson cared little for sectarian religions because of his anticlericalism—that is, he generally held clerics in suspicion. "Jefferson insisted that members of the clerical hierarchy were generally corrupt, greedy, and power-seeking. Together with unscrupulous secular rulers, they grasped for riches and authority."[10]

The key problem for Jefferson was that the inclusion of such a professorship would have meant the inclusion of a professor preaching one particular brand of religion to the exclusion of others. That is just what Dr. Thomas Cooper says to Jefferson in a letter (22 Sept. 1814), prior to Jefferson's reply in early October: "If religion be politically necessary," writes Cooper, "then teach it without regard to the truth of the adopted

---

[7] Thomas Jefferson, "Rockfish Gap Report," in *Thomas Jefferson: Writings*, ed. Merrill D. Peterson (New York: Library of America, 1984), 467.

[8] That view is also shared by J. M. O'Neill. See Robert M. Healey, *Jefferson on Religion in Public Education* (New Haven, CT: Yale University Press, 1962), 5–7.

[9] Mark Beliles and Jerry Newcombe, *Doubting Thomas: The Religious Life and Legacy of Thomas Jefferson* (New York: Morgan James, 2015).

[10] For example, Arthur Scherr, *Thomas Jefferson's Image of New England: Nationalism versus Sectionalism in the Young Republic* (Jefferson, NC: McFarland Books, 2016), 56.

system: but if you are to teach theology in your university on the ground of its truth, who is to judge which System is true? Suppose you teach Ecclesiastical History: any body can read it at home. Who can read it at all, with prejudices in favour of any System?" There was no religious studies program in Jefferson's day, where a professor, schooled in many world religions, could comparatively discuss the merits and demerits of several of those religions with students. And so, the inclusion of such a professorship of divinity would have equated to the academic patronage of one sectarian religion—a contravention of separation of church matters and state matters.

The omission of a professorship of divinity was also due to Jefferson—in spite of attending worship services of various denominations, befriending clergy of various denominations, donating money to various churches, and even recommending sermons by various clergymen, such as Bourdaloue, Massillon, and Sterne—having, as a whole, a hostile attitude toward religious sectarianism and religious clericalism.

One reason for his hostility was historical—religious empleomania, as shown by events such as the sanguinary Crusades, Galileo going before the Inquisition and being forced to abjure his heliocentrism, and even the enmity shown by Anglican ministers during Jefferson's three bids for the presidency at the end of the eighteenth century and the beginning of the nineteenth century. Concerning the Galilean incident, Jefferson writes in his *Notes on Virginia*, "Galileo was sent to the Inquisition for affirming that the earth was a sphere: the government had declared it to be as flat as a trencher, and Galileo was obliged to abjure his error."[11]

Another reason for this hostility was personal. The clergy proved to be an albatross to the success of Jefferson's university. Jefferson was incensed by opposition to his nomination of Thomas Cooper for Professor of Law, whose ties with Unitarianism, a liberal religion whose adherents entertained what were considered by many clerics to be maverick and heretical views, proved to be his downfall. Edwin Gaustad writes, "Cooper quickly

---

[11] Thomas Jefferson, *Notes on the State of Virginia*, ed. William Peden (Chapel Hill: University of North Carolina Press, 1954), 159–60.

became a symbol of what was wrong with Jefferson's religion, and what, unless nipped in the bud, would be wrong with the infant University of Virginia."[12] Jefferson, however, was irate. In a letter to his friend and former secretary William Short (4 Aug. 1820), he vents: "The Presbyterian clergy are the loudest, the most intolerant of all sects, the most tyrannical and ambitious, ready at the word of the lawgiver . . . to put the torch to the pile, and to rekindle in this virgin hemisphere, the flames in which their oracle Calvin consumed the poor Servetus."

A final reason for his hostility was theoretical. Jefferson disdained theory—especially theory unchecked by careful, accumulative observations. In his 1814 letter to Cooper, for instance, Jefferson considers the constraints placed on the teaching of medicine at a third-tier institution: "Perhaps I should concur with you also in excluding the *Theory* [not the *Practice*][13] of medecine." He then writes of the great harm done by his good friend and physician Dr. Benjamin Rush, with "his theory of bleeding, and mercury." Medicine, for Jefferson, is of the rank of religion: "[T]his [theoretical Medicine] is the Charlatanerie of the body, as the other [religion] is of the mind.[14]

Jefferson complains that opposition to the University of Virginia is mostly at the hands of the clergy, who complain that they are "excluded" from the university.[15] To Cooper (2 Nov. 1822), Jefferson says, "a handle has been made of this to disseminate an idea that this is an institution, not merely of no religion, but against all religion."

Jefferson elaborates on a compromise to the controversy that has arisen due to the university's lack of religious instruction. He writes of

---

[12] Edwin Gaustad, *Sworn on the Altar of God: A Religious Biography of Thomas Jefferson* (Grand Rapids: William B. Eerdmans, 1996), 176. Cooper eventually took a job at South Carolina College as Professor of Chemistry in 1820.

[13] The brackets here are Jefferson's; emphasis is mine.

[14] No doubt a play on Socrates's speech in Plato's *Gorgias*, where Socrates contrasts medicine, as a science (*technē*) of the body, with pastry baking, which is a pseudo-science (*empeiria*) of the body, and justice, which is a science of the soul, with oratory, which is a pseudo-science of the soul. Plato, *Gorgias*, trans. Donald Zeyl (Indianapolis: Hackett Books, 1987), 464b–466a.

[15] Joseph C. Cabell to TJ, 7 Jan. 1822.

"the expediency of encouraging the different religious sects to establish, each for itself, a professorship of their own tenets, on the confines of the University, so near as that their students may attend the lectures there, and have the free use of our library, and every other accommodation we can give them." The key here, as Thomas Healey notes, is not so much respect for the expression of diversity of religious opinions, guised in the garbled metaphysical language of each particular sect, with the hope of some profitable end to that expression, but allowing "divinity students registered at other schools [to] take courses in science at the university."[16] Jefferson concludes, "By bringing the sects together, and mixing them with the mass of other students, we shall soften their asperities, liberalize and neutralize their prejudices, and make the general religion a religion of peace, reason and morality." His sentiments that espouse softening, liberalizing, and neutralizing are consistent with something he expressed more than three decades prior in his *Notes on Virginia*: "The way to silence religious disputes, is to take no notice of them."[17] Here, Jefferson refers to a "happy discovery," concerning religious toleration and "harmony . . . unparalleled" in New York and Pennsylvania. Both references fail to mention the positive qualities associated with free religious expression. The focus, instead, is the eschewal of negatives by expunging the metaphysical excrescences from religious sectarianism and removing empleomaniacal religionists from political offices. Religionists of all persuasions are to have their own "religious" spaces, where they are free to discuss and debate fatuous metaphysical religious issues.

"When Once We Quit the Basis of Sensation"
Jefferson's Materialism

The term *philosopher* was generally pejorative in Jefferson's time. To be a philosopher was to be linked with the mostly French eighteenth-century Enlightenment intellectuals, *les philosophes*, who audaciously attacked

---

[16] Thomas M. Healey, *Jefferson on Religion in Public Education* (New Haven, CT: Yale University Press, 1962), 222.

[17] Jefferson, *Notes on the State of Virginia*, 161.

then-present superstitions and misbeliefs through the practical application of science and its methods and reason. Many *philosophes* were also atheists. They championed free presses and free expression of religious belief (or eradication of religion), and particularly attacked religious fanaticism. Some prominent *philosophes* were Voltaire, Rousseau, Diderot, Helvetius, Condorcet, and D'Alembert. Voltaire's *Candide*, for example, is an unsubtle attack in the form of a lampoon of the German philosopher Gottfried Leibniz, who infamously asserted that the world, with its numerous seeming blemishes, was still "la meilleur des mondes possibles."[18]

Jefferson thought and lived in the manner of a *philosophe*. Driven by the notion of the innate goodness of all persons, he continually strove for political, educational, and religious reforms—the three being dependent concerns.

Jefferson never stated whether this world was the best of possible worlds, but he did say the following in a letter to John Adams (8 Apr. 1816): "Yea. I think with you that it is a good world on the whole, that it has been framed on a principle of benevolence, and more pleasure than pain dealt out to us." Yet even the ills are often disguised gifts. Consistent with the thinking of Unitarian ministers and polymaths Joseph Priestley and Richard Price, Jefferson writes to Dr. Benjamin Rush (23 Sept. 1800), "I am in the habit of looking out for what good may arise from them as consolations to us, and Providence has in fact so established the order of things as that most evils are the means of producing some good."[19] Here, and almost everywhere else in Jefferson's writings, sanguineness trumps cynicism.

Like his "trinity of the three greatest men the world had ever produced"—Bacon, Locke, and Newton—Jefferson was a committed empiricist. Empiricism entails beliefs founded upon appeal to the evidence of the human senses. "A patient pursuit of facts, and cautious combination and comparison of them, is the drudgery to which man is subjected by his

---

[18] "The best of possible worlds."

[19] The context concerns the devastating effects of yellow fever in Philadelphia. The passage is often taken as evidence of Jefferson's callous insensitivity to the sufferings of others. Yet he is merely strongly wedded to the goodness of Providence, so there must be a reason—and a good one—for deity to allow such devastation.

Maker, if he wishes to attain sure knowledge," says Jefferson in his *Notes on Virginia*.[20] To Charles Thomson (20 Sept. 1787), he writes: "I wish that the persons who go thither would make very exact descriptions of what they see of that kind, without forming any theories. The moment a person forms a theory, his imagination sees, in every object, only the traits which favor that theory."[21]

Empiricism also entails a commitment to revising or discarding conclusions based on evidence garnered when new and incompatible evidence surfaces, as well as the suspension of judgment when the facts are not suggestive of an explanation. Concerning the latter, Jefferson says to Daniel Salmon (15 Feb. 1808):

> We certainly are not to deny whatever we cannot account for. A thousand phenomena present themselves daily which we cannot explain, but where facts are suggested, bearing no analogy with the laws of nature as yet known to us, their verity needs proofs proportioned to their difficulty. A cautious mind will weigh well the opposition of the phenomenon to everything hitherto observed, the strength of the testimony by which it is supported, and the errors and misconceptions to which even our senses are liable.

Here, the mysterious phenomenon under scrutiny is a stone that has fallen from the clouds—a meteorite.

Following the lead of empiricists Henry Home (better known as Lord Kames) and A. L. C. Destutt de Tracy,[22] Jefferson's epistemology was grounded not on certain indubitable facts, rationally intuited, but on feeling—a type of primitive sensing of the sort Kames called "intuitive

---

[20] This is a footnote by Jefferson to Query VI. Jefferson, *Notes on the State of Virginia*, 76–77.

[21] Jefferson was a steady critic of the medicine of his time, as he believed that it too often was guided more by theory than observation.

[22] See Destutt de Tracy, *Élémens d'Idéologie*, 5 vols. (Bruxelles: Courcier, 1827), III.164, and Lord Kames, *Morality and Natural Religion*, 2nd ed. (London: C. Hitch & L. Hawes, 1758), 259–67.

perception."[23] Appropriating Descartes, Jefferson writes to John Adams (15 Aug. 1820) about his "habitual anodyne": "'I feel, therefore I exist.' I feel bodies which are not myself: there are other existences then. I call them *matter*. I feel them changing place. This gives me *motion*. Where there is an absence of matter, I call it *void*, or *nothing*, or *immaterial space*. On the basis of sensation, of matter and motion, we may erect the fabric of all the certainties we can have or need." The groundwork here is manifestly Epicurean/Newtonian.[24] Matter, void-space, and motion form the basics of the cosmos. With those basic posits, all change in the cosmos can be explicated. There is no need for nonmaterial spirits or body-independent minds.

But what of the mysterious phenomenon of thinking? Moreover, what of God? One might expect Jefferson to agree with philosopher and Anglican theologian Samuel Clarke, who maintained that pure matter was incapable of thinking and that God was immaterial, and whom Jefferson

---

[23] Elsewhere I write: "Intuitive perception is 'the faculty of perception, working silently, and without effort'—*viz.*, a sort of immediate grasp of some truth or conveniency that is guided by sensory data. By intuitive perception, not reason, we come immediately to see our moral duties, our continued identical existence over time, the self-existence and benevolence of deity, and the uniformity and causal framework of the cosmos." M. Andrew Holowchak, *Thomas Jefferson, Moralist* (Jefferson, NC: McFarland, 2017), 29.

[24] For Epicurus, all bodies, even those of the gods, are the products of the accidental collisions of atoms, which, falling through void-space on account of their weight, arbitrarily swerve. Such swerves cause collisions and the collisions over time create complex bodies—even living bodies and the gods. Due to the unceasing bombardment of atoms on larger bodies, all existences, except the gods, are destructible and ephemeral. Yet each god, indestructible, has a point of its creation, but no point of its dissolution. The co-affection of atoms in divine bodies is thus somehow of a permanent sort—impervious to whatever blows they might receive. Epicurus, *Letter to Herodotus*, trans. Brad Inwood and L. P. Gerson (Indianapolis: Hackett, 1994), §§39–40, 62–68. In *Principia Mathematica*, Isaac Newton begins by defining "mass" and "motion," and the forces of or that act on bodies—that is, the "innate force of matter," "impressed force," and "centripetal force." He then writes of "absolute time," "absolute space," "absolute place," and "absolute motion" without offering definitions, because they are "well known to all." Next, he offers his celebrated three laws of motion. Newton's aim throughout is not to wax epistemological or metaphysical. Given the axioms, corollaries, and lemmas of his system, the explanatory power of the system speaks for itself. Isaac Newton, *Principia*, vol. 1: *The Motion of Bodies*, trans. Florian Cajori (Berkeley: University of California Press, 1962), 1–13.

considered the foremost authority on the attributes of God.[25] But he did not. Jefferson was an out-and-out materialist.

Jefferson continues his correspondence with Adams: "I can conceive *thought* to be an action of a particular organization of matter, formed for that purpose by its Creator, as well as that *attraction* in an action of matter, or *magnetism* of loadstone." If the Creator can endow the sun and the loadstone with the power of attraction, then the Creator can endow matter with a capacity to think. Jefferson concludes: "When once we quit the basis of sensation, all is in the wind. To talk of *immaterial* existences, is to talk of *nothings*. To say that the human soul, angels, god are immaterial is to say, they are *nothings*, or that there is no god, no angels, no soul. I cannot reason otherwise."

Jefferson's argument is one of economy—what today we call *Ockham's razor*, though it is a methodological principle that goes back at least as far as Aristotle. Jefferson elaborates in a letter to Adams (14 Mar. 1820):

> When I meet with a proposition beyond finite comprehension, I abandon it as I do a weight which human strength cannot lift, and I think ignorance, in these cases, is truly the softest pillow on which I can lay my head. Were it necessary however to form an opinion, I confess I should, with Mr. Locke, prefer swallowing one incomprehensibility rather than two. It requires one effort only to admit the single incomprehensibility of matter endowed with thought: and two to believe, 1st. that of an existence called Spirit, of which we have neither evidence nor idea, and then 2dly. how that spirit which has neither extension nor solidity, can put material organs into motion.

---

[25] When Jefferson engaged in a conversation with a book peddler, the seller noted that Jefferson began by stating that the best book on the nature of God was written by Samuel Clarke. The book to which Jefferson refers is Clarke's *A Discourse Concerning the Being and Attributes of God* (1704). See Samuel Whitcomb Jr., "A Book Peddler at Monticello," in *Visitors to Monticello*, ed. Merrill D. Peterson (Charlottesville: University Press of Virginia, 1989), 94–95.

For Jefferson, there are problems with materialism, but they pale when compared to the problems with a materialism that allows for immaterial substances and action between the two substances, which are radically unlike.

It is incontestably extraordinary that the lodestone attracts iron objects, yet according to Jefferson, no sober-sided person would explain that attractive capacity by some nonmaterial aspect of that lodestone.[26] To do so would be to add to the initial incomprehensibility. Likewise, thinking is merely the result of a "particular organization of matter." Change that organization and that matter is incapable of thinking. Thus it is unneeded to posit a separate, immaterial substance to account for thinking. To do so would be to create a second mystery when before there was only one.

That is likely the view Jefferson also entertained early in life. In his *Literary Commonplace Book*, Jefferson commonplaces Lord Bolingbroke, who acknowledges the wondrousness of thinking matter:

> [I]t is nonsense, and something worse than nonsense, to assert
> what you assert, that god cannot give the faculty of thinking
> . . . to systems of matter whose essential properties are solidity,
> extension &c. not incoginativity. this term of negation can be no
> more the essence of matter, than that other, immateriality, can
> be the essence of spirit. our ideas if solidity and extension do
> not include the idea of thought, neither do they include that of
> motion; but they exclude neither.[27]

Jefferson's commonplacing of Bolingbroke strongly suggests an uptake of his claims.

Jefferson was also likely influenced by Locke's materialism. He writes to Dr. Thomas Cooper (14 Aug. 1820), "[M]r Locke, on whose authority they [spiritualists or, more narrowly perhaps, Presbyterians] often plume

---

[26] The capacity to attract iron objects is due to the arrangement of atoms on the lodestone.

[27] Thomas Jefferson, *Jefferson's Literary Commonplace Book*, ed. Douglas L. Wilson (Princeton: Princeton University Press, 1989), 26–27.

themselves, openly maintained the materialism of the soul; and charged with blasphemy those who denied that it was in the power of an almighty creator to endow with the faculty of thought any composition of matter he might think fit."

Jefferson could also have been influenced by Joseph Priestley, who says in *Disquisitions Relating to Matter and Spirit*, "Since it has never yet been asserted that the powers of *sensation* and *thought* are incompatible with these (*solidity*, or *impenetrability*, and consequently a *vis intertiæ*, only, having been thought to be repugnant to them), I therefore maintain that we have no reason to suppose that there are in man two substances so distinct from each other."[28]

Jefferson, in his letter to Adams and elsewhere,[29] also appeals for his materialism to the authority of empiricists Destutt de Tracy and Dugald Stewart, as well as "the fathers of the church of the three first centuries generally"—that is, Origen, Macarius, Justin Martyr, Tertullian, Augustine, Basil, Lactantius, Tatian, and Athenagoras—though he admits to being insufficiently acquainted with the writings of those fathers. In a letter to Dr. Thomas Cooper (11 Dec. 1823), Jefferson later acknowledges, in agreement with Cooper's *The Scripture Doctrine of Materialism*, that Jesus was also a materialist.[30]

Those who maintain that God is immaterial, he continues to Adams, are schematizing atheists: "All heresies, being now done away with us, these schismatists are merely atheists, differing from the material atheist only in their belief, that 'nothing made something,' and from the material deist, who believes that matter alone can operate on matter." Consequently, thinking that some immaterial power or intelligence can create something material, or even act on it, is to be an atheist no less than the wholesale materialist who posits that there is no God, not even a material one.

---

[28] Joseph Priestley, *Disquisitions Relating to Matter and Spirit* (London: J. Johnson, 1777), xxxviii. There is no evidence that Jefferson owned the book.

[29] For example, TJ to Thomas Cooper, 14 Aug. 1820.

[30] Thomas Cooper, *The Scripture Doctrine of Materialism* (Philadelphia: A. Small, 1823), 23.

Immatter, whatever sort of strange substance that might be, cannot act on matter.

Thus far, we have, on behalf of Jefferson, a foursquare commitment to materialism and to a material Creator. Consistent with the mechanistic thinking of his day, whatever acts on matter must be material, and so if God crafted the cosmos, God too must be matter.

How, then, did the cosmos come to be created? Jefferson considers the issue in an earlier letter to Greek scholar Charles Thomson (17 Dec. 1786). Jefferson offers a commentary on a book, *An Inquiry into the Original State and Formation of the Earth; Deduced from Facts and the Laws of Nature* by John Whitehurst (1713-1788). In the commentary, he offers his own account of a cosmogony. Here he is working from the notions of the *Scala Naturae*, or Great Chain of Being, and providential economy—that is, that there is a natural progression from the simplest living organisms (infusorians) to the most complex (humans) and that organisms at every level strive to progress to the next level of complexity; thus there can be no gap in the "chain," and each organism ever strives to perfect itself. The *Scala Naturae* and providential economy have their roots in the biological thinking of Aristotle, millennia ago, but the teleology is radically different. For Aristotle, all species of flora and fauna are as they have forever been and will eternally be as they now are. Jefferson here has not yet accepted the legitimacy of organic extinction, which later he would embrace.

Jefferson begins with what he thinks is reasonable for any account of the cosmos by theorists—with an argument from consensus. "They all suppose the earth a created existence. They must suppose a Creator then; and that He possessed power and wisdom to a great degree." Note here that he does not explicitly commit to omniety (e.g., omnipotence, omniscience, and omnipresence). Following the principles of induction that had their roots in Greek antiquity (e.g., Aristotle and the Hippocratic physicians), he merely acknowledges a cause, an incomprehensibly powerful deity, sufficiently large to produce its effect, the incomprehensibly large cosmos. Moreover, Jefferson establishes to his own satisfaction the existence of God, as creator of the cosmos, by argument from consensus—indeed, a flimsy sort of argument. Yet, as we shall see in the next section, the consensus for Jefferson is not warrant for God being the craftsperson of the cosmos, but instead the result of an immediately *sensed* perception that the universe has been created in time and is not self-sufficing.

There are two scenarios that Jefferson considers. First, by assuming that the earth was created "for the habitation of animals and vegetables," two distinct creations seem reasonable. "He [God] first made a chaotic lump and set it into motion, and then, waiting the ages necessary to form itself— that when it had done this, He stepped in a second time, to create the animals and plants which were to inhabit it." The account here is perhaps meant to square with the two accounts given in Genesis (1:1–2:3 and 2:4 ff.).

A second, more economical, scenario seems more reasonable to Jefferson. "As a hand of a Creator is to be called in, it may as well be called in at one stage of the process as another. We may as well suppose He created the earth at once, nearly in the state in which we see it, fit for the preservation of the beings He placed on it." Jefferson again appeals to the consideration of providential economy within the theoretical frame of the *Scala Naturae*.

Jefferson's preference for the second scenario once again draws from providential economy and is very likely Bolingbrokean. Commonplacing Bolingbroke, Jefferson writes at §49, "nothing can be less reconcileable to the notion of an all-perfect being, than the imagination that he undoes by his power in particular cases what his wisdom . . . once thought sufficient to be established for all case."[31] In short, an omniperfect being, or relatively so, has no need for divine intervention, as God gets things right the first time. It is a compelling, provocative argument.

"Fabricator of All Things from Matter and Motion"
Jefferson's God

Jefferson corresponded with Thomson in 1786, and his views of the cosmos changed thereafter, as he was confronted with and assimilated new scientific findings, such as the existence of exploding stars, or what we now

---

[31] Jefferson, *Jefferson's Literary Commonplace Book*, 45.

call *novae* or *supernovae*, and fossilized evidence sufficient to show the extinction of living things. Thus Jefferson came to see that the operations of nature were more complex than he had believed in 1786, though he very likely never wavered from his belief in providential economy—that is, there being only one creation.

Jefferson was somewhat reluctant to articulate his view on the nature of divinity. To Rev. Ezra Stiles (25 June 1819), he states: "The benevolent and sublime reformer of that religion [i.e., Jesus] has told us only that God is good and perfect, but has not defined him. I am, therefore of his theology, believing that we have neither words nor ideas adequate to that definition. And if we could all, after his example, leave the subject as undefinable, we should all be of one sect, doers of good, and eschewers of evil."

Claims such as this incline scholars to maintain that Jefferson had nothing to say about God. Karl Lehman, for instance, asserts: "His explicit statements about matters of creed show only that he himself acknowledged a Supreme Being directing the world. For the rest, they are negative and opposed to what seemed to him to be incompatible with reason: polytheism, superstition, mystical speculation, the dogma of the Trinity. . . . He never stated his ideas about God."[32]

However, Jefferson did hold certain specific views of God (e.g., that God had superlative powers and was corporeal), though he did think it was presumptuous to claim to know God.

Robert Healey takes a different tack. Looking at all the epithets that Jefferson gives for the deity that crafted and sustains the cosmos—"God," "God of the universe," "Creator," "intelligent and powerful agent," "Giver of life," "He who made us," and so on—Healey concludes that this deity is the creator and sustainer of the cosmos, the source of humankind's moral law, and the "supreme judge" of each person in the afterlife.[33] However, he does not indicate that Jefferson frequently fails to capitalize "god" in writings to intimates. This could be a signal that Jefferson's deity is not a personal God

---

[32] Karl Lehmann, *Thomas Jefferson: American Humorist* (Charlottesville: University of Virginia Press, 1985), 35.

[33] Healey, *Jefferson on Religion in Public Education*, 28–30, 34–39.

that listens to and answers human prayers, but is something like a material mechanism, though one with unfathomable intelligence.

In a late-in-life letter to John Adams (11 Apr. 1823), Jefferson has this to say about the nature of deity. He begins, "I hold (without appeal to revelation) that when we take a view of the Universe, in it's parts general or particular, it is impossible for the human mind not to percieve and feel a conviction of design, consummate skill, and indefinite power in every atom of it's composition." The notions of perceiving and feeling again suggest an epistemology similar to Kames and Tracy. This feeling is immediate, not inference based. It is not a matter of arguing from analogy, as David Hume does in *Dialogues Concerning Natural Religion*, conceding that the cosmos is an ordered thing of some sort—whether like an animal, a vegetable, or an artifact—and concluding that it must have an intelligent cause of some sort, whether that cause is one or many.[34] The "consummate skill" and "indefinite power"—Jefferson again here chooses his epithets carefully—merely require a cause sufficiently large to produce an effect. There is no hint in this letter of infinite powers.

Jefferson proffers four arguments for the existence of deity. His first is an argument from design. When we view the universe and see "the movements of the heavenly bodies, so exactly held in their course by the balance of centrifugal and centripetal forces, the structure of our earth itself, with it's distribution of lands, waters and atmosphere, animal and vegetable bodies, examined in all their minutest particles, insects mere atoms of life, yet as perfectly organised as man or mammoth, the mineral substances, their generation and uses, it is impossible, I say, for the human mind not to believe that there is, in all this, design, cause and effect, up to an ultimate cause, a fabricator of all things from matter and motion,"[35]

---

[34] David Hume, *Dialogues Concerning Natural Religion*, ed. Richard H. Popkin (Indianapolis: Hackett, 1998), 39ff.

[35] See also TJ to John Adams (8 Apr. 1816), "When the atheist descanted on the unceasing motion and circulation of matter through the animal, vegetable and mineral kingdoms, gifted with the power of reproduction, the theist, pointing 'to the heavens above, and to the earth beneath, and to the waters under the earth,' asked, if these did not proclaim a first cause possessing intelligence and power." Cf. Kames, "When we at last take in at one view the material and moral worlds, full of harmony, order, and beauty,

there is perceived or felt harmony and order. There is perceived or felt cause and effect. There is perceived or felt ultimate cause. He argues for the immediacy of sensing God's presence. Reason, through analogical arguing, is absent.[36]

Next, Jefferson provides an argument from superintendency. Some stars have disappeared; others have come to be. Comets, with their "incalculable courses," deviate from regular orbits and demand "renovation under other laws." Some species of animals have become extinct.[37] "Were there no restoring power, all existences might extinguish successively, one by one, until all should be reduced to a shapeless chaos."

Third, Jefferson gives an argument from consensus. "So irresistible are these evidences of an intelligent and powerful Agent that, of the infinite numbers of men who have existed thro' all time, they have believed, in the proportion of a million at least to Unit, in the hypothesis of an eternal pre-existence of a creator, rather than in that of a self-existent Universe." Such "unanimous sentiment," he admits, is an argument from likelihood, not a proof, but this argument makes the existence of deity very probable.

---

happily adjusted to answer great and glorious purposes; there is in this grand production necessarily involved the conviction of a cause, unbounded in power, intelligence, and goodness." Lord Kames, *Essays on the Principles of Morality and Natural Religion: Corrected and Improved, in a Third Edition*, ed. Mary Catherine Moran (Indianapolis: Liberty Fund, 2005), 326.

[36] Healey, unaware of the influence of Kames and Tracy on Jefferson, takes such passages as instances where men are "allowed to observe and to use his reason freely." Thus, they make a "rational deduction of God's existence from observable phenomena." If the process were rational and mediate, not perceptual and immediate, the inference would not be deductive, but analogical and inductive. Later he says that "reason used uprightly in conjunction with the sense came to the incontestable conclusion that God did exist." Healey, *Jefferson on Religion in Public Education*, 100–102, 171.

[37] Jefferson came only relatively late to accept animals' extinction. In his *Notes on Virginia*, he clearly believes, following the notions of the Great Chain of Being and of providential economy, that the bones of the mammoth—"found at the Saltlicks, on the Ohio"—are mere relics of an animal still to be found in the northern parts of North America. "Such is the œconomy of nature that no instance can be produced of her having permitted any one race of her animals to become extinct; of her having formed any link in her great wok so weak as to be broken." Jefferson, *Notes on the State of Virginia*, 43–47, 53–54.

It also hearkens back to a special reason for unanimity: a unique, moral sense that perceives deity.[38]

Finally, Jefferson appeals to an argument from authority as evidence for the existence of deity. In John 4:24, Jesus says that God is spirit (*pneuma*). Jefferson points out that *pneuma*, for the ancients, was deemed a material substance, though a tenuous one. He appeals to Origen, who writes similarly of deity. Citing John 1:1–3 directly, Jefferson indicates: "In the beginning God existed, and reason [or mind] was with God, and that mind was God. This was in the beginning with God. All things were created by it, and without it was made not one thing which was made."

What are we to make of such arguments? If something akin to an immediate feeling for certain axial truths of the cosmos (argument 1)—for example, Kames's intuitive perception—then the other arguments are *de trop*, unneeded.[39] Consider what Lord Kames says concerning the futility of arguing for deity:

> To found our knowledge of the Deity upon reasoning solely, is not agreeable to the analogy of nature. We depend not on abstract reasoning, nor indeed on any reasoning, for unfolding our duty to our fellow creatures: it is engraved upon the table of our hearts. We adapt our actions to the course of nature, by mere instinct, without reasoning, or even experience. Therefore, if analogy can be relied on, it ought to be thought that God will discover himself to us, in some such manner as may take in all mankind, the vulgar and illiterate as well as the deep-thinking philosopher.[40]

Why, then, does Jefferson give the three other arguments? The answer is that he is likely following the historical lead of scholars throughout the

---

[38] Healey arguably overemphasizes this argument, without recognition that it is rooted in the moral sense. Healey, *Jefferson on Religion in Public Education*, 98.

[39] For more on the Stoic cosmos, see M. Andrew Holowchak, *The Stoics: A Guide for the Perplexed* (London: Continuum, 2009).

[40] Kames, *Essays on the Principles of Morality and Natural Religion*, 201. See also 207, 210–12.

centuries—a tendency, traceable to antiquity and still extant today, to swamp—that is, to offer as many reasonable arguments for a claim, such as the existence of God, as is possible. Excellent illustrations of swamping while arguing the existence of deity can be found in Cicero's *On the Nature of the Gods* or Descartes's *Meditations on First Philosophy.*

Yet the cogency of such arguments, saponaceous because they are metaphysical, is not the focus here. What is of interest is what they tell us about Jefferson's God. Jefferson's God is the creator and superintendent of the cosmos, Jefferson's God is one, Jefferson's God is material, and Jefferson's God has "consummate skill" and "indefinite power," yet perhaps not omnipotency.

The nodus here is Jefferson's ascription of superintendency, which is at odds with the sentiment in Jefferson's 1786 letter to Thomson, arguing against superintendency. Did Jefferson change his mind over time?

What is at stake is a commitment to deism or theism, or a change of mind from deism to theism. By *deism*, we understand God as a creator or first cause of the cosmos, and a being who, after construction, nowise intervenes thereafter in the course of cosmic events. This view may be called *noninterpositionist* By *theism*, we understand God as a creator or first cause of the cosmos, and a being who, after construction, intermittently intervenes in cosmic events. This view may be called *interpositionism.*[41] The question we must now consider is this: Did Jefferson begin as a deist or noninterpositionist and change to a theist or interpositionist, given the relatively new scientific findings of exploding stars and the legitimacy of extinction (change-of-mind thesis, or T_{CM}), or did he consistently champion deism (deistic thesis, or T_D)?

On the one hand, it is possible that Jefferson's view of the agency of God changed over time—that T_{CM} is true. Early on, he believed that the universe was harmoniously and expertly designed by a divine artificer who thereafter never intervened in cosmic affairs, that there is a chain of beings

---

[41] These concepts are relatively recent, and a distinction between the two terms would have been relatively meaningless to Jefferson.

from uncomplex to complex, that there is a telic tendency of movement of life from simplicity to complexity, and that perceived flaws in the design are attributable to human ignorance, not divine impotency. Later, upon his acceptance of the existence of exploding stars and the extinction of species, articulated in his 1823 letter to Adams, he adopted a more hands-on view of deity (i.e., one that gave the creator a superintending role in addition to that of creator). Charles Sanford endorses this view. "He [Jefferson] believed firmly in a God of providence who was active in his world and was guiding human affairs. His long struggles in the political arena for man's betterment were supported by his belief in a God who guided the affairs of nations."[42]

According to this argument, advances in science forced Jefferson to change his mind about deity. Early on for Jefferson, the *Scala Naturae* and providential economy indicated that the number of species on the planet was fixed and unalterable at the moment of creation. In time, the "paleontologists" of Jefferson's day provided sufficient geological evidence (e.g., the undeniable existence of numerous fossilized species of biota that no longer exist) to compel Jefferson to relinquish that view. The cosmos, it seems, was just not that simple, and the creator was not so economical.

Consider, for illustration, the catastrophism of French naturalist Georges Cuvier. In his *Essay on the Theory of the Earth*, Cuvier argued that the fossils in the various geological strata were the result of periodic catastrophes (e.g., the biblical flood) that devastated the earth and extinguished numerous species of biota. Those remaining species then repopulated the globe.

Yet Jefferson never seems to have taken Cuvier's catastrophist route. Jefferson's own view—expressed succinctly, inchoately, and crudely in an 1823 letter to Adams—is that extinction of species is real but catastrophism is not. There is not only a "superintending power" but also a "restoring

---

[42] Charles B. Sanford, *The Religious Life of Thomas Jefferson* (Charlottesville: University of Virginia Press, 1984), 93.

power," for without it, "all existences might extinguish successively, one by one, until all should be reduced to a shapeless chaos."[43]

According to T_{CM} and upon acceptance of the extinction of species, Jefferson commits himself to theism—the belief that deity, as some sort of tenuous matter, exists both as a creator and superintendent. God (1) is an architect, builder, and hands-on superintendent that plans and builds the cosmos, and then, as it were, lives near it to watch over and repair it; or (2) regulates the cosmos through thorough immersion in it, as in the case of the Stoics, for whom the cosmos was deity (i.e., Zeus).

In addition to Jefferson's 1823 letter to Adams, there is much textual evidence in support of his shift to theism or interpositionism later in life. In many political addresses and public speeches, Jefferson appeals to God for divine guidance. For example, he writes the following to Rev. David Barrow of Kentucky (1 May 1815): "We are not in a world ungoverned by the laws and the power of a Superior Agent. Our efforts are in His hand, and directed by it; and He will give them their effect in His own time." In addition, Jefferson writes to educator George Tickner (25 Nov. 1817) about a retributive deity: "The reason is that Napoleon is being punished for his crimes against the liberties & happiness of the human race. It proves that we have a god in heaven. That he is just, and not careless of what passes in this world. And we cannot but wish to this inhuman wretch, a long, long life, that time as well as intensity may fill up his sufferings to the measure of his enormities."

Though Jefferson's political addresses and public speeches can be explicated by political motives, certain writings, some relatively early, clearly express a certain commitment to supernatural interposition.

In certain writings on slavery, Jefferson, in denouncing the institution, warns of a just God intervening in the course of human events. "When the measure of [slaves'] tears shall be full, when their groans shall have

---

[43] Jefferson's restorative power must have functioned similar to Alcide d'Orbigny's deity. D'Orbigny posited some twenty-seven special creations to compensate for the loss of species during the numerous catastrophes that created the geological strata in which the fossils were found. Alcide d'Orbigny, *Natural History Museum*, accessed May 18, 2017, www.nhm.ac.uk /research-curation/research/projects/dorbigny/dOrbhistory.html.

involved heaven itself in darkness, doubtless," says Jefferson to French politician Jean Nicholas Démeunier (26 June 1786), "a God of justice will awaken to their distress, and by diffusing light and liberality among their oppressors, or, at length, by His exterminating thunder, manifest His attention to the things of this world, and that they are not left to the guidance of a blind fatality." In *Notes on Virginia*, Jefferson appeals to the justice of God "through supernatural interference" from the slaves' perspective. "I tremble for my country when I reflect that God is just: that this justice cannot sleep for ever: that considering numbers, nature and natural means only, a revolution of the wheel of fortune, an exchange of situation, is among possible events: that it may become probable by supernatural interference!"[44]

And so, writes Charles Sanford, "Jefferson went beyond his deistic teachers in attributing love, care, concern, guidance, providence, protection, and wisdom to God, the Creator of the universe, but he agreed with them in stressing the might and power of God. . . . This belief in God's guidance gave Jefferson a confidence which lesser leaders lacked."[45] Karl Lehmann seems to agree: "His explicit statements about matters of creed show only that he himself acknowledged a Supreme Being directing the world." Emphasizing the 1823 letter to Adams, William Wilson is also in the theistic camp. "The evidence of divine existence *is* activity, intentionality, and will. If we detect harmony in the universe we infer (we do not assume or personify anything) an agent." Concerning the construction of Jefferson's adaption of the Bible (explored in more detail in Chapter Three), Wilson adds, "Jefferson's Christ is attempting to point out the active will of God in the world, and how one must seek it, how one must find it, and how one must follow it. One day it will prevail."[46] For Wilson, the warrant

---

[44] Jefferson, *Notes on the State of Virginia*, 163. Tucker takes this as evidence that Jefferson thought belief in God was needed for social order. He maintains that this contradicts what Jefferson said in Query XVII about one's neighbor believing in no God or in twenty gods. David Tucker, *Enlightened Republicanism: A Study of Jefferson's Notes on the State of Virginia* (Lanham, MD: Lexington Books, 2008), 102–3.

[45] Sanford, *The Religious Life of Thomas Jefferson*, 96.

[46] William M. Wilson, "The Myth of Jefferson's Deism," in *The Elusive Thomas Jefferson: Essays on the Man behind the Myths*, ed. M. Andrew Holowchak and Brian W. Dotts (Jefferson, NC: McFarland, 2017), 120, 128.

for this assertion of prevailing, of a final intervention in human affairs, is Jefferson's inclusion of Matthew 24:1, which is Jesus's apocalyptic premonition of the destruction of Jerusalem.

In sum, according to T_{CM}, Jefferson began as a deist or noninterpositionist (someone who believes that God constructed the cosmos and thereafter left it alone) and became a theist or interpositionist (someone who believes God constructed the cosmos and periodically intervenes in cosmic matters to set things right).

On the other hand, it is possible that Jefferson's view of the agency of God never changed over time—that he was always a deist or noninterpositionist (i.e., that T_D is true). According to T_D, God merely created the cosmos much in the same way as it appears today. The disappearance of stars, the aberrant orbits of comets, and the extinction of species are merely to be explained not by a hands-on "restoring power" but instead by a restorative mechanism, weaved by God into the material fabric of the cosmos, in the manner of a builder installing a thermostat in a house to regulate its temperature. Maurizio Valsania endorses this view: "Jefferson did not renounce his opinion that humans . . . are left alone in this world, God dwelling in an untouched physical space, 'not meddling with the concerns of the scale of beings below them', God is a relatively distant figure for him."[47]

What seems beyond question is Jefferson's early commitment to deism. That is shown plainly in his *Literary Commonplace Book*, where he abundantly commonplaces Lord Bolingbroke's religious views from the latter's *Philosophical Works*. Bolingbroke's deity is "sovereignly good, . . . almighty and alwise" (§14) and can effortlessly grant certain types of matter the ability to think (§§11–13). Bolingbroke's god does not intervene in foreordained cosmic events—such as through Christ's miracles (§22 and §26), punishment for the fall of man (§15 and §42), or divine superintendency—but establishes once and for all cosmic harmony, as "nothing can be less reconcileable to the notion of an all-perfect being, than the imagination that he

[47] Maurizio Valsania, "'Our Original Barbarism,'" *Journal of the History of Ideas* 65, no. 4 (2004): 638–41.

undoes by his power in particular cases what his wisdom . . . once thought sufficient to be established for all case" (§49). Moreover, Bolingbroke's deity has not made "man the final cause of the whole creation" (§16 and §46). Bolingbroke's deity does not communicate his existence through revelation or inspiration, or only to one type of people (§16, §§20–22, §24, and §32). His deity does not punish or reward humans in an eternal afterlife, for "justice requires that punishments . . . and rewards . . . [ought to] be measured [o]ut in various degrees and manners, according to the various [c]ircumstances of particular cases, and in due proportion to them" (§52)—that is, justice ought to be meted out in this life. The religious law of Bolingbroke's deity—"the law of nature is the law of god" (§36)—is to be found in nature. "Natural religion represents an allperfect being to our adoration and to our live" and requires humans to "love the lord thy god with all thy heart" (§56).[48]

In keeping with T_D, Jefferson's many political references to the interposition of deity in human affairs and his references to an angry God punishing slave owners are metaphorical expressions of political politeness—of speaking to others in terminology that they can most readily grasp. Jefferson was no stranger to this practice. The wakening of God's justice here is just a matter of retribution that is weaved into the cosmic tapestry of events, ever progressing over time.

Yet there is one good reason to take Jefferson as a noninterpositionist or deist throughout his life: his 1820 bible. Reconstructing the works of the four evangelists in the New Testament in his effort to reconstruct the actual words and life of Jesus, Jefferson was insistent on removing all thaumaturgy—things, he writes to close friend William Short (4 Aug. 1820), in contravention of the laws of nature. "When they tell us of calves speaking, of statues sweating blood, and other things against the course of nature, we reject these as fables not belonging to history." Hence, passages in which Jesus feeds a great crowd with two fish and five loaves of bread (Matt. 15:32–38) or brings back to life a dead young woman (Matt. 9:18–26)

---

[48] Jefferson, *Jefferson's Literary Commonplace Book*.

are excised. By insisting that all thaumaturgy be removed from his bible, Jefferson follows the tradition of Bolingbroke, saying that through Jesus's miracles, god "undoes by his power in particular cases what his wisdom ... once thought sufficient to be established for all cases."[49] In other words, he allows for periodic exceptions to the laws of nature through the miraculous agency of Jesus. Like Bolingbroke, Jefferson believed that God's inscrutable powers allowed him to intervene periodically in human affairs. Such interventions would speak against, not for, the unfathomable powers of God.

Moreover, Jefferson could have taken the path of Joseph Priestley, whose religious works he read and greatly admired. Priestley argued that Jesus was a man who was empowered by God to perform miracles and who was raised from the dead. Priestley acknowledges that much of the argument on behalf of Jesus's divinity is on account of "the death and resurrection of a man, in all respect like themselves, being better calculated to give other men an assurance of their own resurrection, than any super-angelic being"[50]—that is, God granting Jesus, qua man, certain superhuman powers.

Yet Jefferson did not follow Priestley's lead; his deity was always Bolingbrokean.[51] There was no need for God to intervene in cosmic affairs through Jesus's resurrection or his miracles, because God, by virtue of being God, got it right the first time. Given that, what is currently inexplicable about the cosmos might later be explicated by "renovation under other laws," as he says in an 1823 letter to Adams. For Jefferson, there is more to the nomological structure of the cosmos than Sir Isaac Newton has given us.

---

[49] Jefferson, *Jefferson's Literary Commonplace Book*, §49.

[50] Joseph Priestley, *A History of the Corruptions of Christianity* (London: British and Foreign Unitarian Association, 1871), 8.

[51] Colman writes, "As Jefferson's appraisal of Christianity grew softer under the influence of Joseph Priestley, he cannot be said to be a simple follower of his early reading of Bolingbroke. This is especially true with regard to Bolingbroke's assessment of the superiority of pagan over Christian morality, Priestley's influence on Jefferson's view of Christianity cannot be underestimated." John Colman, "Diamonds from Dunghills: Jefferson's Materialism, Free Inquiry, and Religious Reform," *American Political Thought* 6 (2017): 352.

Finally, divine superintendency in the manner of a hands-on deity is unwarranted, because it is unnecessary. For Jefferson, superintendency is readily explicated by a deity of unplumbed intelligence, who has built superintendency into the cosmos in the manner of a builder who fashions a thermostat for a house to regulate its temperature. Theism or interpositionism is not needed.

Concluding Thoughts

As we will explore in the next chapter, Jefferson is clear that one of our two substratal moral or religious duties is love of or "duties to God." How is that love to be expressed, and how are those duties to be discharged?

As others have noted, at times, Jefferson did attend religious services, during which he would sing (he loved to sing) and pray with others. He also befriended several religious clergy and, at times, donated handsomely to churches. However, these instances offer no evidence of transdenominationalism or evidence of any effort on behalf of Jefferson to communicate with God.

Jefferson's God, creator of an enormous cosmos, is not a being to whom a person would sing or pray, though Jefferson did both at times, when in public. Consider, for instance, what Jefferson indicates in his travel notes while touring the south of France, upon witnessing poor people of several villages gathered for daily mass: "Few chateaux. No farm houses, all the people being gathered in villages. Are they thus collected by that dogma of their religion which makes them believe that, to keep the Creator in good humor with his own works, they must mumble a mass every day?"[52] That is not a sentiment of someone who believes in the efficacy of prayer or singing hymns—though, again, Jefferson did both at times. Jefferson's God could take no notice of songs or prayers by creatures, beautifully constructed and essential parts of the cosmos, but nonetheless relatively

---

[52] Thomas Jefferson, "Notes of a Tour into the Southern Parts of France, &c., 3 March–10 June 1787," in *The Papers of Thomas Jefferson*, vol. 11: *1 January–6 August 1787*, ed. Julian P. Boyd (Princeton: Princeton University Press, 1955), 415–64.

inconsequential. Consider what Jefferson says to Virginian politician Miles King (26 Sept. 1814):

> I have trust in him who made us what we are, and knows it was not his plan to make us always unerring. He has formed us moral agents. Not that, in the perfection of his state, he can feel pain or pleasure from any thing we may do: he is far above our power: but that we may promote the happiness of those with whom he has placed us in society, by acting honestly towards all, benevolently to those who fall within our way, respecting sacredly their rights bodily and mental, and cherishing especially their freedom conscience, as we value our own.

The sentiment here is that we demonstrate our reverence for and love of God by doing well what he crafted us to do: to behave benevolently, as social animals, and to study, through science, the magnificent cosmos that God crafted.

In that regard, Jefferson is like philosopher David Hume, who writes, "The life of man is of no greater importance to the universe than that of an oyster."[53] In comparing man to an oyster, Hume is not so much aiming to degrade his fellow humans—to put humans in their place. He is merely noting that deity has given the same attention to the details of all the minutiae of the cosmos. Anyone who claims that the cosmos was created for the sake of humans does not grasp the intricate connection of all parts of the cosmos: from the mighty Texas oak to the eastern oyster, from the tall Kenyan warrior to the rock falling from the clouds. To grasp fully deity and the cosmos deity created, we must begin by setting aside all anthropocentric biases. In that regard, Jefferson was genuinely a *philosophe*.

---

[53] David Hume, "On Suicide," in *Dialogues Concerning Natural Religion with "Of the Immortality of the Soul," "Of Suicide," "Of Miracles,"* ed. Richard H. Popkin (Indianapolis: Hackett, 1998), 100.

CHAPTER TWO

"The Best of All Possible Worlds, If There Were No Religion in It"

Religion, Sectarian and Natural, and Morality

*"It is natural to imagine that [humans] will form a notion
of those unknown beings, suitable to the present gloom and
melancholy of their temper, when they betake themselves to the
contemplation of them. Accordingly, we find the tremendous
images to predominate in all religions; and we ourselves, after
having employed the most exalted expression in our descriptions
of the Deity, fall into the flattest contradiction in affirming that
the damned are infinitely superior in number to the elect."*

—David Hume, *Dialogues Concerning Natural Religion*

T homas Jefferson claimed to be a Christian in the truest sense of the
word—"I am a real Christian . . . a disciple of the doctrines of Jesus"[1]—
that is, one who was moved by and lived pursuant to the teachings of Jesus.
In his "Notes on Religion" (1776), he writes of Jesus's teachings as follows:

> The fundamentals of X^{ty} as found in the gospels are 1. Faith, 2.
> Repentance. That faith is every [where] explained to be a belief
> that Jesus was the Messiah who had been promised. Repentance

---

[1] TJ to Charles Thomson, 9 Jan. 1816.

was to be proved sincerely by good works. The advantages accruing to mankind from our Saviour's mission are these. 1. The knolege of one god only. 2. A clear knolege of their duty, or system of morality, delivered on such authority as to give it sanction. 3. The outward forms of religious worship wanted to be purged of that farcical pomp & nonsense with which they were loaded. 4. An inducement to a pious life, by revealing clearly a future existence in bliss, & that it was to be the reward of the virtuous.

Yet Jefferson also tells us in a letter to William Short (13 Apr. 1820) that though he considers Jesus a great moralist and of sublime wisdom, he does not concur with all that Jesus preaches. For instance, Jesus is a spiritualist who preaches repentancy for misdeeds. Jefferson is a materialist who advocates some sort of retribution for misdeeds. We cannot, thus, merely assume that because Jefferson considered Jesus to be the world's foremost moralist, what Jesus said, Jefferson adopted.

Moreover, Jefferson states plainly in numerous writings that the New Testament cannot be taken literally, as there have been, over the centuries, fabrications, excrescences, and hyperboles weaved into the life and teachings of Jesus—hence his motivation for crafting his own version of Jesus's life and morals, his own harmony (see Chapter Three).

What, then, does it mean for Jefferson to be a "real Christian"? What are the true doctrines of Jesus? Are they identical to the true principles of morality?

In an attempt to answer those questions, this chapter traces out, through letters as well as lists and catalogs of books, Jefferson's distinction between natural and sectarian religions. Natural religion, which is identical to morality, is the commitment to love of God and love of fellow humans.[2] Sectarian religions, in contrast, promote love of God and other

---

[2] In his bible, Jefferson includes Mark 12:31–32, which speaks of love of God and love of one's neighbor as oneself, and then adds Matthew 22:40, which says, "On these two commandments hang all the law and the prophets."

humans, but are sidetracked by all sorts of metaphysical issues that are intended to confound what is manifestly simple to promote the political ambitions of their espousers. Thus Jefferson—though he frequently attended worship, sometimes gave very generous donations to several churches, and befriended several clerics—did not have a high opinion of sectarian religions.

"How to Live Well and Worthily in Society"
Religion and Morality

In the preface, I mentioned the abundant confusion, much of which is polarized, on the issue of Jefferson's religious views in today's literature. The largest reason for much of the confusion—"Jefferson's religious beliefs never cohered," says Paul Conkin[3]—is the general refusal to come to terms with Jefferson's personal definition of religion. It is not that Jefferson had the "correct" notion of religion but instead that in order to arrive at some understanding of Jefferson's thinking, we must start somewhere—with some definition, or at least some conditions necessary for a definition—and analyzing Jefferson's words and writings is as good as any proposed start.

In the 1780s, when he began to take an active interest in Jesus and his teachings, Jefferson always thereafter considered himself to be a Christian in the true sense of the word. In a letter to Dr. Benjamin Rush (21 Apr. 1803), Jefferson objects to "that anti-Christian system imputed to me by those who know nothing of my opinions." He adds: "To the corruptions of Christianity I am indeed opposed; but not to the genuine precepts of Jesus himself. I am a Christian, in the only sense he wished any one to be; sincerely attached to his doctrines, in preference to all others; ascribing to him every *human* excellence; & believing he never claimed any other." So, to be religious was to be a Christian in Jefferson's sense: one committed to acceptance of Christ's teachings—specifically, as we shall shortly see, his moral teachings, stripped of their corruptions. Yet even Jesus, whom

---

[3] Paul K. Conkin, "The Religious Pilgrimage of Thomas Jefferson," in *Jeffersonian Legacies*, ed. Peter S. Onuf (Charlottesville: University Press of Virginia, 1993), 45.

Jefferson came to consider the world's greatest moralist, did not, according to Jefferson and as we see in the 1820 letter to Short, get everything right.

For Jefferson, religion, correctly apprehended, is equivalent to morality. This is generally in accord with philosopher and historian David Hume, an older contemporary of Jefferson, who says the following through the mouth of Cleanthes in his *Dialogues concerning Natural Religion*:

> The proper office of religion is to regulate the hearts of men, humanize their conduct, infuse the spirit of temperance, order, and obedience; and, as its operation is silent and only enforces the motives of morality and justice, it is in danger of being overlooked and confounded with these other motives. When it distinguishes itself, and acts as a separate principle over men, it has departed from its proper sphere and has become only a cover to faction and ambition.[4]

The interlocutor Philo agrees, "It is certain, from experience, that the smallest grain of natural honesty and benevolence has more effect on men's conduct than the most pompous views suggested by theological theories and systems."[5]

The sentiment is that religion is only legitimate when it acts in the service of morality and justice—that is to say, subtly, when it works quietly. However, formal religious systems—political in nature and inveigling people through the mysteries of miracles, such as a dead man coming back to life and water mysteriously and immediately being converted to wine, and other matters at odds with common sense, such as one god being three—are, for Jefferson, anything but quiet and thus are mostly metaphysical nonsense.

Jefferson always shared Hume's view; he believed that religion was between a man and his god—a taciturn, private affair.

---

[4] David Hume, *Dialogues concerning Natural Religion*, ed. Richard H. Popkin (Indianapolis: Hackett, 1998), 82.
[5] Hume, *Dialogues concerning Natural Religion*, 83.

For Jefferson, people, essentially social beings, are adequately equipped with a moral sense to guide them in social situations, as a benevolent deity would not make humans social beings and also create them to be morally deficient. In short, humans have an innate and natural sensual understanding of their moral duties, which are both other-directed and god-directed.[6]

Humans fulfill their duties to humankind by recognizing correct moral action in circumstances in their daily interactions with others. There is no need for moral instruction, as a sense of morally correct action is innate—hence, Jefferson disadvises nephew Peter Carr (10 Aug. 1787) to attend lectures on morality, as our moral conduct is not "a matter of science"—but there is a need to goad and hone morality to incite persons to act when circumstances call for action.[7]

Likewise, humans fulfill their duties to God through study and care of the cosmos in which they were placed.[8] This largely explains Jefferson's appreciation for and love of science. The truths disclosed by science allow humans to get a glimpse of the mind of God. That is why Jefferson, in his travel notes while touring French villages, speaks disparagingly of the mass of French peasants who, having no farmhouses, huddle in villages and "keep the Creator in good humor with his own works" by mumbling "a mass every day." Consider also what Jefferson writes to Angelica Church (27 Nov. 1793) concerning Maria Cosway, who was living in a convent: "I knew that [in addition] to much goodness of heart she joined enthusiasm

---

[6] Healey adds that reason often aids the moral sense by "demonstrating the utilitarian value of correct moral assessment"—hence the need for moral instruction through education. Healey fails to consider Jefferson's many utterances concerning the dangers of rational intrusion. Reason, involved in moral affairs (see TJ to Maria Cosway, 12 Oct. 1786), generally does more harm than good. Healey also mistakenly asserts that humans are "endowed unequally with human attributes . . . such as the moral sense." Jefferson is clear that all humans have (roughly) the same capacity for moral sensing, though the capacity for reasoning is not so equitably God-given (TJ to Thomas Law, 13 June 1814). Robert M. Healey, *Jefferson on Religion in Public Education* (New Haven, CT: Yale University Press, 1962), 171.

[7] See M. Andrew Holowchak, *Thomas Jefferson, Moralist* (Jefferson, NC: McFarland, 2017), chap. 1.

[8] Collins arguably is mistaken when he states that it is reasonable for public schools to teach "fundamental features of morality." Peter Collins, "Jefferson on Philosophy of Religion and Public Education," *Journal of Thought* 31, no. 2, 1996: 51–52.

and religion; but I thought that very enthusiasm would have prevented her from shutting up her adoration of the God of the universe within the walls of a cloister; that she would rather have sought the *mountain-top*."

Outside of the certain core beliefs that all genuinely religious persons share, there are considerable differences in personal religious convictions. Yet none of those differences has any bearing on a citizen's capacity to govern or to be governed. "It does me no injury for my neighbor to say there are twenty gods, or no god. It neither picks my pocket nor breaks my leg," says Jefferson in an oft-quoted passage, generally adjudged indicative of his atheism or infidelity, from his *Notes on Virginia*.[9] Thus, for Jefferson, religious conviction is a personal, not a political, matter.

"The care of every man's soul belongs to himself," writes Jefferson in his "Notes on Religion" in 1776. "Laws provide against injury from others; but not from ourselves." Four decades later (6 Aug. 1816), Jefferson writes similarly to Mrs. Harrison Smith: "I have ever thought religion a concern purely between our God and our consciences, for which we are account-able to Him, and not to the priests. God himself will not save men against their wills." In general, consistent over a lifetime, religious belief is per-sonal, not political. Government has no right to encroach on matters of the soul—religion being chief among them. Government can, if it decides, coerce religious uniformity in behavior, but it cannot bring about unifor-mity of will by doing that. If it coerces uniformity of religion, it oversteps its function, and if the coercions are long and consistent, the citizenry has a right to overthrow the government. Government has no right to intervene in matters of religious belief.

Thus, because it is a personal matter, religion cannot be politicized. When clergy, driven by empleomania, engraft themselves into the "machine of government"—Jefferson tells Jeremiah Moor (14 Aug. 1800), in another

---

[9] Thomas Jefferson, *Notes on the State of Virginia*, ed. William Peden (Chapel Hill: University of North Carolina Press, 1954), 159. See Rev. William Linn, who would later write in mockery of Jefferson, "Let my neighbor once persuade himself that there is no God, and he will soon pick my pocket, and break not only my *leg* but my *neck*." William Linn, *Serious Considerations of the Election of a President: Addressed to the Citizens of the United States* (New York: John Furman, 1800), 19.

instance of his frequently used metaphor of the "machine"—they become a "very formidable engine against the civil and religious rights of man." That speaks much to Jefferson's distrust of the politically ambitious religious clerics both of his day and in the past.

Consequently, for Jefferson, government also functions best when it is silent, and it is most silent when its laws are few. Those governing must be like machines insofar as they grasp and actuate the will of the majority. Consider what Jefferson says to Dr. Benjamin Rush (13 June 1805) about his role as president: "I am but a machine erected by the constitution for the performance of certain acts according to laws of action laid down for me, one of which is that I must anatomise the living man as the Surgeon does his dead subject, view him also as a machine & employ him for what he is fit for, unblinded by the mist of friendship." When government is stentorian and its laws are many, its loudness and the number of its laws are sure signs that the rights of its citizens are being suffocated.

The problem for Jefferson—and history is itself proof of this trend—is that sectarian religion is essentially political, while aboveboard, natural religion is generic, exoteric, and simple. Jefferson writes to James Fishback (draft—27 Sept. 1809) on the latter: "every religion consists of moral precepts, & of dogmas. in the first they all agree. all forbid us to murder, steal, plunder, bear false witness &c., and these are the articles necessary for the preservation of order, justice, & happiness in society." Yet most of the doctrines of a sectarian religion are esoteric; they are not crafted for the sake of honest or benevolent living. Clerics use indecipherable metaphysical claims to their political advantage. They also engage in fatuous disputes. Jefferson continues:

> in their particular dogmas all differ; no two professing the
> same. these respect vestments, ceremonies, physical opinions,
> & metaphysical speculations, totally unconnected with moral-
> ity, & unimportant to the legitimate objects of society. yet these
> are the questions on which have hung the bitter schisms of
> Nazarenes, Socinians, Arians, Athanasians in former times, &

now of Trinitarians, Unitarians, Catholics, Lutherans, Calvinists, Methodists, Baptists, Quakers Etc. among the Mahometans we are told that thousands fell victims to the dispute whether the first or second toe of Mahomet was longest; & what blood, how many human lives have the words "this do in remembrance of me" cost the Christian world!

In such matters, religions do not follow but deviate from nature.

Yet there are certain axial tenets common to all religions that link them together and link religion as a whole to morality. Jefferson tells Elbridge Gerry (29 Mar. 1801) that "the mild and simple principles of the Christian philosophy" have been made feculent by the priesthood, who "sophisticate it, ramify it, split it into hairs, and twist its texts" just so they are then needed to explain it. He adds that the "mild and simple principles of the Christian philosophy" are the principles common to all right-intended religions. He iterates this sentiment in numerous other letters.[10] For instance, Jefferson expresses this same sentiment neatly, succinctly, and beautifully in a letter to Philadelphian merchant and politician Thomas Leiper (21 Jan. 1809):

> My religious reading has long been confined to the moral
> branch of religion, which is the same in all religions; while in
> that branch which consists of dogmas, all differ, all have a differ-
> ent set. The former instructs us how to live well and worthily in
> society; the latter are made to interest our minds in the support
> of the teachers who inculcate them. Hence, for one sermon on a
> moral subject, you hear ten on the dogmas of the sect.

This topic also appears in one of Jefferson's most important letters on morality: "Reading, reflection and time have convinced me that the interests of society require the observation of those moral precepts only in which all religions agree (for all forbid us to steal, murder, plunder, or bear false witness), and that we should not intermeddle with the particular

---

[10] For example, TJ to William Canby, 18 Sept. 1813; TJ to John Adams, 11 Jan. 1817; and TJ to Thomas Parker, 15 May 1819.

dogmas in which all religions differ, and which are totally unconnected with morality," he writes to physician James Fishback (27 Sept. 1809). Jefferson espouses that the principles common to all (reasonable) religions are the axial principles of morality, and that the axial principles of morality are just the fundamental principles of religion. He adds that there are good men in every religion, and when Jefferson found such individuals, he befriended them and often donated handsomely to their churches.

Why, then, are there such disagreements among men concerning the "true" religion? Jefferson answers to Fishback, "The varieties in the structure and action of the human mind as in those of the body, are the work of our Creator, against which it cannot be a religious duty to erect the standard of uniformity." In sum, it is the will of God that people should not think uniformly—that is, be as unreflective as bromides.

That sentiment is an iteration of what Jefferson writes in Query XVII of *Notes on Virginia*. Uniformity of opinion in religious matters is undesirable and harmful. The history of pursuit of religious uniformity has been a history of villainy through sanguinary practices. Jefferson singles out the Crusades. Yet deity has given men reason to debate civilly religious concerns, and because of reason, there is the possibility that if any single sectarian religion should be true, its truth will be discovered in time.[11] The argument—one of numerous others, each quickly thrown out—is a plea for freedom of religious expression and governmental non-involvement in such personal matters (which will be the foci of the final chapter of this text). "Let us too [like Pennsylvania and New York]," continues Jefferson, "give this experiment fair play, and get rid, while we may, of those tyrannical laws," prohibitive of free religious expression.[12]

Yet there is one area of agreement. "The practice of morality being necessary for the well-being of society," he continues in the letter to Fishback, "[deity] has taken care to impress its percepts so indelibly on our hearts that they shall not be effaced by the subtleties of our brain." Each person, endowed with a moral sense, is naturally and intuitively equipped to abide

---

[11] Jefferson, *Notes on the State of Virginia*, 159–61.
[12] Jefferson, *Notes on the State of Virginia*, 161.

by the correct moral code, which Jefferson equates with "the moral precepts of Jesus," divested of the supernatural and metaphysical trappings, which Jefferson maintains were added by corrupters.

Five years later, Jefferson expresses to Miles King (26 Sept. 1814) that deity has so authorized matters that each tree must be judged by its fruit. The suggestion here is not that each action should be judged moral or immoral when it has a fruitful or fruitless outcome. Jefferson, like Aristotle, is referring to actions over the course of a lifetime.[13] He adds that religion is "substantially good which produces an honest life," and for that, each is accountable solely to deity. "There is not a Quaker or a Baptist, a Presbyterian or an Episcopalian, a Catholic or a Protestant in heaven; . . . on entering that gate, we leave those badges of schism behind." The suggestion, if not implication, is that religious clerics are otiose. Allen Jayne states, "Jefferson eliminated all intermediate authorities between God and man as the source of religious truth, such as exclusive revelation or scripture, church or tradition, and most of all, the clergy."[14]

That is precisely what Jefferson states in a letter to John Adams (22 Aug. 1813): All people should follow the Quakers: live without priests, follow their internal monitor of right and wrong,[15] and eschew matters inaccessible to common sense, for belief can only rightly be shaped by "the assent of the mind to an intelligible proposition." This requires a certain degree of maturity of intellect, and that is why Jefferson was adamant that children should not be taught the formal principles of any sectarian religion.[16] Their

---

[13] Aristotle, *Nicomachean Ethics*, trans. H. Rackham (Cambridge: Harvard University Press, [1926] 1990), 2.4.

[14] Allen Jayne, *Thomas Jefferson's Declaration of Independence: Origins, Philosophy, and Theology* (Lexington: University of Kentucky Press, 1998), 151.

[15] A sentiment expressed by John Locke in notes taken by Jefferson in 1776. Jefferson writes, "Christ has said 'wheresoever 2 or 3 are gatherd. togeth. in his name he will be in the midst of them.' this is his definition of a society. he does not make it essential that a bishop or presbyter govern them. without them it suffices for the salvation of souls." Thomas Jefferson, "Notes on Locke and Shaftesbury, 11 October–9 December 1776," *Founders Online*, National Archives, http://founders.archives.gov/documents/Jefferson /01-01-02-0222-0007, accessed June 18, 2017.

[16] Jefferson's favorite historian, Tacitus, writes: "I believe it will be allowed just that such impressions as are most wise and virtuous, and worthy to last, should be first made, not

minds are not yet sufficiently mature enough to consider them critically. They are liable, in today's terms, to brainwashing. I amplify this topic in the last section of the final chapter.

Two common threads exist in all such passages. First, religion is a personal matter. What one believes might bring harm to a believer, but if that harm extends to no others, the believer should not be coerced to think otherwise. Coercion can never bring about consent. Thus government has no right to intervene in such concerns and impose a uniform religious standard. Further, the principles common to all religions are few, exoteric, simple, and the true principles of morality. According to Jefferson, the numerous and esoteric principles that are topics of rigorous religious disputation are metaphysical gobbledygook, beyond the comprehension of any rational being. Esoteric religious principles are created to muddle common understanding and to allow for religious imposition in political matters at the expense of others' civil and religious rights.[17] "A man must be very clear-sighted who can see the impression of the finger of God on any particular one of them," Jefferson writes to Thomas B. Parker (15 May 1819).

Did Jefferson believe in internalizing *all* the teachings of Jesus—that is, were the principles common to all religions just Jesus's teachings, uncorrupted by later power-lusting schizmatizers?

Jefferson's 1822 letter to Dr. Benjamin Waterhouse (June 26) provides particular insight, because here he explains what he considers to be the

---

only because they are most important, but because the most early impressions are likely to abide longest, especially when the understanding finds afterwards cause to approve and retain what the mind had already imbibed. Upon our spirits, whilst yet young and tender, any ideas whatsoever may be stamped, however foolish, however mad, or even pernicious. Nay, such are very easily infused, though very hard to be removed. This is exemplified in the eminent stubbornness of religious errors." Publius Cornelius Tacitus, *The Works of Tacitus. In Four Volumes, To Which Are Prefixed, Political Discourses upon That Author by Thomas Gordon*, 2nd ed., vol. 3 (London: T. Woodward & J. Peele, 1737), accessed July 19, 2017, http://oll.libertyfund.org/titles/786#Tacitus_006703_343.

[17] Owen notes that Jefferson's "primitive Christianity" aligns itself to "indifference to doctrinal questions." One wonders whether "indifference" is too tame and should not be supplanted by "disdain." J. Judd Owen, *American Political Science Review* 101, no. 3 (2007): 500. Luebke claims that Jefferson's anticlericalism was in response to the hostile clerical attacks, during his campaign for the presidency. Fred C. Luebke, "The Origins of Thomas Jefferson's Anti-Clericalism," *Church History* 32, no. 3 (1963): 344–56.

most valuable teachings of Jesus. The "doctrines of Jesus are simple, and tend all to the happiness of man." Those doctrines are threefold: "1. That there is one only God, and he all perfect. 2. That there is a future state of rewards and punishments. 3. That to love God with all thy heart and thy neighbor as thyself, is the sum of religion." Thus, to be a Christian in the sense of being a follower of Christ's teachings is to accept fully the three principles that Jefferson articulates.

Yet, was Jefferson's Christianity that of Christ? Though he considered Jesus to be the world's greatest moralist, Jefferson never countenanced full acceptance of everything Christ taught. As noted at the beginning of this chapter, Jefferson writes to his former secretary and friend, William Short (13 Apr. 1820): "It is not to be understood that I am with [Jesus] in all of his doctrines. I am a Materialist; he takes the side of Spiritualism; he preaches the efficacy of repentance towards forgiveness of sin; I require a counterpoise of good works to redeem it, &c., &c."

Jefferson was with Christ in the letter to Waterhouse only on the third principle, which for him was the essence of religion. He was monotheist, but as we saw in Chapter One, there is little reason to believe that he fully embraced a philosophy proclaiming God's perfection, if perfection implies omniety—omniscience, omnipotence, omnipresence, omnibenevolence, and so forth. Deity as Creator of the cosmos needed only such powers to bring about the cosmos, and it is doubtful, as illustrated by Jefferson's letters to John Adams (8 Apr. 1816 and 18 Dec. 1825), that he believed the cosmos itself was a work of perfection in the sense of being crafted by an all-powerful, flawless being. "It is a good world on the whole," says Jefferson in the earlier letter, "[and] it has been framed on a principle of benevolence, and more pleasure than pain dealt out to us." In that, he was in accord with David Hume and ancient Greek and Roman cosmogonists, who maintained that a cause (God) must be equal to or greater than its effect (the cosmos). And Jefferson did not believe in a future existence beyond this life, as will be discussed in more detail in Chapter Four.

For Jefferson, to be religious, in the true and natural sense, is to love God, one in nature, and show love to one's fellow humans through benevolence-based actions. Yet that is precisely what it means to be moral.[18] As we have already seen, in his *Life and Morals of Jesus*, Jefferson includes Luke 10:27: "Thou shalt love the Lord thy God with all thy heart, and with all thy soul, and with all thy strength, and with all thy mind: and thy neighbour as thyself."[19]

That said, we are now positioned to explore a comment that Jefferson makes in an 1814 letter to Thomas Law (June 13), a prominent citizen of Washington, which has been purposely omitted until now. There he considers the "foundation of morality" and entertains several possibilities: truth, love of God, the aesthetic sense, and egoism. Only the second concerns us. "This [love of God] is but a branch of our moral duties, which are generally divided in to duties to God and duties to man." He then adds: "Whence arises the morality of the Atheist? It is idle to say, as some do, that no such being exists."

This passage is usually taken to mean that there are moral atheists (i.e., that one can be an atheist and still be fully moral). Examining the letter to Thomas Law, Arthur Scherr takes Jefferson's mention of "the morality of the Atheist" as evidence of his philosophy that morality is indifferent to belief in God.[20] Scherr notes that Jefferson mentions the unquestioned virtue of atheists like D'Alembert and Diderot. Mike Zuckert, referring to Jefferson's advisory letter to Carr (10 Aug. 1787), writes, "The moral sense doctrine, in the very crudeness and simplicity in which it is put here, is Jefferson's way of assuring Carr that—contrary to Dostoevsky's famous

---

[18] Collins makes the mistake of thinking morality is "an aspect of religion," comprising love of God and our moral beliefs, "inward motive and intention and benevolence or charity." Peter Collins, "Jefferson on Philosophy of Religion and Public Education," *Journal of Thought* 31, no. 2 (1996): 49, 46. Sheridan says that Jefferson "sometimes insinuated that a number of Jesus's precepts and injunctions were valid only insofar as they were expressions of a universal moral law that predated Christianity and was common to all religions." Eugene R. Sheridan, *Jefferson and Religion* (Charlottesville: Thomas Jefferson Foundation, 1998), 65.

[19] Thomas Jefferson, *The Jefferson Bible* (Washington, DC: Smithsonian Books, 2011), 38. For more, see M. Andrew Holowchak, *Jefferson's Bible: With Introduction and Commentary* (Berlin: DeGruyter, 2018).

[20] For example, Arthur Scherr, "Thomas Jefferson versus the Historians: Christianity, Atheistic Morality, and the Afterlife," *Church History* 83, no. 1 (2014): 60–109.

dictum—the moral life is perfectly secure without God and without religion. It is well provided for by nature."[21]

Yet moral atheism is an unlikely interpretation here, as to be genuinely moral is to fulfill our moral duties to both God and others. That much is incontestable in the letter to Law. So, when Jefferson refers to the "morality of the Atheist," he is merely acknowledging that an atheist can be *behaviorally* similar, if not behaviorally identical, to a true religionist—an atheist can be morality abiding, even virtuous, insofar as his actions toward others are virtuous. For instance, an atheist might be beneficent toward others and act with respect, and perhaps even love, for the cosmos and all things in it. The difference is that the true religionist, qua moralist, will see the hand of God in all that he respects and loves, and that makes a significant difference, even if it is only a cognitive difference. Yet that cognitive difference is mammoth. It separates a true moralist from a morality-abiding atheist.

Love of deity is part of morality because God is the creative intelligence and power responsible for the cosmos. A true moralist, as Jefferson says in a letter to John Adams (8 Apr. 1816), literally sees deity in the cosmos. "When the atheist descanted on the unceasing motion and circulation of matter through the animal, vegetable and mineral kingdoms, gifted with the power of reproduction, the theist, pointing 'to the heavens above, and to the earth beneath, and to the waters under the earth,' asked, if these did not proclaim a first cause possessing intelligence and power." Again to John Adams (11 Apr. 1823), he states, "When we take a view of the Universe, in it's parts general or particular, it is impossible for the human mind not to be percieve and feel a conviction of design, consummate skill, and indefinite power in every atom of it's composition." In both cases, to reiterate Chapter One, there is no argument from analogy; Jefferson, consistent with Destutt

---

[21]Michael Zuckert, "Thomas Jefferson and Natural Morality," in *Thomas Jefferson, the Classical World, and Early America*, ed. Peter S. Onuf and Nicholas P. Cole (Charlottesville: University of Virginia Press, 2011), 66.

de Tracy's epistemology[22] and Lord Kames's "intuitive perception,"[23] writes about the direct *perception* of deity. What we can know of deity through perception is exceptionally, unfathomably large design, skill, and power.

As Jefferson writes in his "Syllabus" (explored in detail in Chapter Three), "He [Jesus] pushed his scrutinies into the heat of man; erected his tribunal in the region of his thoughts, and purified the waters at the fountain head."[24] In consequence, morality is a matter of beneficence but also benevolence. Intention matters, as one can be behaviorally beneficent without being benevolent—that is, one can perform an action consistent with a kindly motive without being moved by kindness. Being morality abiding does not imply being moral, though being moral implies being morality abiding.

Yet neither the moral atheist nor the true moralist, it is critical to add, acts charitably toward others out of fear of punishment in an afterlife. Such is a proper inducement for a child, incapable of mature reasoning, but it is no proper inducement for an adult. To do the right thing for fear of retribution would be to act rightly for the wrong reason—that is, to act wrongly. A true religionist acts morally because he recognizes—that is, he senses—that it is the right and the natural way to act.

"I Am of a Sect by Myself"
Jefferson's Quakerism

In the preceding section, I refer to a letter written to John Adams (22 Aug. 1813). Here, Jefferson says that a true religionist ought to follow the Quakers—that is, follow his own sense of right and wrong, live without priests, and disdain all but the most uncomplex matters of religion, as Jesus's teachings are simple, to the heart, and accessible to all.

---

[22] A. L. C. Destutt de Tracy, *Éléments d'ideologie*, 5 vols. (Bruxelles: Courcier, 1827), 3.164. For more on Jefferson's cosmos, see M. Andrew Holowchak, "'I Cannot Reason Otherwise': Jefferson's Cosmos," in *Thomas Jefferson: Uncovering His Unique Philosophy and Vision* (Amherst, NY: Prometheus Books, 2014).

[23] Lord Kames, *Essays on the Principles of Morality and Natural Religion*, 2nd ed. (London: C. Hitch & L. Hawes, 1758), 265–75, 298–309.

[24] Thomas Jefferson, "Syllabus," in *Writings*, ed. Merrill D. Peterson (New York: Library of America, 1984), 1125.

There are numerous other references to Quakers or Quakerism in Jefferson's writings, and all, with one exception (with criticism forthcoming), are positive. Jefferson had enormous respect for the Quakers' simple way of living and plain and intemerate manner of worshipping.

Yet next to nothing, except passing remarks, has been written about Jefferson's views on Quakerism, and that is unfortunate, given Jefferson's respect for the Quakers. Nonetheless, following Jefferson's criticism of Quakers in a letter to Samuel Kercheval (19 Jan. 1810)—the one exception noted previously—Edwin Gaustad says, "Quakers bothered Jefferson because they seemed still tied to England, the land of their origin." He concludes, "In the world of dogma, Quakers passed Jefferson's test; in the world of politics, they failed."[25] In short, Jefferson lauded the Quakers' manner of religiosity but not their political ties to England.

The Quakers' movement began in seventeenth-century England as a rebellion against the abuses of England's Anglicanism. Some Quakers migrated to America to escape religious mistreatment, only to find religious persecution in America. Rhode Island, Pennsylvania, and New Jersey, however, were relatively tolerant of Quakerism, and for the most part, it thrived in those territories. Quakers practiced a sort of universal priesthood of all who believed—that is, each was his own priest and could communicate directly, as he saw fit, with God, often through the medium of Jesus. Quakers also derived inspiration through reading the Bible. They preached purity of living through emulation of the life of Jesus.

Jefferson, of course, was not a Quaker, because he refrained from any commitment to a sectarian religion, and though Quakerism lacked many of the entrapments of most sectarian religions, Jefferson still considered Quakerism a sectarian religion. "I am of a sect by myself, as far as I know," he tells Ezra Stiles (25 June 1819). Moreover, Jefferson was against partisanship in everything, even politics. "I am not a Federalist," he writes to Francis Hopkinson (13 Mar. 1789), "because I never submitted the whole system of my opinions to the creed of any party of men whatever in religion, in

---

[25] Gaustad, *Sworn on the Altar of God*, 200–201.

philosophy, in politics, or in anything else where I was capable of thinking for myself. Such an addiction is the last degradation of a free and moral agent." Should we follow the example of Christ, however, we would "all be of one sect, doers of good and eschewers of evil."

It is the politics of Christianity, as practiced in his day, to which Jefferson objects. His 1801 letter to Elbridge Gerry (19 Mar.) conveys his belief that religionists over the centuries "have added metaphysical scribble to the mild and simple principles of the Christian philosophy." It has been their job "to sophisticate it, ramify it, split it into hairs, and twist it's texts till they cover the divine morality of its author with mysteries, and require a priesthood to explain them." The way to combat the scribble of empleomaniacal religionists is to eliminate their influence from politics and political hierarchies. Each person must be his own priest. "the Quakers seem to have discovered this. they have no priests, therefore no schisms. they judge of the text by the dictates of common sense and common morality."

Jefferson is adamant that individuals should not be judged by the principles they embrace, but by their actions over the course of their lives. He tells William Canby (18 Sept. 1813) that each will be judged at the gates of heaven as a Quaker preacher—one who holds himself, not some creed, accountable for his actions, for actions over time are the surest proof of principles. "He who steadily observes those moral precepts in which all religions concur, will never be questioned at the gates of heaven, as to the dogmas in which they all differ." In other words, at the gates of heaven, each person is stripped of his sectarianism. He says the same in a letter to Miles King (26 Sept. 1814).

In a letter to Thomas Whittemore (5 June 1822), Jefferson exults the Quakers' lack of "formulas of creed." He states: "the religions of antiquity had no particular formulas of creed. those of the modern world none; except those of the religionists calling themselves Christians, and even among these, the Quakers have none. and hence alone the harmony[,] the quiet, the brotherly affections, the exemplary and unschismatising society of the Friends."

Weeks later, Jefferson extols the merits of Quakerism as he writes to Benjamin Waterhouse (26 June 1822). Unlike most other Christians who willingly "give up morals for mysteries, and Jesus for Plato," they craft no "formulas of creed and confessions of faith." He continues, "[A]greeing in the fundamental doctrines of the gospel, [Quakers] schismatize about no mysteries, and, keeping within the pale of common sense, suffer no speculative differences of opinion, any more than of feature, to impair the love of their brethren."

Quakers, for Jefferson, may be contrasted with Christian Platonizers, who have mythologized the Bible to suit their own empleomaniacal purposes. "The Christian priesthood, finding the doctrines of Christ leveled to every understanding, and too plain to need explanation, saw, in the mysticisms of Plato, materials with which they might build up an artificial system which might, from it's indistinctness, admit everlasting controversy, give employment for their order, and introduce it to profit, power and pre-eminence." For Jefferson, Quakers, in contrast, have demythologized and depoliticized Platonic Christianity. They sought to bring the teachings of Jesus back to their original simplicity, by requiring no creeds and no interpreters of biblical scripture. There is also no question of Jefferson's profound respect for their manner of living—agrarian and uncomplex.

Yet despite the numerous positives of their religion, as Jefferson saw it, Quakers also had their metaphysical religious disputes—for example, debates over religious understanding through the inner light versus reading the Bible, over the viability of the Trinity, and over the need for religious rituals like baptism and communion. And so, Quakerism was not wholly creed free.

Moreover, the Quakers' manner of living, though laudable on account of its simplicity, was too simplistic for Jefferson. For instance, the Quakers, who were chiefly agrarian, administered and received only the rudimentary elements of education—what Jefferson would have considered ward-school education—aimed to give them the basic tools of self-sufficient agrarian living so that each could carry out the Quakers' ethos by embracing community, spirituality, personal responsibility, and stewardship. There was no need of or place for an Isaac Newton to disclose the axial dynamical principles of the physical universe or a William Harvey to explain how blood circulates through the body. Thus, there was no need for the sort of higher education that would give rise to such persons. That, Jefferson certainly recognized, was also a large defect of Quakerism. The axial religious and ethical precepts Jefferson embraced included duties to God, and such duties were properly fulfilled only when humans used to their most complete capacity their God-given talents as scrutators of the cosmos that God created. It is likely that only through the fullest apprehension of the God-created cosmos do humans come closest to the most complete communion with God.

"The 'Tribunal' of 'Reason and Free Inquiry'"
Reason, Free Inquiry, and Religious Truths

In *Notes on Virginia* and in several other writings, Jefferson is clear that the free expression of reason is essential for the divulgence of religious truth.[26] "Reason and free enquiry are the only effectual agents against error," he states in Query XVII. "Give a loose to them, they will support the true religion, by bringing every false one to their tribunal, to the test of their investigation. They are the natural enemies of error, and of error only."[27] He offers two illustrations: "Had not the Roman government permitted free inquiry, christianity could never have been introduced. Had not free inquiry been indulged, at the æra of the reformation, the corruptions of christianity could not have been purged away. If it be restrained now, the present corruptions will be protected, and new ones encouraged." The sentiment here seems to be that there is a true sectarian religion, and reason can be used in its discovery.

In letter of advice to his nephew Peter Carr (10 Aug. 1787), Jefferson tells his nephew to begin inquiring thusly into religious matters: "Fix reason firmly in her seat, and call to her tribunal every fact, every opinion."

---

[26] See also Jefferson, "Notes on Locke and Shaftesbury"; TJ to Benjamin Waterhouse, 26 June 1822; and TJ to James Smith, 8 Dec. 1822.

[27] Jefferson, *Notes on the State of Virginia*, 159.

Here, Carr is tasked to weigh customary beliefs against his knowledge of the workings of nature. After guiding Carr through some particulars, Jefferson adds: "You must lay aside all prejudice on both sides & neither believe nor reject anything because any other persons, or description of persons have rejected or believed it. Your own reason is the only oracle given you by heaven, and you are answerable not for the rightness but uprightness of the decision." The sentiment here is that reason is the right tool, the only tool, for assessing religious claims.

In his 2017 essay "Diamonds from Dunghills," John Colman offers a précis of the ratiocinative program that Jefferson has in mind in such letters. Drawing from Jefferson's discussion of free inquiry and religion in Query XVII of Jefferson's *Notes on Virginia*, Colman writes that "free inquiry would contribute to the reform of religion by separating the 'diamonds' of primitive, or rational, Christianity from the 'dunghill' of revealed religion," with the result of forging an alliance between religion and free inquiry—religion being a subordinate partner in that alliance. "Bringing revealed Christianity before the 'tribunal' of 'reason and free inquiry' would restore primitive, rational Christianity, thereby securing religious liberty in fact, not just in theory."[28] Colman is correct to note that the process is one of restoration, though he fails to expound on why that is the case. He is, unfortunately, also silent concerning just how Jefferson saw that project. His title, however, inevasibly draws us to those letters in which Jefferson describes the stripping process he used—plucking diamonds from dunghills or dung heaps—in constructing his versions of the Bible in 1804 and 1820.

Robert Healey calls Jefferson, on account of the program advocated by Jefferson in the letter to Carr, a "dogmatic rationalist." Though he asks Carr to eschew bias, consider all alternatives, and bring reason forth as adjudicator, "Jefferson's presentation is slanted so that it is almost impossible not to come to his own conclusions. The apparent alternatives are so stated that there is only one possible choice for a sensible man. When Jefferson says,

---

[28] John Colman, "Diamonds from Dunghills: Jefferson's Materialism, Free Inquiry, and Religious Reform," *American Political Thought* 6 (2017): 344.

'You must lay aside prejudice on both sides,' he believes that prejudice is involved in one side only. Mystery, the irrational, the naturally impossible clearly cannot be accepted." And so, Jefferson's own "primitive Christianity" was free of those defects.[29]

Others also argue in a similar way. Eugene Sheridan states: "For Jefferson, human reason, not supernatural revelation or ecclesiastical authority, henceforth became the sole arbiter of religious truth. Thus, through rational investigation he came to believe in a supreme being who created the universe and continued to sustain it by means of fixed, mathematically precise natural laws."[30] Richard Samuelson, taking a Stoical/ Cartesian tack, says that truths for Jefferson were "clear and distinct." Quoting Jefferson that belief is "the assent of the mind to an intelligible proposition," Samuelson adds that "any truth that could not be discovered clearly and distinctly to the human mind via the empirical method was, by definition, not necessary to the good life."[31] Charles Sanford, drawing from Jefferson's *Notes on Religion* in 1776, states that the Savior, following Jefferson, chose to propagate religion by "it's influence on reason."[32] He also indicates that "[r]eason results in a stronger religion than faith and revelation."[33] Sanford includes a section titled "Religion Is Known by Reason" in his first chapter, which essentially sums up his view of Jefferson's religiosity. Edwin Gaustad quotes Jefferson in an 1822 letter on "the progress of reason in its advance towards rational Christianity."[34] Robert Healey maintains that "freedom of thought is a *sine qua non* for the development of true religion." He quotes Jefferson in *Notes on Virginia*: "Reason and free inquiry are the only effectual agents against error. Give a loose to them, they will

---

[29] Healey, *Jefferson on Religion in Public Education*, 175–76.

[30] Eugene Sheridan, Introduction to *Jefferson's Extracts from the Gospels*, ed. Dickinson W. Adams (Princeton: Princeton University Press, 1983), 7–8.

[31] Richard Samuelson, "Jefferson and Religion: Private Belief, Public Policy," in *The Cambridge Companion to Thomas Jefferson* (Cambridge: Cambridge University Press, 2009), 149.

[32] Charles B. Sanford, *The Religious Life of Thomas Jefferson* (Charlottesville: University Press of Virginia, 1984), 20.

[33] Sanford, *The Religious Life of Thomas Jefferson*, 8.

[34] Gaustad, *Sworn on the Altar of God*, 146.

support the true religion by bringing every false one to their tribunal, to the test of their investigation."[35]

Yet such passages and others are often misconstrued by scholars, who are frequently solely interested in Jefferson's take on religion and free inquiry. Wherein lies the misconstrual?

All such scholars neglect to say anything of the moral sense when assessing Jefferson's views on religious truths. Jefferson unambiguously states, in a large number of writings (e.g., TJ to Peter Carr, 10 Aug. 1785, and TJ to Thomas Law, 13 June 1814), that we come to grasp morally correct action by feeling or sensing, not by reason, and that is consistent with the moral-sense and moral-sentiment literature that he read and appropriated. He also states unambiguously (e.g., TJ to James Fishback, 27 Sept. 1809, and TJ to Thomas Law, 13 June 1814) that the truths of religion are just the truths of natural morality—love of and duties to God and love of and duties to others.[36] And so, if the "truths" of morality are morally sensed or felt, then so are the "truths" of religion. What, then, is the role of reason in seeking religious truth if each of us senses religious truths and morally correct action?

Jefferson's point in Query XVII of *Notes on Virginia* and in numerous letters concerning Christianity—consider especially his "Syllabus" as an enclosure in a letter to Dr. Benjamin Rush (21 Apr. 1803)—is that Christ's actions and teachings have been corrupted over the centuries by religious zealots, moved by empleomania—that is, political ambition. Much has been added to what Christ taught in an effort to becloud what is manifestly intemerate and simple. Jefferson's repeated appeal to reason in his many writings is not for the sake of direct disclosure of the truths of religion or morality, but for the sake of weeding out the countless fabrications

---

[35] Healey arguably misconstrues the logic in the wording. Jefferson does not assert that free inquiry—reason being understood as the vehicle of free inquiry, given his quote from Jefferson—is needed for true religion, but the converse. Jefferson argues that reason and free inquiry are sufficient for ascertaining the true religion. Healey, *Jefferson on Religion in Public Education*, 96.

[36] See M. Andrew Holowchak, "Duty to God and Duty to Man: Jefferson on Religion, Natural and Sectarian," *Sophia* 55, no. 2 (2016): 236–61.

or corruptions artificially conjoined to the teachings of Jesus, which because of each person's moral sense will be readily recognizable amid the feculence. In short, reason is a sufficient tool for deracinating religious falsehoods and fatuities—the metaphysical entrapments of religions—and what remains, what survives the deracination of reason, will be the core tenets of religion: duties to God and to man. Thus, the process, in keeping with Colman, really is one of restoration.

"A General Collection as I Think You Would Wish and Might in Time Find Convenient to Procure"
Jefferson's Lists of Books

There is also extratextual evidence that confirms Jefferson's take on the equivalency of morality and true religion via some lists of books that he provides in key letters and the catalog of books in his libraries.

I begin with an early letter to Robert Skipwith, who had married Jefferson's wife's half-sister probably sometime in July 1771.[37] Skipwith writes to Jefferson (17 July 1771) to ask for a catalog of books "suited to the capacity of a common reader who understands but little of the classicks and who has not leisure for any intricate or tedious study."[38] Here, Skipwith is looking for a list of books to read for enjoyment to pass the time, or at least to have for show. It is difficult to know whether Skipwith is being gravely serious or polite to a future member of the family.

Jefferson, of course, takes Skipwith's letter very seriously. He replies some two weeks later (3 Aug. 1771) and cannot stay within the confines of Skipwith's letter. "I sat down with a design of executing your request to form a catalogue of books to the amount of about 50 lib. sterl. But could by no means satisfy myself with any partial choice I could make." Jefferson settles on "a general collection as I think you would wish and might in time find convenient to procure." He offers a list of 148 books under the categories Fine Arts, Criticism of the Fine Arts, Politics and Trade, Religion,

---

[37] John B. Boles, *Jefferson: Architect of American Liberty* (New York: Basic Books, 2017), 41.
[38] Thomas Jefferson, *The Papers of Thomas Jefferson*, vol. 1: *1760–1776*, ed. Julian P. Boyd (Princeton: Princeton University Press, 1950), 74.

Law, Ancient History, Modern History, Natural Philosophy and Natural History, and Miscellaneous. The list does not answer Skipwith's request— which, again, is totally in line with Jefferson's personality—but provides what could well be a first library for a future scholar or a member of the Virginian gentry, who in Jefferson's eye needs to be well-read.

Jefferson places twelve authors and fifteen works under "Religion"; there is no category for morality. He lists the ancients Xenophon, Epictetus, Antoninus, Seneca, and Cicero, as well as the moderns Locke, Bolingbroke, Hume, Kames, Sterne, and Sherlock. Twelve of the works concern morality; three concern religious criticism. The selections, weighted heavily toward morality, suggest that religion is helpful only insofar as it offers moral instruction. To help students free themselves from the constraints of politicized Christianity, there is the study of works critical of canonical Christianity.

Next, in an extraordinarily extensive list to John Minor more than forty years later in 1814—which is an emended list in a letter to Bernard Moore (c. 1773)[39]—Jefferson contrasts "Ethics and Natural Religion" with "Sectarian Religion." The former lists works by Locke, Stewart, Enfield, Condorcet, Cicero, Seneca, Hutcheson, de Raymondis, and Charron. The latter lists the Bible (here, the Old Testament), the New Testament, and critical works of Middleton, Priestley, and Volney, as well as the sermons of the Revs. Sterne, Massillon, and Bourdaloue.

While included in Jefferson's category of Ethics and Natural Religion, the books of Dugald Stewart (*Philosophy of the Human Mind in Search after Truth*) and William Enfield (*The History of Philosophy*) are not straightforwardly ethical. There are two ancient authors listed, both Roman: Seneca was a Stoic. Cicero was an eclectic, who had marked Stoic leanings, as he repeatedly returned to Stoic readings in times of personal crisis. The books by Locke, Condorcet, Hutcheson, de Raymondis, and Charron are ethical works.

---

[39] Thomas Jefferson, *The Papers of Thomas Jefferson*, Retirement Series, vol. 7: *28 November 1813 to 30 September 1814*, ed. J. Jefferson Looney (Princeton: Princeton University Press, 2010), 625–31.

The books under Sectarian Religion are a salmagundi—a strange mixture indeed. There are first the Old and New Testaments. According to Jefferson, both—particularly the Old Testament—contain much nonsense and metaphysical baggage. As he writes in his "Syllabus" in an enclosure to an 1803 letter to Dr. Benjamin Rush (Apr. 21; see Chapter Three), according to Jefferson, the Jewish religion of the Old Testament contains little of merit other than its pronouncement that God is one. "Their ideas of him & of his attributes were degrading & injurious. Their Ethics were not only imperfect, but often irreconcilable with the sound dictates of reason & morality. . . . They needed reformation, therefore, in an eminent degree." Still, the Old and New Testaments are listed not only because they are historically significant religious works but also because they contain certain gems of wisdom—especially the New Testament.

Jefferson also includes Conyers Middleton's and Joseph Priestley's books, which are historical criticisms of the Bible. Condorcet's *Progrès de l'esprit humain* and le Comte de Volney's *Les Ruins* are each a sustained criticism of the politicized Christianity of Jefferson's day through a fictive narrative.

In addition, Jefferson recommends sermons from Rev. Laurence Sterne, a witty and avant-garde novelist and perhaps Jefferson's favorite writer; Rev. Jean Baptiste Massillon; and Rev. Louis Bourdaloue. These sermons contain material that Jefferson certainly found objectionable—as we will further explore in Chapter Three, Jefferson rejected the divinity of Christ and miracles[40]—yet he still lists them.[41] Why is this so? These sermonizers are especially morally engaging. Though not wholly free of the metaphysical entrapments of sectarian religions, they did manage, however, to cut through those entrapments and speak to the heart of each person. Consequently, the fact that Jefferson included sermons of

---

[40] Jefferson here follows the lead of Middleton, Bolingbroke, and perhaps even David Hume.

[41] For more on Jefferson's uptake of the moral content of sermonizers, see M. Andrew Holowchak, *Thomas Jefferson, Moralist* (Jefferson, NC: McFarland, 2017), 121–26.

Christian ministers with metaphysical content indicates forthrightly that he did not believe, as it were, in throwing out the baby with the bathwater.

In sum, these two lists, a decade apart, show that Jefferson considered religious instruction worthwhile inasmuch as it reinforced the principles of morality accessible through the moral sense. Offering a sharp distinction between natural religion and sectarian religion, the cataloging of his list of books to Minor is additional evidence that Jefferson considered as equivalents natural religion and ethics and viewed sectarian religion as a man-made institution, engendered in early history by men's political ambitions.

"I Cannot Live without Books"
Library Catalogs

More significant than Jefferson's lists of books in key letters are the catalogs of books from his various libraries. These catalogs offer invaluable clues about Jefferson's way of thinking regarding the various sciences of his day. Thus another means of uncovering what Jefferson thought about religion is through inspecting those catalogs of books.

It is generally accepted that Jefferson had four libraries. There was his library at Shadwell (1757–70), which contained some 40 books, at first, and as many as 400 at the time of the Shadwell fire (February 1, 1770), which destroyed the house and the library therein. Next, there was his first library at Monticello (1770–1815), his largest and main library, which began after the fire and contained some 6,700 books at its peak. That ended when Jefferson, having fallen deeply in debt, sold 6,487 books to Congress on January 30, 1815—as a consequence of the British having stormed Washington in 1814 and burning down the Capitol on August 24—to create the Library of Congress. Jefferson was given nearly $24,000 in the transaction, a handsome sum, yet one that did not reflect the true value of the books. Then, there was Jefferson's "retirement library" (1815–26), which comprised some 1,600 books and contained works more suited to a man of retirement. Finally, there was his library at Poplar Forest (1811–26), a second residence that functioned as a get-away resort for Jefferson.[42]

Such vast libraries would not have been serviceable without some system for organizing the books. Jefferson eventually settled on a method of cataloging his books by adopting Francis Bacon's tripartition of subjects into History (Memory), Philosophy (Reason), and the Fine Arts (Imagination)—each associated with one of the key three faculties of mind. By 1783, Jefferson had constructed a complete (or relatively so) catalog of his books, based on that tripartition (see Figure 2.1). Numbering 2,640 books at that time,[43] the catalog contained the following breakdown of subtopics under the general rubric of "Philosophy."[44] History and Fine Arts, unrelated to morality and religion, need not concern us here.

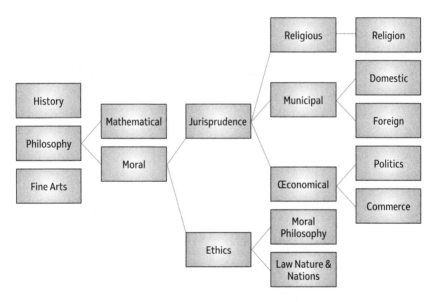

Figure 2.1. "Religion" and "Moral Philosophy" in Jefferson's 1783 catalog of books

---

[42]"Timeline of Jefferson's Life and His Libraries," Thomas Jefferson's Libraries, accessed December 14, 2013, http://tjlibraries.monticello.org/tjandreading/timeline.html.

[43]Thomas Jefferson, "1783 Catalogue of Books," *Thomas Jefferson Papers*, Massachusetts Historical Society, accessed June 25, 2020.

[44]This catalog is essentially the same as that of 1789, though the number of books was increased to some 5,000.

Under "Moral," we find "Jurisprudence" and "Ethics." Ethics comprises "Moral Philosophy" and "Law of Nature & Nations"; Jurisprudence comprises "Religious," "Municipal," and "Œconomical." Concerning the placement of Religion, Douglas L. Wilson writes insightfully, "Jefferson's unusual designation of religion as belonging to jurisprudence shows that he approached religion less as theology, for which he provided no category, and more as a sphere of institutionalized moral suasion."[45]

More can be said about this organization system. Religion's subsumption under Jurisprudence suggests that Jefferson here approaches Religion as a man-made or political institution, not a natural institution. Hence, by "Religion" he likely means here "Sectarian Religion," as he says in the letter to John Minor. The linkage of "Moral Philosophy" with "Law of Nature & Nations" suggests Moral Philosophy is a sort of natural religion.

Jefferson's retirement library catalog (see Figure 2.2) begins with the same three main Baconian categories—History, Philosophy, and Fine Arts—yet he subtilizes the groupings here in a less complex way. Under Philosophy (Reason), he lists "Mathematics" and "Ethical." Under Ethical, one finds "Morality," "Moral Supplements," and "Social Organization." "Ethics" is the sole subcategory of Morality; "Religion" and "Law" the sole subcategories of Moral Supplements. "Politics" falls under Social Organization.

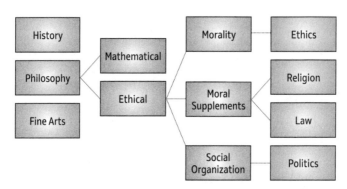

Figure 2.2. "Religion" and "Ethics" in Jefferson's retirement library

---

[45] Douglas L. Wilson, *Jefferson's Books* (Charlottesville: Thomas Jefferson Memorial Foundation, 1996), 43.

In the 1783 catalog, "Religion" comes under "Religious Jurisprudence." In the retirement library, it is linked again with "Law," under "Moral Supplements," and kept apart from "Ethics." Once again, the linking of Religion to Law suggests "Religion" likely means "Sectarian Religion."

In Jefferson's 1783 catalog, "Moral Philosophy" is both a higher category than "Ethics" and subsumable under it. In the retirement library, "Ethical Philosophy" is a higher category than "Morality," though "Ethics" is placed under "Morality." There is nothing in Jefferson's writings to suggest a distinction between "Ethics" and "Morality." The insouciant manner in which he uses the terms suggests in these catalogs, and elsewhere, that the two could be used interchangeably.

Here the following question redounds: Is the simplified scheme of the retirement library indicative of a maturation of Jefferson's thinking on categorization?[46]

One must be guarded and not make too much of that simplification. The retirement library was principally not for serious use—"I cannot live without books," said Jefferson to John Adams (10 June 1815), "but fewer will suffice where amusement, and not use, is the only future object"— but for enjoyment or moral motivation. And so the books he collected were weighed heavily toward history and morality, with a weighty dose of Greeks and Romans—Cicero, Tacitus, Epictetus, and even the much abhorred Plato.[47] As granddaughter Ellen Randolph Coolidge said, "I

---

[46] Wilson notes that the 1783 catalog was too complex to be serviceable, and thus he broke down his books as follows: (1) Ancient History; (2) Modern History; (3) Physics; (4) Natural History; (5) Technical Arts; (6) Ethics; (7) Jurisprudence; (8) Mathematics; (9) Gardening, Architecture, Sculpture, Painting, Music, and Poetry; (10) Oratory; (11) Criticism; and (12) Polygraphical. Wilson, *Jefferson's Books*, 43.

[47] In an 1814 letter to Adams (July 5), Jefferson writes of the arduous task of reading Plato's *Republic*. "Having more leisure there [at Poplar Forest] and here for reading, I amused myself with reading seriously Plato's republic. I am wrong however in calling it amusement, for it was the heaviest task-work I ever went through. . . . While wading thro' the whimsies, the puerilities, and unintelligible jargon of this work, I laid it down often to ask myself how it could have been that the world should have so long consented to give reputation to such nonsense as this?" For more on Jefferson's execration of Plato, see M. Andrew Holowchak, "Jefferson's Platonic Republicanism," *Polis* 31, no. 2 (2014): 369–86.

saw him more frequently with a volume of the classics in his hand than with any other book."[48] Under "Religion," about one-third of all books are related to the Bible—especially biblical criticism. That should not come as a surprise. From Jefferson's early days, when commonplacing the thoughts of Lord Bolingbroke on the latter's criticisms of the Bible, throughout his life, he retained a keen interest in biblical criticism.

In sum, Jefferson's recommended reading lists and library catalogs provide some additional insight into his notion of the equivalency of "Natural Religion" and "Morality" or "Ethics."

Concluding Thoughts

"There has been in almost all religions a melancholy Separation of religion from morality," writes Unitarian minister Richard Price to Jefferson (26 Oct. 1788)—a sentiment that could only have been dear to Jefferson. Here Price laments the deplorable state of religion in his day. The politics of religion and the empleomania of religionists have obfuscated the real meaning of religion. Clerics, wedded to empleomania over the centuries and not to morality, have sought to dress religion in metaphysical plasters in order to advance political ambition and gain political power. "I have never permitted myself to meditate a specified creed," says Jefferson to Thomas Whittemore (5 June 1822). "[T]hese formulas have been the bane & ruin of the Christian church, it's own fatal invention which, thro' so many ages, made of Christendom a slaughter house, and at this day divides it into Casts of inextinguishable hatred to one another."

Throughout his life, Jefferson sought to divest power-lusting religious clerics of that power by several means, including the introduction of several bills with the aim of religious reform; the changes he imposed on the College of William & Mary; and even through the construction of his own adaption of the Bible, divest of what he considered to be supernatural and nonsensical, which he at times wished to see published, if only under a pseudonym. However, unlike Jesus, Jefferson did not propose his reforms

---

[48] Henry S. Randall, *The Life of Thomas Jefferson* (New York: Derby & Jackson, 1858), vol. 3, 346.

subtly through parabolic words, but unsubtly through his deeds over the course of his lifetime.

Jefferson was no friend to sectarian religion. Late in his life, he writes the following to John Adams (5 May 1817):

> If by religion we are to understand sectarian dogmas, in which no two of them agree, then your exclamation on them is just, 'that this would be the best of all possible worlds, if there were no religion in it.' But if the moral precepts, innate in man, and made a part of his physical constitution, as necessary for a social being, if the sublime doctrines of philanthropism and deism taught us by Jesus of Nazareth, in which all agree, constitute true religion, then, without it, this would be, as you say, 'something not fit to be named' even, indeed, a hell.

In a lengthy conversation with a bookseller at Monticello, when the conversation turned to religion and the energetic researches of American clergy of various denominations, Jefferson reputedly and succinctly replied, "The Clergy were all _____"—the blank being filled by Jefferson with a word, certainly derogatory, in a language unrecognizable to the seller.[49]

Jefferson's involvement in religious worship, his occasional contributions to several churches, and his graciousness and friendliness toward many religious clerics did not stem from his appreciation of sectarian religions, but merely his acknowledgment that religious services could have profound moral content and that many religious clerics were upstanding, moral men, in spite of their nugatory metaphysical beliefs.

Jefferson's description of the congregations in the village of Charlottesville provides what, for him, is an exemplary illustration of worship without fanaticism: "In our village of Charlottesville, there is a good degree of religion, with a small spice only of fanaticism," he tells Unitarian Dr. Thomas Cooper (2 Nov. 1822). In the village, there were four sects that met at the courthouse for worship, and each had the run of the building

---

[49] Samuel Whitcomb Jr., "A Book Peddler at Monticello," *Visitors to Monticello*, ed. Merrill D. Peterson (Charlottesville: University Press of Virginia, 1993), 95.

for one Sunday of every month. "Here, Episcopalian and Presbyterian, Methodist and Baptist, meet together, join in hymning their Maker, listen with attention and devotion to each others' preachers, and all mix in society with perfect harmony."

Though he often declaimed vigorously against Trinitarianism, for Jefferson, what mattered was not so much whether God was one or three, but rather the sort of persons that a religion churned out. For him, one was always to judge a tree by its fruit.

CHAPTER THREE

"After the Fogs Shall Be Dispelled"

Jefferson and the Bible

When Thomas Jefferson assumed the presidency, there was wide-spread fear, cultivated mostly by High Federalists and their fish, who did what they could to keep Jefferson from the nation's highest office. Like Socrates—put on trial for his life for avowedly believing in no gods and in gods other than the traditional Greek gods, for making weak arguments seem strong (i.e., being a Sophist), and for examining things in the sky and in the earth (i.e., being a *physiologos*, or a philosopher of nature)[1]—Jefferson was, as it were, put on trial for being an atheist, for having unconventional and dangerous religious views, and because of his enthusiastic interest in science, for being a person most ill-suited for political office.

Here I will offer a few illustrations of the acrimony surrounding Jefferson's potential presidency. Yale president Timothy Dwight fulminated against Jefferson and his Jeffersonians—"the illuminati, the philosophers, the atheists, and the deists." He declaimed in a loud manner, "We may see the Bible cast into a bonfire, the vessels of the sacramental supper borne by an ass in public procession, and our children, either wheedled or terrified,

---

[1] Plato, *Five Dialogues: Euthyphro, Apology, Crito, Meno, and Phaedo*, trans. G. M. A. Grube (Indianapolis: Hackett, 2002), *Ap.* 17b–c, *Euthyp.* 3b, and *Cr.* 18b–c and 23d.

uniting in chanting mockeries against God."[2] Rev. John M. Mason, a friend of Alexander Hamilton, published "The Voice of Warning to Christians on the Ensuing Election" in 1800. He condemned Jefferson and "[h]is solicitude for wresting the Bible from the hands of their children—his notoriously unchristian character—his disregard of all the evidences of divine worship—his utter and open contempt of the Lord's day." He adds that Jefferson was a person "who writes against the truths of God's word; who makes not even a profession of Christianity; who is without Sabbaths; without a sanctuary; without so much as a decent external respect for the faith and worship of Christians."[3] Lawyer Theodore Dwight posited, "Murder, robbery, rape, adultery, and incest will be openly taught and practiced, the air will be rent with the cries of distress, the soil will be soaked with blood, the nation black with crimes."[4] In New York, Rev. William Linn stated flatly, "The election of any man avowing the principles of Mr. Jefferson would . . . destroy religion, introduce immorality, and loosen all the bonds of society." He added, "The voice of the nation in calling a deist to the first office must be construed into no less than a rebellion against God."[5] Finally, an editor of *Gazette of the United States* (10 Sept. 1800), a prominent Federalist paper, wrote, "To be asked by every American, laying his hand on his heart, as: 'Shall I continue in allegiance to God—and a Religious President; Or impiously declare for Jefferson—and No God!!!'"[6]

Jefferson, of course, was still elected president despite the controversy, and he assumed the nation's highest office from 1801 to 1809. Once elected, he astonished both Republicans and Federalists by asking members of both parties to lick their wounds and come together as members of a people, united under the principles of liberty, free inquiry, and toleration

[2] Gordon S. Wood, *Empire of Liberty: A History of the Early Republic, 1789–1815* (Cambridge: Oxford University Press, 2009), 586.

[3] Henry Stephens Randall, *The Life of Thomas Jefferson* (Philadelphia: J.B. Lippincott & Co., 1781), 568.

[4] Wood, *Empire of Liberty*, 586.

[5] Noble E. Cunningham Jr., *In Pursuit of Reason: The Life of Thomas Jefferson* (Baton Rouge: Louisiana State University Press, 1987), 225.

[6] Edward J. Larson, *A Magnificent Catastrophe: The Tumultuous Election of 1800* (New York: Simon & Schuster, 2008), 173.

of diversity. "Let us reflect that, having banished from our land that religious intolerance under which mankind so long bled and suffered, we have yet gained little if we countenance a political intolerance as despotic, as wicked, and capable of as bitter and bloody persecutions." He added: "Every difference of opinion is not a difference of principle. . . . We are all Republicans, we are all Federalists."[7]

Moreover, once elected, Jefferson did not burn the citizens' Bibles, but as previously noted, he did begin to construct his own version of the Bible by picking out what he took to be the actual teachings of Jesus and leaving behind excrescences; he completed that task in 1804. Dissatisfied with the result, he again undertook an expanded version of the project in 1819—expanded because he included text illustrative of the life of Jesus—and this was completed in 1820.

Why did Jefferson, a man who consistently preached that religion was a personal affair, construct his own version of the Bible? Given his lifelong asseverations that each person's religiosity is between him and his God, the answer could only be that he sought personal motivation or edification.

But, in this chapter, I offer a different answer. I advance what I admit is a highly contentious thesis—that Jefferson's bible was not constructed merely for personal edification. Given the significance of the Bible to many across the globe in his day and given the importance that Jesus came to have in Jefferson's thinking on morality, Jefferson aimed to do for religion what John Baxter did for history. As John Baxter republicanized David Hume's *History of England*—thought to be insidiously Tory by Jefferson and especially dangerous because of Hume's mesmeric mastery of composition—Jefferson aimed to deterge the Bible. Not finding much worth salvaging in the Old Testament except the commitment to monotheism, his interest was only in the four Gospels—"mutilated, misstated, & often unintelligible"[8]—as he

---

[7] Thomas Jefferson, "First Inaugural Address," in *Thomas Jefferson: Writings*, ed. Merrill D. Peterson (New York: Library of America, 1984), 493.

[8] Thomas Jefferson, "Syllabus," in *Thomas Jefferson: Writings*, ed. Merrill D. Peterson (New York: Library of America, 1984), 1124.

wished to have a proper account of the genuine teachings of Jesus and a true story of his life.

What was Jefferson's motivation for reconstructing the New Testament? In his study of the life and teachings of Jesus, Jefferson came to consider Jesus to be the model citizen, the cynosure, of a Jeffersonian republic, insofar as the universal benevolence he preached was the proper religious and moral grounding needed for a Jeffersonian republic—a government truly by and of the people. Yet that assessment was based on a Jeffersonian reading of the four Gospels in which, inter alia, miracles were disallowed, Jesus's divinity was disavowed, and Jesus did not rise from his grave. He proposed that these elements were a corruption of the Gospels by "schismatising followers" for political purposes. The real Jesus, a man of matchless benevolence and wisdom, could only be seen—"the world will see, after the fogs shall be dispelled . . . the immortal merit of this first of human Sages"[9]—if the corruptions were removed. Thus, and in spite of some statements to the contrary, Jefferson did consider publishing his adaption of the Bible, if only under an assumed name.

"Inspiration Is Become a Mystery"
The Enduring Influence of Lord Bolingbroke

As noted previously, Jefferson was a significant religious reformist, whose actions could be likened in some respects to those of Jesus. One could say that, in time, Jefferson came to morally admire Christ more than any other individual. Jesus universalized morality by challenging customarily held religious beliefs and practices, based on derogatory notions of God and religious segregation. Jesus corrected the Jews' deism by providing a more just notion of his attributes and governance; he championed universal philanthropy, based on benevolence; and he made intention a part of morality. He achieved these goals by the use of parables, designed to make a lasting impression by their often difficult-to-discern messages.

---

[9] TJ to Francis Adrian Van der Kemp, 25 Apr. 1816.

Perhaps Jefferson saw himself as doing something similar. Though lacking the profound verbal skills of the parabolist Christ, he acted through his pen. He put forth several bills—such as the Bill for the More General Diffusion of Knowledge and Bill for Religious Freedom—with the aim of political reforms to enhance human liberty through regard for the personhood of all citizens. He repealed primogeniture and entails, wrote a declaration that was founded on a vision of the equality and freedom of all people, and devoted some forty years of his life to public service at expense of his personal well-being, which includes his work on the University of Virginia. Religious reform for Jefferson was axial, as Jeffersonian republicanism was founded on a future-looking moral vision of a global community of nations, each with amicable relations with every other.

Though Jefferson consistently maintained that government ought not to align itself to the interest of any particular sectarian religion, he did not believe that secular governing was godless governing. The partnership of republican governing and science, which was essential to Jeffersonian republicanism, was essentially religious. Why is that? Jefferson believed that the study of and advancements in particular sciences equated to the study of and greater apprehension of the mind of deity. Consider, for instance, Newton's law of universal gravitation and his three laws of motion. They were laws that God implanted in the cosmos, and disclosure and apprehension of those principles provided a glimpse into the mind of God. Moreover, working to improve the lives of individuals via regard for human rights—life, liberty, and pursuit of happiness, especially— was a matter of advancing God's progressive cosmic plan,[10] with strong Federalism seen as a hinderance of this goal.

Jefferson, we now know, composed two bibles: *The Philosophy of Jesus* (*PJ*, 1804) and *The Life and Morals of Jesus of Nazareth* (*LMJ*, 1820). Of those, only the latter survives, though a relatively precise reconstruction of

---

[10] For more, see M. Andrew Holowchak, Introduction to *Jefferson's Political Philosophy and the Metaphysics of Utopia* (London: Brill, 2017).

the former has been prepared by Dickinson Adams.[11] Moreover, it is generally assumed, especially since no one knew about the existence of *LMJ* until Jefferson had passed—"[he] kept its existence a secret from everyone but Frederick A. Mayo, who bound it"[12]—that *LMJ* and its progenitor were constructed for personal enjoyment. Jefferson, with his deterged version of the four Gospels, could read of Jesus and his teachings without having to sift through mounds of feculent material to get at the "diamonds" contained therein. That much is true, but Jefferson always had in the back of his mind, and sometimes at the front it of it, the publication of the books— especially the *LMJ*, since it was a more polished and complete version of the former. He considered Jesus the model Jeffersonian republican and needed an account of Jesus and his teachings that reflected this sentiment. If this is indeed the case, here Jefferson had a political motivation for his adaptions, though of a nonharmful sort, since he was morally motivated. He considered Jeffersonian republicanism to be the political embodiment of Jesus's true teachings.

There is a general scholarly consensus that Jefferson's interest in Jesus changed over time. There is what I call Jefferson's *literary-criticism phase* of his younger days and a *naturalized-religion phase* of his later years.[13]

In his literary-criticism phase, Jefferson's interest in the Bible is critical—biblical criticism being a skill he might have learned from his early education with Rev. James Maury.[14] For Jefferson, the Bible is a significant

---

[11] Adams worked from the two Bibles Jefferson used to reconstruct his booklet. One was a 1791 version of the King James Bible (Dublin: George Grierson); the other was a 1799 version of the King James Bible (Dublin: Grierson). He also had in his possession "dual copies of the title page and the list of the Gospel verses Jefferson included." Dickinson W. Adams, "The Reconstruction of 'The Philosophy of Jesus,'" in *Jefferson's Extracts from the Gospels,* ed. Dickinson W. Adams (Princeton: Princeton University Press, 1983), 45–46.

[12] Dickinson W. Adams, "'The Life and Morals of Jesus': A History of the Text," in *Jefferson's Extracts from the Gospels,* ed. Dickinson W. Adams (Princeton: Princeton University Press, 1983), 125.

[13] Following my account in *Thomas Jefferson's Bible, With Introduction and Critical Commentary* (Berlin: DeGruyter, 2018), 9–12.

[14] See Thomas E. Buckley, S.J., "Placing Thomas Jefferson and Religion in Context, Then and Now," in *Seeing Jefferson Anew: In His Time and Ours* (Charlottesville: University of Virginia Press), 132–33.

work of literature that impacted the lives of millions, in spite of numerous hyperboles and absurdities. It is as good a book as any for honing one's critical skills and perhaps even the ideal book for a budding scholar.

Jefferson begins censoriously and skeptically early in life—critically preoccupied with the merits of the Bible qua historical book and qua book of moral instruction. Evidence for that exists in his *Literary Commonplace Book*,[15] where Jefferson copies or paraphrases fifty-four passages from Lord Bolingbroke's *Philosophical Works* (§§4–34 and §§36–58), in which Bolingbroke is critical of the Bible. Here it is beneficial to examine thoroughly Bolingbroke's religious views, given that Jefferson was a committed Bolingbrokean throughout his life.

In *Philosophical Works*, Bolingbroke attempts to discredit all such happenings that contravene the laws of nature and belie common experience or common sense. First, there is Bolingbroke's assault on miracles. "The missionary of supernatural religion appeals to the testimony of men he never knew, and of whom the infidel he labors to convert never heard, for the truth of those extraordinary event which prove the revelation he preaches." In contrast, "the missionary of natural religion can appeal at all times, and every where, to present and immediate evidence, to the testimony of sense and intellect" (§26). Miracles, commonplaces Jefferson, are inconsistent with divine perfection. The powers of God are such that what deity has created at one time is in no need of repair at another (§49).

Bolingbroke next rejects the immateriality of the soul or mind (§§8–11). He begins with the inscrutable problem of how mind, deemed immaterial, can act on body, material, and the converse. As bodies are characterized by solidity and extension, Bolingbroke asks just what the essential properties of immatter or spirit are. Immatter seems recognizable only by "what it is not"—that is, it has no discernible properties and so it is a substance *hors ligne*, bizarre. Finally, Bolingbroke asserts, "It is nonsense, and something worse than nonsense, to assert . . . that god cannot give the faculty of thinking, a faculty in the principle of it entirely unknown to us,

---

[15] Thomas Jefferson, *Jefferson's Literary Commonplace Book*, ed. Douglas L. Wilson (Princeton: Princeton University Press, 1989).

to systems of matter whose essential properties are solidity, extension &c. not incogitativity."

Bolingbroke challenges the notion that God made humans in his image and likeness. "The monotheist, who beleives [sic] that there is but one god, and ascribes to this god, whom he should conceive as an all-perfect being, the very worst of human imperfections, is most certainly ignorant of the true god, & as opposite to true theism as the atheist: nay he is more injuriously so" (§17). Along similar lines, Bolingbroke states that it is absurd to think, because "man is the principal inhabitant of this planet," that "this plane[t] alone, was made for the sake of him." He adds: "the ass would be scorched in Venus or Mercury, and be frozen in Jupiter and Saturn. Will it follow that this temperat[e] planet was made for him to bray and to eat thistles in it[?]" (§46).

Bolingbroke also dismisses the notion of divine retribution through reward and punishment in an afterlife:

[T]he miserable state of wicked men in hell is an exercise of justice delayed, but exercises so severely at last, that it would [e]xceed vastly all the necessary degrees of terror, if any of these creatures remained after it in an undetermined condition wherein terror might have it's effect.—justice requires that punishments, and we must say the same of rewards, the two sanctions of all laws, be measured [o]ut in various degrees and manners, according to the various [c]ircumstances of particular cases, and in a due proportion to them. (§52)

He adds that even if the immortality of the soul could be proven, it would not follow that "there should be a state of rewards and punishments" (§54). The implication is that eternal punishment is not only unjust but also incongruent with the notion of the goodness and wisdom of deity. The problem concerns infinity and retribution. There is no conceivable act so execrable—not even the annihilation of all forms of life on the planet—that it merits eternal punition. There is no conceivable act so laudable that it merits eternal reward. Rewards and punishments must fit the deeds of humans.

Bolingbroke rejects Trinitarianism as inconceivable and impossible. The ground for Trinitarianism (§20), Bolingbroke asserts, was "better prepared by philosophy, by that of Plato particularly, and by the polytheistic notions of divine natures, some in the godhead, and some out of it." With the rejection of Trinitarianism, there is no room for Christ's divinity.

Bolingbroke also assails against divine intervention through divine inspiration. "Inspiration is become a mystery . . . that is an inexplicable action of the divine on the human mind." He continues, "[W]e must not assume for truth, what can be proved neither a priori, not a posteriori." That includes the notion of any mystery, divine inspiration included. Later (§27), Bolingbroke says, "can any man be said to apprehend a proposition which contains a mystery, that is something unintelligible; or any thing more than the sound of words? will not the argument against beleiving become still stronger, if a proposition is repugnant to any principles of truth, which we have before admitted on evident demonstration?" Here it is a belief in divine revelation, which rails against reason, that is problematic (§22).

There is then the notion of God sending Christ to form a new covenant with humans. Bolingbroke claims that Jesus did not adequately effect that covenant. Jesus "executed his commission imperfectly," as "he left them at the same time without sufficient information concerning that faith in him, and that obedience to his law," which were needed for redemption. If so, then "how many new covenants might there not be? how often, I say it with horror, might not god change his mind?" Divine confusion or indecisiveness is inconsistent with divine perfection (§30). Later, Bolingbroke adds that if redemption is "the main fundamental article of the christian faith," then that faith is absurd, for the fall of man is "absolutely irreconcileable to every idea we can frame of wisdom, justice, and goodness, to say nothing of the dignity of the supreme being" (§42).

Next, Bolingbroke finds the idea of God sacrificing Christ for the sins of man fatuous. He asks us to imagine a great prince who governs "a wicked and rebellious people." In considering whether to pardon or punish them, "he orders his only and beloved son to be put to death to expiate their sins, and to satisfy his royal vengeance." What sort of satisfaction could that bring the prince? (§44). The notion of a divine sacrifice of God's son in expiation for the sins of humankind is impossible for Bolingbroke—a method of expiation that is unrelated to the crime.

Those commonplaced passages, which seem to have occupied much of Jefferson's cogitations on the Bible in his young life, almost certainly reflect Jefferson's early views on Christianity. As a young man, Jefferson examines the Bible merely or mostly as a text that amply allows for the exercise of his critical faculties. Following Bolingbroke and embracing a Bolingbrokean conception of deity and a skeptical approach to religious texts—a stance that he never fully abandoned—Jefferson's critical investigation here focuses on what he considers to be false or absurd, and there seems to be little regard for what, if anything, is salvageable from the Bible.[16] According to one scholar, "Bolingbroke, applying his own form of methodological doubt to religion, provided Jefferson with ample precedent for questioning most of the basic doctrines of Christian theology and most of the basic assumptions about Christian history." From his twenties to his forties, "Jefferson found answers more in politics than in religion."[17]

Jefferson and Jesus
"The Most Remarkable of Antient Philosophers"

Jefferson's views of the Bible and Christ would change drastically as he aged. Early in his forties, Jefferson begins a volte-face concerning the merits of the Bible, specifically the New Testament. Eugene Robert Healey and Eugene Sheridan call this a "religious crisis," which, for both, occurred early in the 1760s. However, there is no need to assume that some form of

---

[16] See Robert Healey, *Jefferson on Religion and Public Education* (New Haven, CT: Yale University Press, 1962), 18, and Eugene R. Sheridan, Introduction to *Jefferson's Extracts from the Gospels*, by Thomas Jefferson, ed. Dickinson W. Adams (Princeton: Princeton University Press, 1983), 5–7.

[17] E. S. Gaustad, "Religion," in *Thomas Jefferson: A Reference Biography*, ed. Merrill D. Peterson (New York: Charles Scribner's Sons: 1986), 278–79.

crisis was behind Jefferson's shift, and it is likely that this change occurred gradually.[18] Here, Jefferson begins his naturalized-religion phase, which would last until the end of his life. Jesus becomes, for Jefferson, more than a curious historical religious figure. Influenced by men such as Richard Price, Adam Weishaupt, and especially Joseph Priestley, Jefferson begins to see Christ not only as a great moralizer but as a great man—the world's foremost moralist.

In 1786, Jefferson travels to London and meets Richard Price, maverick Unitarian sermonizer, mathematician, and moralist. The two certainly discuss religious affairs, and they begin a polite epistolary exchange on political matters, which shortly turned to religion. Jefferson writes the following to Price (12 July 1789): "Is there any thing good on the subject of the Socinian doctrine, levelled to a mind not habituated to abstract reasoning? I would thank you to recommend such a work to me. Or have you written any thing of that kind?" Enclosing a work of Dr. Nathaniel Lardner ("Two Schemes of a Trinity Considered, and the Divine Unity Asserted"), some letters of Joseph Priestley, and other writings in his reply, Price writes the following on August 3, 1789:

> In consequence of your desire that I would convey to you some tracts on the Socinian doctrine, I desire your acceptance of the volume of Sermons and the pamphlets that accompany this letter. The first part of Dr. Priestley's letters I cannot immediately get; but it shall be sent to you by the first opportunity. The pamphlet entitled [*sic*] *Two Schemes of a Trinity* &c. is reckoned by the Socinians one of the best of all the publications in favour of their doctrine. You will see that Dr. Priestley and I differ much, but we do it with perfect respect for one another. He is a materialist and fatalist and we published some years ago a correspondence on these Subjects.

---

[18] Eugene R. Sheridan, *Jefferson and Religion* (Charlottesville: Thomas Jefferson Foundation, 1998), 15.

Yet it is the Unitarian minister and scientist Joseph Priestley who would make the largest impression on Jefferson. Priestley published two significant books in the 1780s—*An History of the Corruptions of Christianity* (1782) and *An History of Early Opinions concerning Jesus Christ Compiled from Original Writers, Proving That the Christian Church Was at First Unitarian* (1786)—and Jefferson owned and read both. Priestley believed that Jesus was mortal, not divine, but God gave him certain superhuman powers to perform miracles and resurrect from the grave after his death in order to spread the Father's message. However, Priestley rejected the Trinity, atonement, and original sin. His works, especially the former, which Jefferson recommends to several correspondents in recommended reading lists,[19] had a lasting influence on Jefferson. We can presume that Jefferson appropriated much of what Priestley wrote concerning the corruptions of the Bible.

In a letter to Bishop James Madison (31 Jan. 1800), cousin to the politician and future president of the same name, Jefferson expresses a keen interest in Jesus as a philosopher. He writes about the beliefs of German philosopher and founder of Illuminism Adam Weishaupt.

> Wishaupt [*sic*] . . . is among those (as you know the excellent
> Price and Priestly also are) who believe in the indefinite perfect-
> ibility of man. he thinks he may in time be rendered so perfect
> that he will be able to govern himself in every circumstance so
> as to injure none, to do all the good he can, to leave govern-
> ment no occasion to exercise their powers over him, & of course
> to render political government useless. . . . Wishaupt believes
> that to promote this perfection of the human character was
> the object of Jesus Christ. that his intention was simply to rein-
> state natural religion, & by diffusing the light of his morality, to
> teach us to govern ourselves. his precepts are the love of god &
> love of our neighbor. and by teaching innocence of conduct, he

---

[19] For example, TJ to Joseph C. Cabell, Sept. 1800; TJ to Richard Mentor Johnson, 10 Mar. 1808; TJ to unknown, ca. 4 Oct. 1809; and TJ to Gen. John Minor, 30 Aug. 1814.

expected to place men in their natural state of liberty & equality. he says, no one ever laid a surer foundation for liberty than our grand master, Jesus of Nazareth.

This letter, which is often overlooked, sheds light on Jefferson's thoughts concerning naturalized religion. Like Weishaupt and Enlightenment thinkers like Condorcet, Rush, and Mercier, Jefferson believed in the indefinite perfectibility of humans, both intellectually and morally. Like Weishaupt, Jefferson believed that Jesus was essentially a religious and moral reformist, whose intention was to promote human perfection by reinstating natural religion: liberty and equality through the love of God and love of others. As president, he expresses those sentiments in a letter to Priestley more than a year later (21 Mar. 1801): "The Christian religion, when divested of the rags in which they have enveloped it, and brought to the original purity and simplicity of its benevolent institutor, is a religion of all others most friendly to liberty, science, and the freest expansion of the human mind."

For Jefferson, the teachings of Jesus, if cleansed of their corruptions and fully adopted, would prove to be a naturalized religion that would lay the surest foundation for liberty in America by ensuring the country's moral stability.[20] Had Jesus's teachings never been sullied, he says to Unitarian Thomas Wittemore (5 June 1822), "the whole civilized world would at this day have formed but a single sect."

Numerous other religionists and Enlightenment thinkers also sought a naturalized religion, purged of the corruptions of the Christianity of Jefferson's day, to be a religion of liberty and equality. Consider, for example, Dr. Benjamin Rush, who writes in a letter to Jefferson (22 Aug. 1800): "I have always considered Christianity as the strong ground of Republicanism. Its Spirit is opposed, not only to the Splendor, but even to the very forms of monarchy, and many of its Precepts have for their Objects, republican liberty & equality, as well as simplicity, integrity Oconomy in government. It is only necessary for Republicanism to ally itself to the

---

[20] A point made by Sheridan about Jefferson's investment in Jesus's teachings. Sheridan, Introduction to *Extracts from the Gospels*, 19.

Christian Religion, to overturn all the corrupted political and religious institutions of the World."[21] Rush, *pace* Jefferson, was not looking to reform Christianity—it was perfect as a religion in every respect—but merely to align it to republicanism.

In 1803, Jefferson sent Rush a singular enclosure in a letter. Previously, around 1798 or 1799,[22] Jefferson promised to inform Rush concerning his own religious beliefs. On April 21, he fulfills that promise. The enclosure is Jefferson's "Syllabus of an Estimate of the Merit of the Doctrines of Jesus, Compared with Those of Others" (hereafter, "Syllabus")—a précis that aims to flesh out and compare the moralities of certain ancient philosophers, of the Jews, and of Jesus.

The motivation for this ambitious project was Priestley's *Socrates and Jesus Compared* (1803)—a short and scholarly unimpressive book when contrasted with Priestley's other religious writings. Yet the book overwhelmed Jefferson—but not because of the quality of the scholarship.[23]

Jefferson writes to Priestley (9 Apr. 1803) about the pleasure he experienced upon receiving and reading the booklet. Jefferson writes of his desire to see Priestley take up the subject "on a more extensive scale." He recalls his pledge to Rush in 1798 or 1799 to sketch out his "view of the Christian system." Since that pledge, Jefferson has been entertaining a sketch of a book, comparing "a general view of the moral doctrines of the most remarkable of the antient philosophers," "a view of the deism and ethics of the Jews," and "a view of the life, character, doctrines of Jesus." The project would aim to show the deficiencies of the Jewish system and the superiority of Jesus's views compared with those of the greatest of the ancient moralists. Jefferson divulges that idea in this letter to Priestley, noting: "This is the

---

[21] Writes Isaac Kramnick of Tocqueville: "The gradual unfurling of equality in social conditions is [for Tocqueville] . . . a providential fact which reflects its principal characteristics; it is universal, it is lasting and it constantly eludes human interference; its development is served equally by every event and every human being." Isaac Kramnick, Introduction to *Democracy in America*, by Alexis de Tocqueville, trans. Gerald E. Bevan (New York: Penguin Books, 2003), 15.

[22] TJ to Joseph Priestley, 9 Apr. 1803.

[23] A point noticed too by Wills. Garry Wills, "Jefferson's Jesus," *The New York Review of Books*, accessed June 12, 2017, www.nybooks.com/articles/1983/11/24/jeffersons-jesus/.

outline; but I have not the time, still less the information which the subject needs. It will therefore rest with me in contemplation only."[24]

In his letter to Rush on April 21 of the same year, Jefferson states that the "Syllabus" was intended as an outline of a book to be completed by "some one of more leisure and information for the task, than myself." He is, after all, president of the United States at the time, with considerably more pressing issues to consider.

The "Syllabus" tells us much about the development of Jefferson's thinking about Christ and natural religion—about how his mind-set shifted on the matter. It also tells us much about Jefferson's moral views—about the relative influences of the Old Testament, the New Testament, and the ancient moralists on the development of his thinking.

Jefferson begins with "the moral principles inculcated by the most esteemed of the sects of ancient philosophy," and he limns Pythagoras, Epicurus, Epictetus, Socrates, Cicero, Seneca, and Antoninus. Those philosophers give us precepts for self-governance—"the government of those passions which, unrestrained, would disturb our tranquillity of mind"—yet they are defective in our other-regarding duties. "They embraced, indeed, the circles of kindred & friends, and inculcated patriotism or the love of our country in the aggregate, as a primary obligation: toward our neighbors & countrymen they taught justice, but scarcely viewed them as within the circle of benevolence. Still less have they inculcated peace, charity & love to our fellow men, or embraced with benevolence the whole family of mankind." The ancients, it seems, had much that is worthwhile to say concerning the virtues related to our behavior toward others, but they had no notion of beneficence, untainted from the aim of personal gain—that is, equanimity.

Jefferson then turns to the system of Jewish morality, which he covers in a brachylogous manner. He writes:

---

[24] Sheridan maintains that Priestley's book prompted Jefferson to consider his project in the "Syllabus." He writes, "Jefferson was so impressed by Priestley's use of the comparative method in *Socrates and Jesus* that he decided it would also be an excellent way for him to present his own unorthodox religious views." Sheridan, *Jefferson and Religion*, 32–34.

1. Their system was Deism; that is, the belief of one only God. But their ideas of him & of his attributes were degrading & injurious.
2. Their Ethics were not only imperfect, but often irreconcilable with the sound dictates of reason & morality, as they respect intercourse with those around us; & repulsive & anti-social, as respecting other nations.[25] They needed reformation, therefore, in an eminent degree."[26]

Without question, Jefferson thought little of the Old Testament.

Last, Jefferson turns to Jesus, about whom he has much to say. Jefferson begins, "In this state of things among the Jews Jesus appeared." The sentiment seems sufficiently innocent, but its significance ought not be neglected. Here, Jefferson wishes to situate Jesus. Jesus was a Jew. Born into Jewish culture, he was educated in Jewish morality. And so, though his views are in some sense a radical departure from Jewish morality, they are in another sense an extension and correction of them.

Jesus was not blessed by circumstance—his parentage was obscure, his condition was poor, and his education was nil. "Yet his natural endowments great; his life correct and innocent: he was meek, benevolent, patient, firm, disinterested, & of the sublimest eloquence."[27] He preached but wrote nothing, and he did not have a Xenophon or an Arrian to write down what he taught, as did Socrates and the Stoic Epictetus. "The committing to writing his life & doctrines fell on the most unlettered & ignorant men; who wrote, too, from memory, & not till long after the transactions had passed." Jesus died at thirty-three years of age, which, according to Jefferson, was long before his reason "attained the maximum of its energy." He preached

---

[25] Jefferson's critique, we know from a subsequent letter to Adams (12 Oct. 1813), draws much from that of William Enfield, who writes in his *History of Philosophy*, "What a wretched depravity of sentiment and manners must have prevailed before such corrupt maxims could have obtained credit!"

[26] For more on the defects of Jewish morality, see TJ to John Adams, 12 Oct. 1813.

[27] Priestley writes, "The circumstances of the parents of Jesus, and his low occupation till he appeared in public, exclude the supposion [*sic*] of his having had any advantage of liberal education." Joseph Priestley, *Socrates and Jesus Compared* (Philadelphia: P. Byrne, 1803), 37.

for no more than three years, which by Jefferson's standards gave him no
time to systemize his thinking—to develop "a complete system of morals."[28]

For these reasons, among others, Jefferson believed that Jesus's doctrines "were defective as a whole, and fragments only of what he did deliver
have come to us mutilated, misstated, & often unintelligible." In addition
to those problems, there are the "corruptions of schismatising followers,
who have found an interest in sophisticating & perverting the simple doctrines he taught by engrafting on them the mysticisms of a Grecian sophist
[Plato], frittering them into subtleties, & obscuring them with jargon, until
they have caused good men to reject the whole in disgust, & to view Jesus
himself as an impostor."

Those defects notwithstanding, "a system of morals is presented to us,
which, if filled up in the true style and spirit of the rich fragments he left us,
would be the most perfect and sublime that has ever been taught by man."

Jefferson considered Jesus to be a great religious reformist, listing four
reasons for this. First, "he corrected the Deism of the Jews, confirming
them in their belief of one only God, and giving them juster notions of his
attributes and government." Second, he amended a defect in the ancient
philosophers by "inculcating universal philanthropy, not only to kindred
and friends, to neighbors and countrymen, but to all mankind, gathering
all into one family, under the bonds of love, charity, peace, common wants
and common aids."[29] Third, he preached a morality not only of action but
of intention. "He pushed his scrutinies into the heart of man; erected his
tribunal in the region of his thoughts, and purified the waters at the fountain head." Finally, "he taught, emphatically, the doctrines of a future state,
which was either doubted, or disbelieved by the Jews; and wielded it with
efficacy, as an important incentive, supplementary to the other motives to
moral conduct."

---

[28] Cf. Bolingbroke, whom Jefferson commonplaces, "It is not true that Christ revealed
an entire body of ethics." Jefferson, *Literary Commonplace Book*, §28.

[29] Aristotle, for instance, believed that the Greeks were a superior sort of people, and it
is highly unlikely that his ethical views were applicable to any persons other than Greeks.

The influence of Priestley on Jefferson's "Syllabus" in places is overall substantial, but one must not overemphasize that debt—as scholars are wont to do—which is more motivational than substantive. We may presume, because of Jefferson's enthusiasm for Priestley's religious writings, that Jefferson took on board most of what Priestley wrote in his *History of the Corruptions of Christianity.* Yet, as we shall shortly see, he did not take on everything. As a careful reading of his bible shows, Jefferson rejected Priestley's notions that Christ was empowered by deity to perform miracles, that Christ rose from the grave, that deity "interested himself in the affairs of men by occasional interpositions,"[30] that there would be a judgment day, that revelation and not reason proved the existence of deity, and that the epistles of Paul were viable.

In Jefferson's bible, we see the enduring influence of Bolingbroke, not Priestley—a point that is missed by nearly all scholars. Priestley's influence was mostly motivational. *Socrates and Jesus Compared* had a profound influence on Jefferson only because he had been mulling over a comparative but more expansive project for a long time, at least since his pledge to Rush. Upon their acquaintance, Jefferson was certain his project could now be undertaken by a much more capable scholar in Priestley.

Busy as president and not considering himself qualified for the task of fleshing out his "Syllabus," Jefferson convinces Priestley to compose the book, and Priestley agrees to do so. Jefferson thanks the learned Priestley for taking up the topic (29 Jan. 1804): "I rejoice that you have undertaken the task of comparing the moral doctrines of Jesus with those of the ancient Philosophers." He concedes that Priestley, unlike himself, "is so much in possession of the whole subject." Yet knowing what he did about Priestley's views of Jesus (e.g., that Jesus, though a man, was empowered to perform miracles and to raise himself from the grave after death), Jefferson had to have certain reservations concerning the finished product. Priestley's book is titled *Doctrines of Heathen Philosophy, Compared with Those of Revelation*, published in 1804—the same year of his death.

---

[30] Priestley, *Socrates and Jesus Compared*, 31.

Writing to John Adams about Priestly's work on August 22, 1813, Jefferson notes: "[T]he branch of the work which the title announces, is executed with learning and candor, as was everything Priestley wrote, but perhaps a little hastily; for he felt himself pressed by the hand of death." But Jefferson could not hold back his disappointment about one particular omission: "a comparison of the morality of the Old Testament with that of the New."[31] Yet he understands why Priestley omitted that comparison. "He would have been eaten alive by his intolerant brethren, the Cannibal priests. And yet, this was really the most interesting branch of the work."[32]

"It Is a Document in Proof That I Am a Real Christian"
Jefferson's Bibles

Probably on account of his dissatisfaction with Priestley's book, Jefferson begins his own bible in 1804. The book aims to merely disclose the true moral teachings of Jesus. Dissatisfied with the outcome, he would undertake the project more extensively in 1819 and include what could be salvaged concerning the life of Jesus.

Much has been written on Jefferson's bibles—how they were composed and what motivated him to write them. Much of the literature is unflattering, most often because Jefferson had the audacity to tinker with a sacred text.

The opinions of J. Lesslie Hall of William & Mary College reflect a typical response to Jefferson's endeavors. In 1913, he says that Jefferson—"a mere amateur, a mere dabbler in religion"—"mutilated" the Bible. "His opinions on religious subjects are worth no more than the writer's opinions as to conducting a spool-cotton factory." Of Jefferson's numerous "edits," Hall says, "Is this the kind of criticism that Jefferson applied to political papers and documents?"[33]

---

[31] TJ to Benjamin Barton, 14 Feb. 1805.

[32] See also TJ to Benjamin Smith Barton, 14 Feb. 1805.

[33] J. Lesslie Hall, "The Religious Opinions of Thomas Jefferson," *Sewanee Review* 21, no. 2 (1913): 175.

Some forty years later, Arthur Barksdale Kinsolving, rector emeritus of St. Paul's Church in Baltimore, states that Jefferson had a remarkable capacity to study nature but was wholly ignorant when it came to supernature. "Jefferson's horizontal mind and his marvelous writings in the secular order are among the most remarkable left by any man for generations before and after him. But his vertical knowledge, his knowledge of the supernatural, is conspicuously defective." Why are Jefferson's religious views taken seriously? "Thomas Jefferson's marked eminence as an observer and chronicler of phenomena in the horizontal sphere . . . gave him a certain measure of authority vertically"[34]—a dangerous direction for him, a secularist, to take.

Charles Sanford, in *The Religious Life of Thomas Jefferson*, states that Jefferson's bible was shaped by idiosyncratic standards of selection and rejection. His "own preferences colored the enthusiasm with which he tossed aside as 'rubbish' certain verses of the New Testament and treasured as 'diamonds' other verses found beside them." He goes on to say that Jefferson's preference for eschewing the divinity of Christ "resulted from his aversion to religious argumentation and his practical desire to find an agreed-upon basis for moral and social reform."[35]

Paul Conkin cites Jefferson's Tartuffery, dilettantism, and gullibility. "His enthusiasm led him to accept Priestley uncritically. In religion, as in his political thought, Jefferson tended to paper over the problematic or inconsistent elements in the thought of his heroes, and thus always ended up with such an eclectic mix of ideas as to defy systematic ordering. He was a creature of mood and sentiment much more than a rigorous thinker."[36]

---

[34] Arthur Barksdale Kinsolving, "The Religious Opinions of Thomas Jefferson," *Historical Magazine of the Protestant Episcopal Church* 20, no. 3 (1951): 327.

[35] Charles B. Sanford, *The Religious Life of Thomas Jefferson* (Charlottesville: University of Virginia Press, 1984), 110.

[36] Paul K. Conkin, "The Religious Pilgrimage of Thomas Jefferson," in *Jeffersonian Legacies*, ed. Peter S. Onuf (Charlottesville: University of Virginia Press, 1993), 35.

Daniel Boorstin writes, "The Jeffersonian had projected his own qualities and limitations into Jesus, whose career became is vivid symbol of the superfluity and perils of speculative philosophy."[37]

In "Thomas Jefferson and His Bible," Marilyn Mellowes asserts, "Mr. Jefferson's Jesus, modeled on the ideals of the Enlightenment thinkers of his day, bore a striking resemblance to Jefferson himself." Thus, in constructing his bible, Jefferson was looking for himself, not Jesus.[38]

The argument implicit in these critiques, and explicit in the comments of Sanford, Boorstin, and Mellowes, is that in attempting to get at the historical Jesus, Jefferson has given us a Jeffersonized Jesus—a Jesus to suit Jefferson's own purposes. Consequently, in reading *LMJ*, we learn more about Jefferson than Jesus.

In May 1803, Jefferson receives Priestley's *A Harmony of the Evangelists in English* and *A Harmony of the Evangelists in Greek*. It was not uncommon at the time for deistic scholars—especially Unitarians, who were singled out for denying the divinity of Jesus—to compose harmonies. Shortly after having composed his "Syllabus," Jefferson begins work on his own harmony of the Gospels—his booklet, *The Philosophy of Jesus of Nazareth, Extracted from the Account of His Life and Doctrines as Given by Matthew, Mark, Luke and John, Being an Abridgment of the New Testament for the Use of the Indians, Unembarrassed with Matters of Fact or Faith beyond the Level of Their Comprehensions* (hereafter, *PJ*)—a forty-six-page, cut-and-paste compilation of the moral teachings of Jesus. There is no scholarly consensus on what Jefferson means by *"for the Use of the Indians."* Did Jefferson wish for the book to be copied and used as an introductory biblical text for the edification of American Indians? If so, why then does he tell John Adams (12 Oct. 1813) that the book was made "for my own use"? Jefferson does offer the book to his friends Benjamin Rush (8 Aug. 1804) and Francis

---

[37] Daniel J. Boorstin, *The Lost World of Thomas Jefferson* (Chicago: University of Chicago Press, 1993), 157.

[38] Marilyn Mellowes, "Thomas Jefferson and His Bible," *Frontline*, April 1998, accessed May 28, 2017, www.pbs.org/wgbh/pages/frontline/shows/religion/jesus/jefferson.html.

A. Van der Kemp (25 Apr. 1816), and he tells Van der Kemp that he can make use of this text for his own research, so long as Jefferson can remain anonymous. That could, of course, have been meant as an evasive maneuver, in the event that the book, known to be put together by Jefferson, got into the wrong hands. Eugene R. Sheridan argues that Jefferson had in mind "the Federalists and their clerical allies."[39] That seems reasonable, but on the assumption of the truth of his statement to Adams about the book being used for his own edification, the joke was merely for self-amusement, and that seems strange—atypical of Jefferson.

No known copy of *PJ* survives; nonetheless, we know of the existence of this work through references to it in several of Jefferson's letters, as provided shortly. A reconstruction of the booklet was meticulously undertaken by Dickinson W. Adams, working from a list of the Gospels' verses that Jefferson used when constructing the work, as well as an inspection of the two copies of the New Testament from which he clipped the verses.[40] According to Sheridan, as indicated in his noteworthy introduction to the reconstruction, Jefferson's motivation for the book was not only to rebut the charge of atheism raised against him by calumniators, but also to solve the political factionalism and social disharmony that threatened to dissolve republican government. Jefferson aimed "to set forth a demystified form of Christianity that he deemed appropriate for a society that had chosen to live according to republican principles."[41] Sheridan posits that his aim was publication—not self-use.

Edwin Gaustad disagrees with this sentiment. "The retired President did not produce his small book to shock or offend a somnolent world; he composed it for himself, for his devotion, for his assurance, for a more restful sleep at nights and a more confident greeting of the mornings."[42]

---

[39] Eugene R. Sheridan, Introduction to *Extracts from the Gospels,* ed. Dickinson W. Adams (Princeton: Princeton University Press, 1983), 28.

[40] Two copies were needed, for by clipping a passage on one page, he might destroy a passage needed from the other side of the page. Dickinson W. Adams, "The Reconstruction of 'The Philosophy of Jesus,'" in *Extracts from the Gospels,* 45–47.

[41] Sheridan, Introduction to *Extracts from the Gospels,* 13.

[42] Gaustad, *Sworn on the Altar of God,* 131.

Following Jefferson's letters on his reasons for crafting the booklet, *PJ* was incomplete. In keeping with the aim of his "Syllabus," Jefferson intended to compare the real teachings of Jesus to the morality of the Jews and the morality of the ancient philosophers. Later letters show that Jefferson also wished to include a translation of Gassendi's *Syntagma* and a translation of Epictetus—most likely his short work *Enchiridion*—in an effort to contrast the teachings of Jesus with those of Epicurus and the Stoics.[43]

Several references to Jefferson's *PJ* exist in his letters and key writings. In his January 29, 1804, letter to Joseph Priestley, we recall, Jefferson thanks Priestley for agreeing to take up his project—that is, turning his "Syllabus" into a book. He states that he had sent for two Greek testaments from Philadelphia to begin the project, "but I shall now get the thing done by better hands." On August 8, 1804, Jefferson tells Benjamin Rush of his "mere and faithful compilation"—"the Philosophy of Jesus of Nazareth." This letter is a clear indication that Jefferson had completed his own harmony by August.[44] Jefferson sends a copy of his "Syllabus" to John Adams (12 Oct. 1813). He writes of his stripping process: "I have performed this operation for my own use, by cutting verse by verse out of the printed book, and arranging the matter which is evidently his and which is as easily distinguished as diamonds in a dunghill." Jefferson also tells Rev. Charles Clay (29 Jan. 1815) about *PJ*, adding that the book is not intended for publication. One year later (9 Jan. 1816), Jefferson writes to Charles Thomson of the latter's "Synopsis of the Four Evangelists." He adds that he too has made "a wee little book from the same materials, which I call the Philosophy of Jesus." He adds, in a manner that suggests publication, "It is a document in proof that I am a real Christian, that is to say, a disciple of the

---

[43] TJ to Charles Thomson, 9 Jan. 1815, and TJ to William Short, 31 Oct. 1819.

[44] Jefferson never sent Rush a copy of the booklet, probably because Rush stated to Jefferson (29 Aug. 1804) that it was necessary to acknowledge the divinity of Christ in order to render "his *death* as well as his *life* necessary for the restoration of mankind." The tension between Rush and Jefferson over the divinity of Christ remained unresolved when Rush died.

doctrines of Jesus."[45] Later in the same year, Jefferson writes to Francis A. Van der Kemp (25 Apr. 1816) about the haste with which *PJ* was constructed. "It was too hastily done, however, being the work of one or two evenings only, while I lived at Washington, overwhelmed with other business, and it is my intention to go over it again at more leisure. This shall be the work of the ensuing winter." He adds, "To this Syllabus and Extract [*PJ*], if a history of his life can be added, written with the same view of the subject, the world will see, after the fogs shall be dispelled, . . . the immortal merit of this first of human Sages."[46] Finally, Jefferson mentions *PJ* to his friend and former secretary William Short (31 Oct. 1819). "I attempted [*PJ*] too hastily some 12. or 15. years ago. It was the work of 2. or 3. nights only, at Washington, after getting thro' the evening task of reading the letters and papers of the day." With "one foot in the grave," he now finds such tasks "idle." At this time, he obviously has not yet taken up the project, as he told Van der Kemp he would do.

The letters indicate that Jefferson's reconstruction of Jesus's teachings in *PJ* was very likely both personally and politically motivated. He wished to draw personal inspiration from the booklet, as indicated by his remark to Adams in the 1813 letter that the book was composed "for my own use," but

---

[45] Michael Peña challenges Jefferson's claim to being a real Christian. "What does it mean to be a disciple of Jesus? The disciples tried not only to follow the teachings of Jesus, but also to emulate the way he lived. Many have done this by giving away their riches, and in more extreme cases, becoming willing martyrs. However, as Judaizers of the Christian faith often point out—Jesus was a practicing Jew. Included in Jefferson's bible is the fact that Jesus was circumcised. He often quoted the prophets. He prayed at the temple and at the synagogues. He observed Jewish feasts and Jewish holidays such as the Passover. He kept the Jewish dietary restrictions. He even referred to a Gentile woman as a dog (Mt: 15:26—Jefferson omits this). If we are to emulate Jesus in a literal sense, then this in many ways implies behaving like a Jew." Michael Peña, "Jefferson and Religion" (unpublished essay, April 2015), in possession of author.

[46] Jefferson wished to see Van der Kemp undertake the fleshing out of his "Syllabus." Van der Kemp subsequently sent Jefferson (1 Nov. 1816) a detailed syllabus of what he proposed to write. The syllabus—with a focus on revelation and not reason, and inclusive of numerous sentiments with which Jefferson would have disagreed (Jesus's virgin birth, Jesus being both a real human and part of the godhead, Jesus's resurrection, the reality of miracles, "unquestionable proof" of a future state, and Jesus dying for the sin of the human race)—must have militated against Jefferson's excitement concerning Van der Kemp's capacity to undertake Jefferson's comparative project.

as the 1800 letter to Bishop Madison suggests, he likely also thought that a compendium of Jesus's philosophical message, extracted from the Bible and demythologized, might prove both a catholicon for the ignorance of his time and a foundation for aboveboard republicanism. In order for those aims to be actualized, the book would need to be published, if only under a pseudonym. Again, the phrase "the world will see," in his letter to Van der Kemp, strongly suggests publication as a motive—at least at that time.[47]

The Life and Morals of Jesus of Nazareth (hereafter *LMJ*) was composed in 1819 or 1820—the late-1819 letter to Short, in which Jefferson describes the task of reconstructing the New Testament as "idle," is one reason for preferring 1820 to 1819 as the year of completion. Another is that *LMJ* was not fashioned "too hastily," as it gives every indication of meticulous construction.[48] Moreover, in a subsequent letter (1 Dec. 1819), Short is apparently concerned with fleshing out Jefferson's skeletal "Syllabus," or in Jefferson's own words to John Adams (12 Oct. 1813), "to fill up this skeleton with arteries, with veins, with nerves, muscles and flesh." Says Short: "I see with real pains that you have no intention of continuing the abstract for the Evangelists which you begun at Washington. . . . I know nothing which could be more so [agreeable], and at the same time more useful to others."[49] This last sentence suggests that the two, at some point or another, discussed publication of the book for general enlightenment.

The new title indicates that Jefferson's express intendment with the second compilation, of eighty-two pages in length, is broader—to salvage from the New Testament not only the moral teachings of Jesus but also some account of the life of Jesus by removing all such passages that are unconcerned with these matters. It is an aim that Jefferson had wished to

---

[47] Sheridan maintains that *PJ* was intended for publication, but by the time of *LMJ*, Jefferson gave up the aim of publication. Sheridan, *Jefferson and Religion*, 36, 63.

[48] See M. Andrew Holowchak, *Thomas Jefferson's Bible, With Introduction and Critical Commentary* (Berlin: DeGruyter, 2018).

[49] The compilation is never mentioned in his correspondence, and it became evident to family members only after Jefferson's death. See Eugene R. Sheridan, Introduction to *Extracts from the Gospels,* 38.

achieve all along. Not only does Jefferson wish to rescue the teachings of Jesus; he also wishes to show that what can be salvaged of his life shows him to be a true sage—a true Jeffersonian republican.

Jefferson used four languages for his project. Greek and Latin text appeared on the left side of the book, and English and French text appeared on the right, with each page being eight by four and three-quarters inches.[50]

We can consider Jefferson's *LMJ* to be far more ambitious than his *PJ* for several reasons. First, and as the titles imply, while the aim of *PJ* is solely normative—Jefferson wishes to extract from the Bible Jesus's ethical system, or as much of a system as can be extracted—in *LMJ*, Jefferson's aims are normative and historical. He aims to discover, insofar as the New Testament will allow, not only what Jesus taught, but also who Jesus was and what Jesus did.[51] Second, adding the historical dimension would seem to make for differences in Jefferson's *modus agendi*. *PJ*, it seems, is to be created by extraction, and essaying to extract the true teachings of Jesus does not necessarily commit Jefferson to any view of what is not extracted. In contrast, because *LMJ* also involves historical intendment, it is to be created both by extraction and by scrapping. Jefferson's intention in *PJ* is to cull all such passages that are philosophical, but *LMJ* has the additional task of removing passages that are historically improbable—that is, thaumaturgical events. Finally, since the aim of *PJ* is philosophical, its text is arranged topically, while the text of *LMJ*, constrained by regard for historical accuracy, is constrained by chronological considerations and by the need for fluidity of prose to bring alive the personage of Jesus.

In several letters, Jefferson claims that this process of selection/deselection is as easy as plucking "diamonds from dunghills."[52] His process of selection/deselection was guided by two theses of deselection—unnaturalness and inconsistency. The *unnaturalness thesis* requires that all passages at variance with the laws of physical nature should be stripped.

[50] Janice Stagnitto Ellis, "Conservation," in Thomas Jefferson, *The Jefferson Bible, Smithsonian Edition* (Washington, DC: Smithsonian Books, 2011), 39.

[51] *PJ* does begin, in section 1, with some account of the life of Jesus.

[52] TJ to John Adams, 12 Oct. 1813 and 24 Jan. 1814; TJ to F. A. Van der Kemp, 25 Apr. 1816; and TJ to William Short, 31 Oct. 1819.

The *inconsistency thesis* says that all passages inconsistent with a historical personage's character (here Jesus), based on satisfactory testimony, should be stripped.[53] Finally, there are Jefferson's principles of selection, advanced in a letter to William Short (4 Aug. 1820)—*sublimity, purity,* and *guileless-ness.* When Jefferson comes across verses that simply express notions of a nonanthropocentric Supreme Being; of principles of simple and pure morality; and of a moralist who is humble, innocent, simple-mannered, and indifferent to ambition or worldly gain, he selects them for inclusion in his bible.

There were also certain methodological principles at play during the selection/deselection process: redundancy, transition, and complementarity. According to the *redundancy thesis*, when a passage from one Gospel merely rehashes an account contained in another, the less fuller of the accounts is overpassed. According to the *transition thesis*, should a line or lines from an inferior account concerning some aspect of Jesus or his teachings, if added to the superior account, (1) foster transition from some elided text to make the transit smooth across the abyss created by the lacuna in the elided text or (2) aid in the transition between two different stories in one of the Gospels, then that line or those lines should be included. Finally, according to the *complementary thesis*, all such passages from an inferior account, concerning some aspect of Jesus or his teachings, that are not contained in the superior account; do not fall prey to the principles of selection/deselection; and, when added to the superior account, offer a more complete depiction of the life and morals of Jesus, should be added to the superior account.[54]

Because Jefferson used four languages, fitting them on relatively small pages, he could not concern himself with the best available translations. Font size was a desideratum. He chose a school text of the Greek Bible and a Latin trot of the same Greek text—so those texts lined up—and a French

---

[53] Holowchak, *Thomas Jefferson's Bible.*
[54] Holowchak, *Thomas Jefferson's Bible.*

translation by a Swiss Protestant.[55] Gary Wills states that the finished product was anything but scholarly:

> [Jefferson] penned only one note into the book. . . . He made only two changes in the English of the King James, for stylistic elegance, not accuracy. He showed no interest in debate over cruxes famous even in his day, such as the meaning of that odd word translated as "daily" in the Lord's Prayer. In accord with the misconceptions of his time, he thought the Gospels were composed earlier than the Pauline Epistles, and that Matthew was the earliest Gospel.[56]

Such criticisms are misguided. They might suggest some dilettantism, but as scrutiny of the construction of *LMJ* shows, the book was put together by someone with great familiarity with, and profound respect for, the deterged content of the four Gospels.[57] Jefferson might not have been a biblical critic of the size of Price or Priestley, but he knew the four Gospels well and constructed *LMJ* with prodigious regard for minutiae. What else would one expect from Jefferson, if not exactitude?

Though Jefferson's aim in his "Syllabus" was to show that Jesus was no masquerader but a nonpareil philosopher, he did not agree philosophically with Jesus on all moral matters. He writes to William Short (13 Apr. 1820): "It is not to be understood that I am with him in all his doctrines. I am a Materialist; he takes the side of spiritualism: he preaches the efficacy of repentance towards forgiveness [of sin], I require a counterpoise of good works to redeem it &c, &c"—" &c, &c," indicative of more areas of disagreement.

---

[55] Goodspeed notes that Jefferson uses Leusden's Greek text (first published, Utrecht, 1675, though Jefferson likely used a later version, dated 1794), Benedictus Arius Montanus's Latin text (which appeared in the 1794 Wingrave printing of the Greek-Latin pairing, used by Jefferson), and a version of Jean Frederic Ostervald's French Bible (Paris, 1802). Edgar Goodspeed, "Thomas Jefferson and the Bible," *Harvard Theological Review* 40, no. 1 (1947): 71–76.

[56] Wills, "Jefferson's Jesus," 6.

[57] See TJ to Dr. Joseph Priestley, 29 Jan. 1804. For more on the meticulousness of the project, see Holowchak, *Thomas Jefferson's Bible*. See also Ellis, "Conservation," 37–46.

What, then, does Jefferson find so enticing about Jesus and his teachings? He continues to Short, "It is the innocence of his character, the purity & sublimity of his moral precepts, the eloquence of his inculcations, the beauty of the apologues in which he conveys them, that I so much admire." Thus, Jesus is the paradigm Jeffersonian republican and a model citizen of Jefferson's ideal political system; his "principles" of morality, love of others, and love of God are the fundamental moral tenets of Jeffersonian republicanism—principles to which his political ideals are answerable.

Overall, *LMJ* betrays the influence of Joseph Priestley—one of Jefferson's "heroes," as Conkin says in a dilettantish manner—but shows much more the influence of Lord Bolingbroke. Whereas Priestley believed that Jesus, a mortal, was empowered to perform miracles and resurrect after his death, Jefferson's Jesus is a mere man, without a virgin birth, without a capacity to perform actions inconsistent with the laws of nature, and without the ability to rise from his grave. Jefferson's Jesus and his deity are Bolingbrokean, not Priestleyan. This idea has often been overlooked or downplayed by Jeffersonian scholars, with the exception of Douglas Wilson.[58]

But what of the claim that the Jesus of Jefferson's bible is Jeffersonized? First, *LMJ* contains passages like Jesus's prophesy about the decimation of Jerusalem (Matt. 24:1). Jefferson did not believe in prophesy. Why, then, does he include the passage? Perhaps he does so because he believes that the story came from the lips of Jesus (i.e., that it is not something added by his religious schismatizers).

Second, Jefferson writes to Short (13 Apr. 1820) that there are significant differences between his own religious views and those of Jesus. Jesus believed in the forgiveness of misdeeds; Jefferson believed in redemption for misdeeds. Jesus was a spiritualist; Jefferson was a materialist. Jefferson sums: "The syllabus is therefore of his doctrines, not all of mine. I read them as I do those of other ancient and modern moralists, with a mixture of approbation and dissent."

---

[58] Douglas L. Wilson, "Jefferson and Bolingbroke: Some Notes on the Question of Influence," in Garrett Ward Sheldon and Daniel L. Dreisbach, *Religion and Political Culture in Jefferson's Virginia* (Lanham, MD: Rowman & Littlefield, 2000), 107–18, esp. 109.

I end this chapter with these fitting words of scholar Charles Maybee: "In the format which Jefferson chose, the book is not to be read simply as *his* view of Jesus, but as the *true* Bible itself, displacing the one of the church.... This is the first and most obvious indication that Jefferson intended something more by his creation than a book for his own nightly reading table."[59]

Concluding Thoughts

Jeffersonian republicanism was a novel, morality-grounded political philosophy. To achieve the sort of political stability that his republicanism—characterized by the fullest political participation of all citizens, self-sufficiency of the general citizenry, governance of the intellectual and moral elite, and partnership of politics and science, inter alia—required, Jefferson felt that the citizenry should be steeped in a nonsectarian, naturalized religion. That naturalized religion was merely the God-implanted morality that resides in the hearts of all persons—the "precepts" of the moral sense that, for centuries, have been corrupted by the empleomania and esoteric tenets of religious clerics. For Jefferson, Jesus, through his exoteric teachings, was merely aiming to remove religion from the reach of human political ambition, from the rationalizations of the minds of humankind, and place it back in humans' hearts, where, excluding no one, it was within the reach of all. In *LMJ*, Jefferson was merely striving to reclaim those intemerate, exoteric teachings and place them within the reach of all persons through Jesus's unique use of parables, via a deterged version of the New Testament.

---

[59] Charles Mabee, "Jefferson's Anti-clerical Bible," *Historical Magazine of the Protestant Episcopal Church* 48, no. 4 (1979): 474.

CHAPTER FOUR

"With All Is Swelling Pomp, a Boyish Fire Work"

Jefferson and the Afterlife

"The mystery of human existence lies not in just staying alive, but in finding something to live for."
—Fyodor Dostoyevsky, *The Brothers Karamazov*

As is often the case with his late-life correspondences and writings, John Adams begins his 8 December 1818 letter to Jefferson in buttery style: "While you live, I Seem to have a Bank at Monticello on which I can draw for a Letter of Friendship and entertainment when I please." The letter immediately turns mystical and metaphysical:

> I know not how to prove physically that We Shall meet and know each other in a future State; Nor does Revelation, As I can find give Us any positive Assurance of Such a felicity. My reasons for believing, it, as I do, most undoubtingly, are all moral and divine.
>
> I believe in God and in his Wisdom and Benevolence: and I cannot conceive that Such a Being could make Such a Species as the human merely to live and die on this Earth. If I did not believe a future State I Should believe in no God. This Universe

[*sic*]; this all; this To Πᾶν; would appear with all its Swelling Pomp, a boyish Fire Work.

And if there be a future State Why Should the Almighty dissolve forever all the tender Ties which Unite Us So delightfully in this World and forbid Us to See each other in the next?

Adams's thoughts on the afterlife betray an anthropocentric lean that Jefferson, as we saw in Chapter One, could never have embraced. Adams has no difficulty in thinking the myriad other species of life are nonpurposive, yet that cannot be the case for humans. The sentiment is, very likely, that on account of humans' intelligence, of human cognizance of the cosmos and themselves, a God-given life without an afterlife is merely a charade. The "tender Ties" that each individual makes with others in the course of a lifetime and the striving of each person to learn what he can of himself, of other living things, and of his place in the cosmos would be signals of a sadistic deity, deriving some sort of perverse pleasure in observing humans' Sisyphean strivings. The reference to Tὸ Πᾶν (The All), readily recognizable to Jefferson or anyone else with moderate exposure to ancient philosophy, is a reference to the cosmology of the Greek philosopher Epicurus, for whom human existence was the result of a mere accident—the random colliding and binding of atoms—and for whom there was no meaning, or *telos*, to human existence.[1] For Epicurus, the lack of a human end was no reason for lamentation. Each person was to seek peace of mind (*ataraxia*) through the quiet pursuit of pleasure and avoidance of pain.

Adams's sentiment, which is anything but Epicurean, is in keeping with his temperament: discomfited, fragile, testy, and mercurial. Jefferson was also somewhat discomfited and fragile—at least when it came to public perception of him in his political years—but he was neither testy nor mercurial. He was not prone to argument; nor was he wont, pace the perception of him derived through reading today's secondary literature, to

---

[1] Epicurus, *Letter to Herodotus, The Epicurus Reader*, trans. Brad Inwood and L. P. Gerson (Indianapolis: Hackett, 1994), §2.39–66.

frequent changes of mind. His view of the afterlife, as I aim to show in this chapter, was likely consistent throughout his life.

This chapter is an examination of Jefferson's views on the hereafter. I begin with the secondary literature, which points chiefly in two directions: either that Jefferson believed in an afterlife or that he vacillated so frequently in his writings that nothing definitive can be concluded. I end with what I take to be certain telling evidence that strongly suggests that Jefferson, from boyhood till the end of his life, did not believe in an afterlife.

"The Issue Is Not Devoid of Doubt"
Scholarly Befuddlement

As noted in Chapter Two, Jefferson tells Benjamin Waterhouse (26 June 1822) that the doctrines of Jesus are threefold: that God is one and all-perfect, that there exists a future state of rewards and punishments, and that the sum of religion is to love completely God and love one's neighbor as oneself. Yet, as Jefferson explains to his friend and former secretary William Short (4 Aug. 1820), though Jesus was likely the greatest moralist and religious reformist that the world has ever seen, it is not reasonable to believe everything he taught. Is the doctrine of a future state of reward and punishments one of Jesus's teachings that ought to be repudiated?

Jefferson's view of life after death is a matter of great disagreement among scholars. First, some scholars maintain that Jefferson always believed or tended to believe in an afterlife. That view is more prevalent in the literature than any other.

Charles Sanford asserts plainly that Jefferson never wavered on the issue—that, throughout his life, he was a strong proponent of the hereafter. According to Sanford, as Jefferson believed in being judged for how one lived, he also believed in an afterlife: "One idea about life after death that persisted throughout all of Jefferson's writings on the subject was a belief that people were judged for the quality of their lives."[2] As a lawyer, Jefferson recognized the indispensability of seeking justice, but he recognized that

---

[2] Charles B. Sanford, *The Religious Life of Thomas Jefferson* (Charlottesville: University of Virginia Press, 1984), 144.

justice did not always prevail; hence his belief in an afterlife, where justice was divinely meted out. "As a student of law and history and a practicing lawyer and statesmen, he saw the importance of a belief in eternal judgment for encouraging a moral life of service to society."[3]

Sanford also cites several letters and addresses—but there are not as many as Sanford leads us to believe there are—in which Jefferson appeals to an afterlife. He appeals, for instance, to a letter to Thomas Law (13 June 1814). In part quoting Jefferson, Sanford asserts: "'The prospects of a future state of retribution for the evil as well as the good done while here' [are] among the moral forces necessary to motivate individuals to live good lives in society."[4] He then adds: "Jefferson had begun with the conviction that God had created in man a hunger for the rights of equality, freedom, and life and a desire to follow God's moral law. It was only a small step further to believe that God had also created man with an immortal soul."[5] Sanford also appeals to Jefferson's puzzlement over grief in a letter to Benjamin Rush (23 Sept. 1800). "All of our other passions, within proper bounds, have an useful object, but what is the use of grief in the economy [of nature]?"[6] The conclusion Sanford seems to see as implicit is that an afterlife makes human grief sensible; otherwise, it is an enormous enigma.

Robert Healey asserts that Jefferson consistently held a belief in an afterlife. The chief reason is "its value as an incentive to virtue and moral living." He adds, "Remarks reflecting his belief in life after death came with ever increasing frequency from 1787 until his death," both "in private correspondence" and "public utterances." He proposes that Jefferson's belief in an afterlife also gave him personal comfort: "Jefferson's concept of heaven is its prospect of reunion."[7]

---

[3] Sanford, *The Religious Life of Thomas Jefferson*, 145.

[4] Sanford, *The Religious Life of Thomas Jefferson*, 145. This is a critical misread, as Jefferson lists a belief in a future state only among other correctives for someone born without a moral sense.

[5] Sanford, *The Religious Life of Thomas Jefferson*, 152.

[6] Sanford, *The Religious Life of Thomas Jefferson*, 155.

[7] Robert M. Healey, *Jefferson on Religion in Public Education* (New Haven, CT: Yale University Press, 1962), 31–32.

Eugene R. Sheridan acknowledges that Jefferson entertained doubts concerning an afterlife, "but, on the whole, hope triumphed over despair." Sheridan expatiates on his hope-triumphed-over-despair argument: "Belief in the one true god and adherence to the morality of Jesus would lead, Jefferson hoped, so some sort of reward in a life after death, He praised Jesus for preaching the doctrine of a life in the hereafter to encourage virtue in the here and now and presumably accepted the teaching himself of this very reason." He cites Jefferson's late-in-life letter to a namesake, Thomas Jefferson Smith (21 Feb. 1825), in which he enjoins, in a future-oriented manner, the newly born person to love God and behave virtuously so that "the life into which you have entered [will] be the Portal to one of eternal and ineffable bliss." Sheridan adds, "Since Jefferson rejected the orthodox doctrine of hell but approved Jesus's teaching that God would mete out punishments as well as rewards after death, he presumably believed with the Universalists that in time all persons would be reconciled with the deity."[8]

Paul Conkin, who (as noted in Chapter Three) believed Jefferson's religious views were a product of sloppy and uncritical thinking, says that Jefferson adopted a belief in the afterlife for reasons of consolation: "He nourished consoling beliefs about the universe and at times enjoyed a sense of wonderment and awe. He spent a lifetime agonizing over the foundations of morality. He sought types of wisdom, wanted a healthy mind, and always was confident of life after death, a belief that gave him consolation and also one that seemed necessary as a support for public morality."[9]

Given that, for Jefferson, the mind or soul is some sort of matter, Carl Richards asserts that the question of an afterlife reduces to the question of whether psychic matter is indissoluble—whether, for Jefferson, there can be an instauration of matter, once decayed. Richards states that Jefferson believed in the dissolution of the soul upon the dissolution of the body, but he adds that Jefferson believed in the resurrection of the body after

---

[8] Eugene R. Sheridan, Introduction to *Jefferson's Extracts from the Gospels*, ed. Dickinson W. Adams (Princeton: Princeton University Press, 1983), 40–41.

[9] Paul K. Conkin, "The Religious Pilgrimage of Thomas Jefferson," in *Jeffersonian Legacies*, ed. Peter S. Onuf (Charlottesville: University Press of Virginia, 1993), 20.

death.[10] The view is in keeping with Priestley's view of the hereafter (see Chapter Five). Priestley, a committed and through-and-through materialist, thought that there was a life after death insofar as there would be for each person a reconfiguration of bodily matter at some point after death. With bodily reconfiguration, the soul would once again emerge.

John Ragosta argues succinctly that Jefferson's insistence, pace Calvin, that we are to be judged by our deeds by a rational creator "suggests some belief in an afterlife," though he admits the issue "is not devoid of doubt."[11] In an encyclopedia entry titled "Thomas Jefferson and Religion," he writes, "While there is doubt among some historians, he also apparently had some belief in an afterlife; he certainly saw belief in a future state of rewards and punishment as a useful social device."[12]

In a 1933 paper, William Gould states: "It was [Jefferson's] conviction that God would judge men according to the use they made of the reason he had given them, and that a state of reward or punishment awaited them as a result of their decisions. God, he was confident, was desirous of making all men eternally happy, and had prepared for those who submitted to his will a life 'of eternal and ineffable bliss.'"[13]

Ari Helo, in *Thomas Jefferson's Ethics and the Politics of Human Progress*, argues for Jefferson's belief in an afterlife. Jefferson's deism included a belief in the afterlife as well. "He made passing remarks about his hope of entering the Elysium fields [*sic*] with at least John Adams as his companion, and even of receiving thanks for his lifelong advocacy of human happiness on earth."[14]

---

[10] Carl J. Richard, "A Dialogue with the Ancients: Thomas Jefferson and Classical Philosophy and History," *Journal of the Early Republic* 9, no. 4 (1989): 439.

[11] John Ragosta, "Thomas Jefferson's Religion and Religious Liberty," in *Religious Freedom: Jefferson's Legacy, America's Creed* (Charlottesville: University of Virginia Press, 2013), 21–22.

[12] John Ragosta, "Thomas Jefferson and Religion," in *Encyclopedia Virginia*, Virginia Humanities, 4 Nov. 2015, https://www.encyclopediavirginia.org/Jefferson_Thomas_and_Religion.

[13] William Gould, "The Religious Opinions of Thomas Jefferson," *Mississippi Valley Historical Review* 20, no. 2 (1933): 205.

[14] Ari Helo, *Thomas Jefferson's Ethics and the Politics of Human Progress* (Cambridge: Cambridge University Press, 2015), 173.

Jon Meacham follows suit when he claims, "Jefferson believed in the existence of a creator God and in an afterlife." And again, "Jefferson had a fairly detailed vision of the afterlife, seeking comfort from the present pain of the loss of loved ones in the expectation that they would meet again beyond time and space." He cites an 1823 letter to Adams (Apr. 11) in which Jefferson expresses a friendly sentiment concerning the possibility of meeting Adams after death "in Congress, with our antient Colleagues."[15]

Finally, John Boles writes that Jefferson patterned his life after Jesus's: "His was a rationalized, minimalist [religious] creed: he believed in one all-powerful God, the moral teachings of Jesus, and the afterlife."[16] Boles, unfortunately, offers no discussion of Jefferson's belief in an afterlife. One is led to believe that Jefferson, patterning his life after Jesus's life, merely appropriated Jesus's belief in the afterlife.

In addition, some assert that Jefferson's writings on the afterlife are such a hotchpotch that nothing can be definitively asserted. Among these, we find three of the most prominent Jeffersonian scholars: Malone, Peterson, and Koch.

Dumas Malone says that Jefferson devoted much time in his youth to thinking about the afterlife, but later in life, he was content to rest his head on the "pillow of ignorance."[17] Citing a letter to Rev. Isaac Story (5 Dec. 1801) on the transmigration of souls, Malone writes of a young Jefferson's fondness for "the speculations which seemed to promise some insight into that hidden country," but Jefferson adds that such speculations "left me in the same ignorance in which they had found me," so he has "for very many years ceased to read or to think concerning them." Malone adds, "During his inquiring youth and young manhood he did not find the answers; and, characteristically, he addressed himself to the problems of this world which reason can better understand."[18]

---

[15] Jon Meacham, *Thomas Jefferson: The Art of Power* (New York: Random House, 2012), 471.

[16] John Boles, *Jefferson: Architect of American Liberty* (New York: Basic Books, 2017), 363.

[17] TJ to John Adams, 14 Mar. 1820.

[18] Dumas Malone, *Jefferson the Virginian* (Boston: Little, Brown and Company, 1948), 107.

Merrill Peterson is too noncommittal. Also drawing from Jefferson's 1801 letter to Isaac Story, he states succinctly, "Rather than seeking 'the country of spirits,' he preferred to rest his head on 'that pillow of ignorance which the benevolent Creator has made so soft for us, knowing how much we should be forced to use it.'"[19]

After quoting Jefferson's 1819 letter to Rev. Stiles (June 25), Adrienne Koch indicates that it is not possible to know with any degree of certitude Jefferson's religiosity. "The desire for privacy, . . . coupled with a frank admission that there is no knowledge of the specific attributes of God or of the manner in which his superintendence over the world was being exercised, were sufficient reasons for Jefferson's avoidance of everything resembling theological discussion." Thus, "one looks in vain, therefore, for answers to the genuinely puzzling question about Jefferson's 'particular principles' of religion: for example, his beliefs on the states of future rewards and punishments."[20]

E. S. Gaustad maintains in a 1984 paper that the immortality of the soul was, for Jefferson, just compensation for morality. He says: "Like most deists Jefferson saw the doctrine of immortality as being, in some generalized and impersonal sense, a necessary guarantor of morality. Justice and goodness must ultimately prevail, else this is not a moral universe. Since in this life that they do prevail is not always conspicuously evident, then it must be the case that the moral demands of man's nature are met by some 'future state of rewards and punishments.'"[21] Yet, in a later publication, he recants and settles on an ignorance of Jefferson's position. "The precise nature of one's existence after death remained unclear, even dark. And in that darkness Jefferson affirmed that he was content 'to trust for the future to him who has been so good for the past.' If there was ever a subject in

---

[19] Merrill D. Peterson, *Thomas Jefferson and the New Nation: A Biography* (Oxford: Oxford University Press, 1970), 960–61.

[20] Adrienne Koch, *The Philosophy of Thomas Jefferson* (Gloucester, MS: Peter Smith, 1957), 38.

[21] E. S. Gaustad, "Religion," in *Thomas Jefferson: A Reference Biography*, ed. Merrill D. Peterson (New York: Charles Scribner's Sons, 1984), 290.

which persons peered through a glass darkly, that subject was the exact shape or nature that life takes after death."[22]

In addition, a few scholars (including Arthur Scherr and me) have taken Jefferson to reject the notion of an afterlife. Noting John Adams's position—"if I did not believe in a future state, I should believe in no God"—Arthur Scherr argues (echoing the sentiment in Chapter One of this work) that there is no link between morality and belief in God. Jefferson's "Lucretian and . . . Epicurean" metaphysics prohibited belief in an afterlife. "At no time did Jefferson seriously express expectations of immortality. His empiricist epistemology and materialist metaphysics would probably have ruled out adoption of such a belief."[23] In an earlier publication, Scherr states that Jefferson "probably considered belief in an afterlife puerile." Following Jefferson's claim that the true principles of religion are common to all religions, Scherr merely notes that belief in an afterlife is not common to all religions, and he concludes, in a tight syllogism, that Jefferson did not believe in an afterlife.[24]

I have also argued in several previous publications that Jefferson did not believe in life after death,[25] for reasons provided shortly.

"Murmur Not at the Ways of Providence"
Evaluation of the Secondary Literature

This section begins with an analysis of some of the arguments for Jefferson's belief in an afterlife that appear in the literature.

First, there is the argument of Healey that Jefferson often appeals to the afterlife in numerous letters and in public messages and addresses. The

---

[22] Gaustad, *Sworn on the Altar of God*, 142.

[23] Thomas Jefferson, "Immortality, and the Fear of Death: A Reconsideration," *Cithara* 56, no. 1 (2016): 44–67.

[24] For example, Arthur Scherr, "Thomas Jefferson versus the Historians: Christianity, Atheistic Morality, and the Afterlife," *Church History* 83, no. 1 (2014): 82–83, 85, and 93, respectively.

[25] For example, M. Andrew Holowchak, "The Fear, Honor, and Love of God: Thomas Jefferson on Jews, Philosophers, and Jesus," *Philosophical Forum* 18, no. 1 (2013): 49–71, and "Duty to God and Duty to Man: Jefferson on Religion, Natural and Sectarian," *Sophia* 55, no. 2 (2010): 236–61.

instances of this are too numerous for a full expression, so a few illustrations will suffice.

What are we to make of Jefferson's references to the afterlife in his letters? For instance, in 1763, Jefferson writes philosophically to his boyhood friend John Page (July 15):

> The most fortunate of us all in our journey through life frequently meet with calamities and misfortunes which may greatly afflict us: and to fortify our minds against the attacks of these calamities and misfortunes should be one of the principal studies and endeavors of our lives. The only method of doing this is to assume a perfect resignation to the divine will, to consider that whatever does happen, must happen, and that by our uneasiness we cannot prevent the blow before it does fall, but we may add to it's force after it has fallen. These considerations and others such as these may enable us in some measure to surmount the difficulties thrown in our way, to bear up with a tolerable degree of patience under this burthen of life, and to proceed with a pious and unshaken resignation till we arrive at our journey's end, where we may deliver up our trust into the hands of him who gave it, and receive such reward as to him shall seem proportioned to our merit.

Again, he writes to George Outlaw (24 June 1806), who has written President Jefferson on behalf of "the several Baptist churches of the North Carolina Chowan association held as Salem": "Be so kind as to present my thanks to the churches of your association, & to assure them of my prayers for the continuance of every blessing to them now & hereafter." To John Adams (5 July 1814), Jefferson states, "Plato . . . is peculiarly appealed to as an advocate of the immortality of the soul; and yet I will venture to say that were there no better arguments than his in proof of it, not a man in the world would believe it." Given the counterfactual expression, Jefferson commits himself to what he believes are better arguments for the immortality of the soul than Plato's.[26] Also, he ends a lengthy political letter to Philadelphian Thomas Leiper (1 Jan. 1814) with "I pray god to bless you here and hereafter." Next, he tells his namesake Thomas Jefferson Smith (21 Feb. 1825): "Murmur not at the ways of Providence. So shall the life into which you have entered, be the portal to one of eternal and ineffable bliss." Here, context and correspondent are critical (as we will return to shortly).

What of Jefferson's mention of an afterlife in public messages and addresses? Jefferson, for instance, speaks of a universal religion in his First Inaugural Address. He speaks of Americans as "enlightened by a benign religion, professed, indeed, and practiced in various forms, yet all of them inculcating honesty, truth, temperance, gratitude and love of man; acknowledging and adoring an overruling providence, which by all its dispensations proves that it delights in the happiness of man here and his greater happiness hereafter."[27]

It is unsurprising that Jefferson should sometimes appeal to the afterlife in letters and in public messages and addresses. In some instances, this is merely a matter of politeness, and in other instances, it is a dissimulation of a sort. Jefferson sometimes mentions the afterlife in his letters as a gesture of politeness—for instance, to John Adams, for whom disbelief in an afterlife was a sufficient reason to part from life. Yet Jefferson also was fully aware that his religious views were not commonly embraced and was careful to speak and write to others in terms they could readily apprehend—hence, reference to the afterlife in his Second Inaugural Address. If that should be regarded as hypocrisy, it is hypocrisy of a relatively innocuous sort.

Yet, we must remain guarded here. In every reference to an afterlife, whether explicit or elliptical, Jefferson writes in a brachylogous manner, and that terseness is significant and evidence of a lack of conviction on

---

[26] Yet such better arguments might still be fallacious. Scherr infers that the lack of mention of any better arguments here is evidence of "the concept of immortality as 'nonsense.'" Arthur Scherr, "Thomas Jefferson, Immortality, and the Fear of Death: A Reconsideration," *Cithara* 56, no. 1, (2016): 50.

[27] Thomas Jefferson, "First Inaugural Address," in *Jefferson: Writings*, ed. Merrill D. Peterson (New York: Library of America, 1984), 494.

the topic. He never freely enters into a discussion of the hereafter, even with intimates, as he does with God, whom he considers mostly inscrutable.[28] In consequence, such references should not be taken as evidence of belief—for belief, as Jefferson formally wrote to Adams, is assent to a rationally intelligible proposition, and the notion of an afterlife seems not to be rationally intelligible (at least not in the metempirical manner in which it had been historically discussed). Hence, we are in position to understand Malone and Peterson on the soft pillow of ignorance.

We now turn to evaluate the scholarly arguments on behalf of Jefferson's take on the afterlife. Note that this exploration will intentionally omit a discussion of arguments regarding Jefferson's possible agnosticism, as in aiming to show that pro-afterlife arguments are uncogent and anti-afterlife arguments are cogent, claims of agnosticism become immaterial.

I begin with a critical investigation of some of the arguments for Jefferson's belief in an afterlife.

It is commonly asserted that Jefferson thought that the belief in an afterlife was an indispensable inducement for morally correct behavior. Charles Sanford, for instance, writes, "It is significant that Jefferson included the 'prospects of a future state' among the ingredients he thought necessary for inculcating moral behavior among people." He then cites Jefferson's 1814 letter to Law, where Jefferson states just that, as evidence. Sanford then adds:

> As a student of law and history and a practicing lawyer and
> statesman, he saw the importance of a belief in eternal judg-
> ment for encouraging a moral life of service to society. In his
> moral advice to others, he *constantly* [my italics] stressed the
> importance of the expectation of an eternal reward. In letters
> to two young people who were named after him [TJ to Thomas
> Jefferson Smith, 21 Feb. 1825, and TJ to Thomas Jefferson
> Grotian, 10 Jan. 1824], for example, he included the thought of

---

[28] TJ to John Adams, 15 Aug. 1820.

eternal reward of "ineffable bliss." In a much earlier letter to his young daughter Patsy [11 Dec. 1783], Jefferson gave similar advice to always "obey your conscience in order to be prepared for death."[29]

To acknowledge that belief in an afterlife conduces toward morally correct behavior is not to show that there is an afterlife, or even that Jefferson himself was committed to an afterlife. It merely shows that Jefferson thought the hoi polloi needed such an inducement to behave well, and behaving in a morality-abiding manner, necessary for social order and justice, is not behaving morally. Appeals to Jefferson's exposure to legal study and practice are unavailingly uncongent. The syllogism implicit in the first sentence is this: belief in an afterlife promotes virtuous behavior; virtuous behavior diminishes the number of miscreants; so, without belief in an afterlife, the criminal courts would be overcrowded with miscreants. Yet that argument, as an argument for Jefferson's belief in an afterlife, is paralogistic. To establish that Jefferson believed in an afterlife, one would need an argument such as this: justice is not always observed in criminal courts; God is preeminently just; so, God will reward virtue and punish vice in an afterlife.

The problem with that argument is that Jefferson never mentions a deity that rewards and punishes in an afterlife. Even his mention of a vengeful God in Query XVIII of his *Notes on Virginia* does not reference punition in a hereafter. He writes of an angry God, punishing American slaveholders for their practice of slavery: "I tremble for my country when I reflect that God is just: that his justice cannot sleep for ever: that considering numbers, nature and natural means only, a revolution of the wheel of fortune, an exchange of situations, is among possible events: that it may become probable by supernatural interference!"[30]

---

[29] Sanford, *The Religious Life of Thomas Jefferson*, 145.

[30] Thomas Jefferson, *Notes on the State of Virginia*, ed. William Peden (Chapel Hill, NC: University of North Carolina Press, 1954), 163.

Moreover, Jefferson commonplaces Bolingbroke in several places on the absurdity of an afterlife that is retributive in nature. In §36, Jefferson writes:

> [N]either the people of Israel, nor their legislator perhaps, knew anything of [a]nother life, wherein the crimes committed in this life are to be punished;—if Moses know that crimes were to be punished in [a]nother life he deceived the people in the covenant they made by his intervention with god. if he did not know it, I say it with horror, the consequence, according to the hypothesis I oppose must be that god deceived both him and them. in either case a covenant or bargain was made, wherein the conditions of obedience and disobedience were not fully, nor the consequence fairly stated.[31]

In §42, Bolingbroke writes of redemption: "if the redemption be the main fundamental article of the christian faith, sure I am, that the account of the fall of man is the foundation of his fundamental article, and this account is, in all it's circumstances, absolutely irreconcileable to every idea we can frame of wisdom, justice, and goodness, to say nothing of the dignity of the supreme being."[32] In §52, Bolingbroke writes of the injustice of eternal punition:

> the miserable state of wicked men in hell is an exercise of justice delayed, but exercised so severely at last, that it would [e]xceed vastly all the necessary degrees of terror, if any of these creatures remained after it in an undetermined condition wherein terror might have it's effect.—justice requires that punishments, and we must say the same of rewards, the two sanctions of all laws, be measure [o]ut in various degrees and manners, according to the various [c]ircumstances of particular cases, and in a due proportion to them.

---

[31] Jefferson, *Jefferson's Literary Commonplace Book*, 40–41.
[32] Jefferson, *Jefferson's Literary Commonplace Book*, 45.

Commonplacing Bolingbroke—and I have argued elsewhere that Bolingbroke's religiosity shaped Jefferson's thinking more than any other thinker[33]—is not proof that Jefferson did not believe in an afterlife, but rather evidence that he did not believe in an afterlife of reward and punition. Like Bolingbroke, Jefferson also believed that eternal reward or eternal punition—where reward and punition are measured in accordance with deeds—would be out of character for a just God.

Here one could also consider Sanford's argument that "Jefferson had begun with the conviction that God had created in man a hunger for the rights of equality, freedom, and life and a desire to follow God's moral law. It was only a small step further to believe that God had also created man with an immortal soul."[34] This argument too is paralogistic—it might be a small step, but it is still a step. Yet this step might *not* be so small, and I suspect that it is not. God also created other creatures with certain hungers and desires to act as their God-crafted nature bid them to act. Are we then to presume that they also have immortal souls? Is that also not just another step for each of those creatures? We have only to return to certain passages of Bolingbroke, commonplaced by Jefferson (see Chapter One), indicating that humans have no special significance in the cosmos and that humans ought not to anthropomorphize deity (§§16 and 46).[35]

Finally, there is Sanford's argument regarding grief.[36] Recall that Sanford quotes Jefferson in a letter to Adams: "All of our other passions, within proper bounds, have an useful object, but what is the use of grief in the economy [of nature]?"

First, Sanford takes liberties with the quote, and that sort of liberty occurs not infrequently in his book. It should read: "All our other passions, within proper bounds, have an useful object. And the perfection of the moral character is, not in a Stoical apathy, so hypocritically vaunted, and so untruly too, because impossible, but in a just equilibrium of all the

---

[33] M. Andrew Holowchak, *Thomas Jefferson's Bible, With Introduction and Commentary* (Berlin: DeGruyter, 2018), 9–12.

[34] Sanford, *The Religious Life of Thomas Jefferson*, 152.

[35] Jefferson, *Jefferson's Literary Commonplace Book*, 29, 43–44.

[36] Sanford, *The Religious Life of Thomas Jefferson*, 152–56.

passions. I wish the pathologists then would tell us what is the use of grief in the economy, and of what good it is the cause, proximate or remote."

Moreover, there are further issues beyond the liberties taken in Sanford's use of the passage, wherein he omits an ellipsis to show missing text. Sanford is right to assert that Jefferson's consternation concerns a cosmos, constructed by a deity who, in his mind—and here Jefferson is no different from numerous other cosmologists of his day—makes everything for some end. If all human attributes are for the sake of some end, then so too is grief.

This difficulty was not discovered by Jefferson; it was a puzzle for ancient teleological philosophers in Greco-Roman antiquity. Cicero (106–43 BC), for instance, discusses grieving in his *Tusculan Disputations.* Introducing and critically discussing the views of six philosophers or schools of thinking from antiquity on grieving, he concludes that grieving is not natural but human caused. "Whatever evil distress has, it's not due to nature, but brought to a head by a judgment of the will and by a mistaken belief that some great evil has happened." Sums Cicero, "Thus, the evil of grieving comes from belief, not from nature."[37]

Sanford notes that Jefferson winds up agreeing with Adams that grief is not without purpose. God gave grief to men to allow for some command of passions and prejudices, as well as instruction in patience, resignation, and tranquility. Sanford says, "A reconciliation to one's own death because of loneliness for lost family and friends was the only use Jefferson could find for grief." He adds, "Stoic philosophy was not enough to answer the questions of life after death."[38] And so, Sanford grants that nothing here is evidence for an afterlife. Thus, he devotes some four and one half pages to a discussion of grief, titled "The Uses of Grief," as a subsection to a section titled "Ideas of Life after Death," and ultimately concludes that this discussion tells us nothing about Jefferson's view of the afterlife.

---

[37] Cicero, *Tusculan Disputations*, trans. J. E. King (Cambridge: Harvard University Press, [1927] 1945), 3.70 ff.
[38] Sanford, *The Religious Life of Thomas Jefferson*, 156.

Contextomy is also a common issue throughout Sanford's work. One striking example cites a letter to Jefferson's nephew Peter Carr (10 Aug. 1787) as epistolary evidence of Jefferson's belief in an afterlife: "'The hope of a happy existence in a future state increases the appetite to deserve it.'" Yet the sentence reads otherwise: "If that there be a future state, the hope of a happy existence in that increases the appetite to deserve it." Allowing the consequent (i.e., the "then" part of the "if-then" statement) to stand by itself as a declarative assertion changes the sentence's meaning. An assertion, conditioned in Jefferson's words, becomes an unconditioned assertion.

We now turn to consider the arguments of others who have written less voluminously on the subject of Jefferson's views on the afterlife.

There is Eugene Sheridan's hope-triumphed-over-despair argument. That argument is not bolstered by any textual evidence; he offers no passages that would make the view plausible. Recall that Sheridan writes that Jefferson "approved Jesus's teaching that God would mete out punishments as well as rewards after death"—approved because Jefferson kept it in his own bible—and so he himself must have appropriated that view. Yet Jefferson included many passages in his version of Jesus's teachings (e.g., the fall of Jerusalem and the notion of forgiveness) that he did not embrace. Sheridan's argument makes sense only if Jefferson constructed his bible to suit his own moral purposes instead of aiming to get at the real teachings and genuine life of Jesus. And, as I have argued in Chapter Three, Jefferson's bible is not necessarily a source book of Jefferson's own moral beliefs.

Paul Conkin, noting that Jefferson "nourished consoling beliefs about the universe and at times enjoyed a sense of wonderment and awe," asserts that Jefferson "always was confident of life after death." Yet he provides no primary source material to back this claim and falls back merely on the notion that Jefferson *could* have found consolation in his belief in an afterlife.

We turn next to Boles's claim that Jefferson believed in an afterlife because he patterned his life after Jesus, who believed in an afterlife. In many respects, Jefferson did pattern his life after Jesus—though I suspect the Stoics were a larger influence[39]—yet as he tells William Short (13 Apr. 1820), he did not follow Jesus in all things. And I quote again, "It is not to be understood that I am with [Jesus] in all of his doctrines. I am a Materialist; he takes the side of Spiritualism; he preaches the efficacy of repentance towards forgiveness of sin; I require a counterpoise of good works to redeem it, &c., &c." So, we cannot merely assume Jefferson's belief in an afterlife because Jesus preached that there was one. All things considered, if we know that Jefferson took up most of what Jesus preached, that Jesus preached the existence of an afterlife, and that we have no further relevant evidence that has a bearing on Jefferson's views of the afterlife, then we would have more reason than not to adopt the stance that Jefferson did, in fact, believe in an afterlife. Yet, as I will demonstrate shortly, there is further relevant evidence that has a bearing on this issue.

Carl Richards's argument on the subject is intriguing because it harkens back to Priestley's influence on Jefferson. Richards, we recall, worked within the frame of Jefferson's materialism. He maintains that Jefferson believed in an afterlife because he embraced the view of bodily resurrection sometime after death.[40] With resurrection of the body, and given the soul being itself some sort of matter, uniquely configured, then the soul too is capable of revivification. The question is this: Where does Jefferson specifically say that the body will be resurrected after death? We cannot merely presume that Jefferson believed in bodily resurrection because Priestley did. As discussed in the previous chapter, Jefferson's religious views were radically different from those of Priestley in key respects. Jefferson owed much more to Bolingbroke than Priestley.

As noted previously, William Gould argues that God gave humans reason and that each person will be judged pursuant to his use, or misuse, of his rational faculty. Wishing all persons to be eternally happy, God rewards those individuals who submit to his will with an eternal and

---

[39] See M. Andrew Holowchak, *Thomas Jefferson, Moralist* (Jefferson, NC: McFarland, 2017), chap. 9.

[40] Scherr mistakenly asserts that championing materialism rules out the possibility of an afterlife. Scherr, "Thomas Jefferson, Immortality, and the Fear of Death," 62.

ineffably blissful afterlife. Here, Gould draws from Jefferson's exhortatory letter to his nephew Peter Carr (10 Aug. 1787). Yet, in this letter, Jefferson merely advises his nephew to explore rationally all aspects of a religious view. He merely tells Carr that if reason leads him to believe in a future state, then "the hope of a happy existence in that increases the appetite to deserve it." Jefferson sums, "Your own reason is the only oracle given you by heaven, and you are answerable not for the rightness but uprightness of the decision." Jefferson is not telling Carr what to believe but how to go about religious exploration: "Fix reason firmly in her seat."

In addition, there is Scherr's argument stemming from the axial principles of religion. The true principles of religion are common to all religions, yet belief in an afterlife is not common to all religions, and so Jefferson did not necessarily believe in an afterlife. This argument is seemingly aligned with Jefferson's 1814 letter to Law (June 13), where he asserts that only duties to God and duties to humans are the true principles of morality.[41] While Scherr acknowledges this, he takes certain liberties with Jefferson's letter. According to Scherr, while Jefferson clearly states that morality comprises "duties to God and duties to men" in that letter, "the former [for Jefferson is] a less essential aspect of the moral life than [is] the latter." The addendum is rather puzzling. If two things, A and B, are essential aspects of some third thing, C, what does it mean for something to be more, or less, essential? For instance, every recipe for ale requires water, malt, and yeast.[42] Is any single ingredient *more* necessary than any other? Thus, allowing for degrees of essentiality, is, for Scherr, a dodge. He seemingly wishes to allow for the possibility that Jefferson is a moral atheist, which, as I have shown in Chapter Two, is not plausible. An atheist can act in a morality-obedient manner, but to do so without mindfulness of one's duties to God is, for Jefferson, not the same as *being* moral.

Again, we might also note that Jefferson often and incautiously states that all religions embrace the core principles of duties to God and men, and

---

[41] Cf. TJ to George Logan (12 Nov. 1816), where Jefferson says the sum of all religion is "fear god and love thy neighbor."

[42] One can make ale without hops, though that is seldom done.

that is, clearly, not the case. Much rests, however, on a settled definition of "religion." In his 1822 letter to Waterhouse (June 26), when confronted with "the demoralizing dogmas of Calvinism," which makes nothing of "love of our neighbor," Jefferson merely asserts that Calvinism is "a counter-religion made up from the *deliria* of crazy imaginations." So, Jefferson, if he were wedded to the hereafter, would likely offer a similar reply—that any religion which dismisses the afterlife is not a true religion.

Scherr also asserts: "At no time did Jefferson seriously express expectations of immortality. His empiricist epistemology and materialist metaphysics would probably have ruled out adoption of such a belief."

And, finally, Scherr's statement (unsupported by any primary resource) that Jefferson "probably considered belief in an afterlife puerile" needs no commentary, as it is merely asserted, not supported.

"That Eternal Separation Which We Are Shortly to Make"
Evidence of a Singular Sort

In the previous section, I analyze Boles's argument that, *ceteris paribus*, if Jefferson tended to uptake the teachings of Jesus and if there is no telling evidence one way or the other vis-à-vis Jefferson's view of the afterlife, then we are in a position to assert with some degree of confidence that Jefferson believed in an afterlife, simply because Jesus did. The argument, while inductive, is far from foolproof, but the evidence of the premises gives us more reason than not to accept the conclusion (i.e., Jefferson's belief in the afterlife) as true.

Yet the problem with inductive arguments is that they are always susceptible to additional evidence. That additional evidence can often transform a strongly supported conclusion into one that is weakly supported. Consider the following argument:

Angelique, who likes Barnabus, is being escorted to the costume ball by him.

Barnabus tends to be gentlemanly at social events.

So, Angelique will have fun at the costume ball.

Now consider the argument with certain relevant additional evidence:

Angelique, who likes Barnabus, is being escorted to the costume ball by him.

Barnabus tends to be gentlemanly at social events.

At this ball, there is an open bar with Barnabus's favorite drink, the Bloody Mary.

Whenever Barnabus is around Bloody Marys, he gets drunk and acts aggressively.

So, Angelique will have fun at the costume ball.

With the evidence provided by the third and fourth premises, it is now very unlikely that Angelique will have fun at the costume ball. It is now likely that she will have a dreadful time. It is the same, I aim to show, with Jefferson and the afterlife.

First, we can dismiss Jefferson's references to an afterlife in public messages and addresses. They are irrelevant. They are evidence of both personal politeness and some measure of political posturing, not a cognitive commitment. The same can be said for Jefferson's references to the afterlife in numerous letters where politeness is certainly a key factor. Jefferson's uncharacteristic terseness on the subject of the afterlife in such references is evidence that they should be taken *cum grano salis*. Moreover, Jefferson's polite references to the afterlife are not as numerous as Sanford leads us to believe.

Yet there are letters of a different sort that must be weighed differently and taken more seriously. Why is this so?

As shown in many letters, Jefferson was always reticent about expressing his religious views to others. First, he constantly preached that religion was a personal, not public, issue. For religionists, religious expression is between them and their God. Jefferson believed that the rights of nonbelievers should also be respected. Second, had his personal views become public, he would have been subject to prodigiously more ridicule than he hitherto had been—especially in his election years as president.

Yet there exists weighty epistolary evidence in the form of four key letters from Jefferson to trusted intimates—and the fact that those letters are to intimates, to trusted sources, is critical. The first letter shows Jefferson's early skepticism concerning belief in an afterlife. The last three letters are evidence of his conviction that there is no afterlife. These four important letters offer evidence that Jefferson has lifted his head from the pillow of ignorance, as mentioned in his letter to Isaac Story (15 Aug. 1801), because the science of his day had begun to shed light on what Jefferson had earlier perceived to be a wholly metempirical concern.

The first is a very early letter from Jefferson to his boyhood friend John Page (26 July 1764), indicative of his early skepticism about the soul leaving the body "at the instant of death."[43] At just twenty-one years old, Jefferson recounts a story from a magazine that concerns a man who drowned and was submerged in water for some twenty-four hours. The man, though presumed dead, was brought back to life by a method "to give the vital warmth to the whole body by gentle degrees, and to put the blood in motion by inflating the lungs." We are taught, he continues to Page, that when the bodily organs completely cease to function, the "soul leaves the body." He sums, "But does not this story contradict this opinion?" Here the suggestion is that the soul is inseparable from the body, and it hints at Jefferson's commitment to Bolingbrokean materialism. The soul could be revitalized only because the bodily material, which comprises it, had not sufficiently decomposed.

In a letter to John Adams (14 Mar. 1820), Jefferson references the works of Dugald Stewart, A. L. C. Destutt de Tracy, and Pierre Jean George Cabanis. He considers Stuart and Tracy "the ablest Metaphysicians living," by which he means "[i]nvestigators of the thinking faculty of man." "Stuart

---

[43] Scherr acknowledges and discusses the letter. Arthur Scherr, "Thomas Jefferson versus the Historians: Christianity, Atheistic Morality, and the Afterlife," *Church History* 83, no. 1 (2014): 62.

seems to have given it's natural history, from facts and observations; Tracy it's modes of action and deduction, which he calls Logic, and Ideology." Yet it is Cabanis who has done the real empirical groundwork. In his seminal work, *On the Relations between the Physical and Moral Aspects of Man* (1802), which was a bombshell in materialist psychology, Cabanis "has investigated anatomically, and most ingeniously, the particular organs in the human structure which may most probably exercise that faculty." Following such thinkers, Jefferson offers an argument in two parts. First, he proceeds analogically. Thought is to the material organ of the mind as magnetism is to a needle or elasticity is to a spring—merely a product of the matter thus structured. Dissolve the matter and the magnetism and elasticity consequently cease. It is likewise with thought. "On ignition of the needle or spring, their magnetism and elasticity cease. So on dissolution of the material organ by death, its action of thought may cease also, and that nobody supposes that the magnetism or elasticity retire to hold a substantive and distinct existence. These were qualities only of particular conformations of matter; change the conformation, and its qualities change also." The passage proffers an argument, via analogy, that the mind is merely a certain configuration of matter. Destroy that unique material configuration and you destroy the mind.

The question now becomes whether matter can be so structured that thought can occur. Following Locke, Jefferson considers the arguments of spiritualists, who deny that "certain forms of matter" have a capacity for thought. He again appeals to metaphysical simplicity and asserts, "When I meet with a proposition beyond finite comprehension, I abandon it as I do a weight which human strength cannot lift, and I think ignorance, in these cases, is truly the softest pillow on which I can lay my head." Immediately, he adds, "Were it necessary, however, to form an opinion, I confess I should, with Mr. Locke, prefer swallowing one incomprehensibility rather than two." In sum, matter endowed with thought is less incomprehensible than "an existence called spirit, of which we have neither evidence nor idea, and then . . . how that spirit, which has neither extension nor solidity, can put material organs into motion."

The overall argument is similar to one found in Unitarian minister Joseph Priestley's *Disquisitions on Matter and Spirit*. For Priestley, matter and the power of attraction are coextensive. Each body, called an atom[44] but divisible, has parts, which "must be infinitely hard, and therefore must have powers of mutual attraction infinitely strong, or it could not hold together, that is, it could not exist as a solid atom." Priestley adds, "From whatever source these powers are derived, or by whatever being they are communicated, matter cannot exist without them; and if that superior power, or being, withdraw its influence, the substance itself necessarily ceases to exist, or is annihilated." Thus, solidity is a consequence of certain powers, "if there be any foundation for the plainest and best established rules of reasoning in philosophy."[45]

In his later-life letters to John Adams (8 Jan. 1825) and to Francis Adrian Van der Kemp (11 Jan. 1825), Jefferson excitedly references experiments by Flourens and Cabanis on vertebrates. Writing to John Adams, Jefferson calls Jean Pierre Flourens's *Experiences sur le système nerveux* "the most extraordinary of all books." After removing the cerebrum of some vertebrates, Flourens finds that "the animal loses all it's senses of hearing, seeing, feeling, smelling, tasting, and is totally deprived of will, intelligence, memory, perception," though it retains the power of locomotion, given external stimuli. After removing the cerebellum from some vertebrates, he found that "the animal retains all it's senses, faculties & understanding, but loses the power of regulated motion, and exhibits all the symptoms of drunkenness." Puncture of the *medulla elonga* results in instantaneous death. He sums: "Cabanis had proved [in his 1802 work], from the anatomical structure of certain portions of the human frame, that they might be capable of receiving from the Creator the faculty of thinking. Flourens proves that the cerebrum is the thinking organ, and that life and health may continue, and the animal be entirely without thought, if deprived

---

[44] A strange use of the word, as *atomos* means "uncuttable or indivisible thing" in Greek, and the notion was introduced to indicate the smallest possible entity.

[45] The difference is that Priestley believed in an afterlife insofar as a body decomposed could be recomposed by deity. Joseph Priestley, *Disquisitions Relating to Matter and Spirit* (London: J. Johnson, 1777), 2–8, 160–64.

of that organ." Jefferson adds with rodomontade: "I wish to see what the spiritualists will say to this. whether, in this state, the soul remains in the body deprived of it's essence of thought, or whether it leaves it as in death and where it goes?"

Three days later, Jefferson writes to François Adrian Van der Kemp about Flourens's experiments, which demonstrate that the cerebrum is the "organ of thought" and "possesses alone the faculty of thinking." He expresses a desire to know whether the soul remains in the body when the brain is deprived of thought and, if it does leave, where it goes, if the thoughtless body still lives. The implication, once again, is that certain powers of the soul are localized in certain parts of the material brain. If those parts are materially disfigured, destroyed, or removed from the body, the animal loses those powers. Jefferson sums:

> [T]his is a terrible tub thrown out to the Athanasians. they
> must tell us whether the soul remains in the body in this state,
> deprived of the power of thought? or does it leave the body, as
> in death? and where does it go? can it be recieved into heaven
> while it's body is living on earth? these and a multitude of other
> questions it will be incumbent on them to answer otherwise
> than by the dogma that every one who believeth not with them
> without doubt shall perish everlastingly. the Materialist, fortified
> by these new proofs of his own creed, will hear with derision
> these Athanasian denunciations.

These letters to Adams and Van der Kemp offer compelling evidence of Jefferson's commitment to the dissolution of mind upon the death of a person. Regarding such letters, Charles Sanford remarks: "Matter had many mysterious properties, such as magnetism gravity, and the power of the brain to think. Why not immortality for human beings?"[46] Yet that logic does not follow the analogical strain of Jefferson's argument.

---

[46] Sanford, *The Religious Beliefs of Thomas Jefferson*, 82.

The aforementioned letters to Adams and Van der Kemp are not decisive—Jefferson knows that they must be considered with due caution—but they offer abundant evidence of doubt in Jefferson's mind concerning the soul's capacity to survive without the body. Given the cerebrum is the seat of sensation, perception, intelligence, memory, and thought, and given that the cerebellum is responsible for regulated motion, all the functions attributed to the soul seem to be explicable by the material brain. The conclusion seems plain that the soul is just the brain and the cerebrum is the intellective soul—a reductive view that is consistent with the drift of thinking that appears in much of the literature on contemporary philosophy of mind.[47]

More can be added to the evidence provided by these four intriguing letters to Jefferson's intimates. There are Jefferson's parting words with his wife, Martha; the excessive grief he exhibited after Martha's passing; his reaction to the death of his sister Jane; his changes of the Bible; and his reticence to share his own religious beliefs with anyone—even members of his family.

We first turn to consider the parting words shared between Jefferson and his moribund wife, which were taken directly from Laurence Sterne. With Martha Jefferson moribund, she and Jefferson copy prose from Laurence Sterne's *Tristram Shandy* to a sheet of paper:

Time wastes too fast: every letter
I trace tells me with what rapidity
life follows my pen. The days and hours
of it [. . .] are flying over our heads like

---

[47] That was also the view of Jefferson's dear friend Dr. Thomas Cooper. Cooper had sent Jefferson a copy of his new manuscript on materialism, which Jefferson acknowledged on March 29, 1824—in his final letter to Cooper. In Cooper's booklet, writing under the name of "A Layman" and following the works of Cabanis and Tracy, he argues similarly that the attributes of the soul are just those of the brain—that is, that there is no such thing as an immaterial soul. "The Soul therefore is not immortal." Cooper also convinced Jefferson that the notion of an afterlife in the four Gospels related only to the day of judgment, and that day concerns the resurrection of the soul only insofar as there is bodily resurrection on that day. Thomas Cooper, *A View of the Metaphysical and Physiological Arguments in Favour of Materialism* (Philadelphia: A. Small, 1824), 12, 24.

[light] clouds of windy day never to return—
more every thing presses on—*and every*
time I kiss thy hand to bid adieu, every absence which
follows it, are preludes to that eternal separation
which we are shortly to make!

The italicized part of the passage on the folded paper is in Jefferson's hand; the first half is in the writing of Martha. The paper, when found after Jefferson's death, contained a lock of Martha's hair. Were Jefferson, and his wife, committed to belief in an afterlife, this shared moment of intimacy would not have included a reference to "that eternal separation we are shortly to make." One could, of course, take that to mean "separation of soul from body *en route* to the afterlife," but that is, I think, taking too much liberty with words, which unfortunately happens much too often in Jeffersonian scholarship. The passage is not hopeful, but sorrowful.

Furthermore, we must consider if the excessive grief Jefferson suffered upon Martha's passing in 1782 was not indicative of one who believed he would meet his wife again in the hereafter upon his own death. His grief was excessive because it was grounded in a recognition of no possibility of reunion.[48] Daughter Martha, who was certainly devastated herself, wrote of their final days and her father's grieving subsequently.

During my mother's life he (Jefferson) bestowed much time
and attention on our education—our cousins, the Carrs, and
myself—and after her death, during the first month of desolation which followed, I was his constant companion while we
remained at Monticello. . . . As a nurse no female ever had more
tenderness nor anxiety. He nursed my poor mother in turn with
aunt Carr and her own sister—sitting up with her and administering her medicines and drink to the last. For four months that
she lingered he was never out of calling; when not at her bedside,
he was writing in a small room which opened immediately at

---

[48] This point was brought to my attention by Arthur Scherr.

the head of her bed. A moment before the closing scene, he was
led from the room in a state of insensibility by his sister, Mrs.
Carr, who, with great difficulty, got him into the library, where
he fainted, and remained so long insensible that they feared
he never would revive. The scene that followed I did not witness, but the violence of his emotion, when, almost by stealth,
I entered his room by night, to this day I dare not describe
to myself. He kept his room three weeks, and I was never a
moment from his side. He walked almost incessantly night and
day, only lying down occasionally, when nature was completely
exhausted, on a pallet that had been brought in during his long
fainting-fit. My aunts remained constantly with him for some
weeks—I do not remember how many. When at last he left his
room, he rode out, and from that time he was incessantly on
horseback, rambling about the mountain, in the least frequented
roads, and just as often through the woods. In those melancholy
rambles I was his constant companion—a solitary witness to
many a burst of grief, the remembrance of which has conse-
crated particular scenes of that lost home beyond the power of
time to obliterate.[49]

The intensity and duration of Jefferson's reaction to his beloved wife's
death, it is reasonable to assert—and most scholars are in agreement on
this—betray the depth of feelings he had for her. It would be strange for a
man of such high intelligence to grieve so if he was indeed committed to
a belief in the hereafter.

There is also Jefferson's reaction to the death of his much-beloved
sister, Jane. When Jane, unwed, prematurely died on October 1, 1765, at
twenty-five years of age, Jefferson was crushed. Writes great-granddaughter
Sarah N. Randolph: "The loss of such a sister to such a brother was irrep-
arable; his grief or her was deep and constant; and there are, perhaps few

---

[49] Sarah N. Randolph, *The Domestic Life of Thomas Jefferson, Compiled from Family
Letters and Reminiscences* (New York: Harper & Brothers, 1871), 62–63.

incidents in the domestic details of history more beautiful than his devotion to her during her life, and the tenderness of the love with which he cherished her memory to the last days of his long and eventful career."[50] He crafted an epitaph:

Ah, Joanna, puellarum optima,
Ah, aevi virentis flore, praerepta,
Sit tibi terra laevis;
Longe, longeque valeto.[51]

There is no evidence that Jefferson's grief upon Jane's passing was such as it was when his wife died, yet we must assume, given Jefferson's great love of his sisters and the similarities between Jane and Martha Wayles Skelton,[52] that Jefferson grieved greatly on her passing. Along with the untimely death of his best friend Dabney Carr, it was one of the great early losses of his life. Jefferson lost not only a sister, but also his soul mate, and in the last line of his epitaph, he writes "farewell forever and forever," which implies an eternal separation.

Next, we return to Jefferson's bible. Here, Jefferson did not include any mention from the Gospels of Jesus being raised from his tomb after his death. Jefferson could readily have chosen Priestley's path—that Jesus, though a man, was given by God certain superhuman powers, one of which being a capacity to overcome death, in an effort to be a moral inducement to others. Acknowledging that the hoi polloi require a belief in the afterlife to encourage virtuous behavior, he could have, at least, included Christ's rising from his tomb as a moral goad for the masses. Yet he did not, and the reason seems simple: he did not believe in the possibility of an afterlife.

Finally, though Jefferson somewhat guardedly shared snippets of his religious views with intimates such as William Short and John Adams,

---

[50] Sarah N. Randolph, *The Domestic Life of Thomas Jefferson* (Cambridge: University Press, 1939), 22.

[51] Roughly, "O Jane, best of youthful women, / Ah, taken prematurely in the prime of youthful vigor, / May the earth be light on you; / farewell forever and forever."

[52] See M. Andrew Holowchak, *Thomas Jefferson: Psychobiography of an American Lion* (Hauppauge, NY: Nova Science, 2019), chap. 1.

he refused to share anything with members of his own family. In his 1787 letter to Peter Carr, he bids his nephew to examine both the view that Christ was a god, capable of supernatural deeds, and the stance that Christ was a mere mortal, merely capable of extraordinary wisdom. Christ's nature is a matter for Carr to decide for himself. Grandson Thomas Jefferson Randolph said after the passing of his grandfather, "Of his peculiar religious opinions his family know no more than the world."[53] One grandchild, biographer William S. Randall notes, quoted Jefferson in reply to a request to reveal his own religious views. "If I inform you of mine, they will influence yours—I will not take the responsibility of directing any one's judgment on this subject."[54]

Religious belief, then, had implications. Had Jefferson firmly believed in an afterlife, his refusal to convey that belief is difficult to grasp. Following Pascal's wager and in believing, then, as he would have believed, members of Jefferson's family would have had everything to gain: promises of future reward and of escape from eternal perdition. Jefferson's refusal to share his religious beliefs only makes sense if he indeed did not believe in an afterlife. Jefferson—following the lead of Bolingbroke, who recognized that eternal punishment is inconsistent with divine goodness—likely thought an afterlife was largely improbable but still possible. Should he be wrong about the afterlife, then others to whom he would have communicated his views might eternally suffer. Moreover, even if he should not be wrong, others who could not suffer through life without the promise of an afterlife—consider John Adams, as we have seen—would endure far more hardship in this life. Yet Jefferson seemed sure of one thing: that integrity of forming judgments through the fullest use of reason was more important than chancing upon the right opinion without integrity. No deity at the gates of heaven would fault a person for the fullest use of reason.

---

[53] William S. Randall, *The Writings of Thomas Jefferson*, vol. 3 (Philadelphia: J. B. Lippincott, 1871), 561.

[54] Randall, *The Writings of Thomas Jefferson*, vol. 3, 561.

Concluding Thoughts

And so, what can we reasonably conclude? Jefferson's letters from the 1820s concerning experiments on animals' brains and his bible, which was completed in 1820, strongly intimate a clear commitment to no belief in an afterlife at that time. His writing "farewell forever and forever" on the death of sister Jane, and of the "eternal separation" he and his wife, Martha, were about to endure prior to her death in 1782, largely suggest his lack of belief in the afterlife. Jefferson's 1764 letter to Page is at least good evidence of his early skepticism concerning the afterlife. Thus, the best evidence that we have offers us no reason to think that he ever seriously considered the notion of life after death. The most we can say is that he might have been open to the possibility of life after death very early in life, and that is not saying much.

Thus, while Jesus was committed to love of God, duties to one's fellow man, and belief in an afterlife as the core principles of morality, Jefferson was very probably committed only to love of God and duties to one's fellow man.

CHAPTER FIVE

"Cerberus, with One Body and Three Heads"

Jefferson's Unitarianism

"The doctrine of Transubstantiation implies a physical impossibility, whereas that of the Trinity, as unfolded in the Athanasian Creed, implies a mathematical one; and to this only we usually give the name of contradiction."

—Joseph Priestley

J efferson frequently spoke out concerning his aversion to the adoption of any sectarian religion. "I have never permitted myself to mediate a specified creed," he writes to Rev. Thomas Whittemore (5 June 1822). "[T]hese formulas have been the bane and ruin of the Christian church, its own fatal invention which through so many ages, made Christendom a slaughter house, and to this day divides it into castes of inextinguishable hatred of one another." Yet, later in life, he habitually spoke favorably of one particular religion, Unitarianism, and even claimed to be a Unitarian. He states in a letter to James Smith (8 Dec. 1822), "I confidently expect that the present generation will see Unitarianism become the general religion of the United States." The sentiment certainly implies approbation and personal sanction of Unitarianism.

Are we here faced with just another instance of Jefferson's avowed "monumental" confusion,[1] "blithe hypocrisy,"[2] or Tartuffery? How can one consistently speak favorably of a particular religion, even wish to see it as the adopted religion of a fledgling country, and yet steadfastly refuse to accept any particular religion?

In this chapter, I offer an answer, and a relatively simple one, to these questions. With a focus on the Unitarianism of Rev. Richard Price and Rev. Joseph Priestley—they were Unitarians who had views with which Jefferson had some familiarity—I begin with a précis of the Unitarian movement. Next, I turn to Jefferson's budding interest in Unitarianism. In the final section, I address the following questions: Was Unitarianism, for Jefferson, a sectarian religion? If so, did Jefferson later in life come to sanction "a specific creed" by sanctioning Unitarianism? If not, precisely to what did Jefferson's sanction of Unitarianism amount? An inspection of Jefferson's writings on Unitarianism shows that the answers to such questions are astonishingly simple.

"These Sacred Blessings Will Spread"
Unitarianism in Jefferson's Day

Unitarianism, a religious movement that began in 1565 in Transylvania, sprang up, as its name shows, in response to Trinitarianism. Unitarians rejected the notion of three gods in one, and thus, they also rejected the divinity of Christ. While Jesus might have been a superhumanly powerful being, he was not the son of God. They also rejected other dogmata, such as predestination, original sin, and the inerrancy of the authors of the Bible.

Unitarianism, as a religion of reason and not of revelation, partnered neatly with the rampant deism and rationalism of the Enlightenment and, consequently, attracted deists and rationalists who otherwise would give no expression to their religiosity.[3] "As an open religion, insistent on the

---

[1] Winthrop Jordan, *White over Black: American Attitudes toward the Negro, 1550–1812* (Baltimore: Penguin, 1969), 453.

[2] Robert Dawidoff, "The Jefferson Option," *Political Theory* 21, no. 3 (1993): 438.

[3] Earl Morse Wilbur, *A History of Unitarianism* (Cambridge, MA: Harvard University Press, 1952), 47–48.

right of all to free enquiry in religion, Unitarianism had no set creeds," writes Ruth Watts, "and throughout the 19th century was subject to varying internal divisions." She continues:

> Yet Unitarians were characterized by their denial of the Trinity and of original sin, their affirmation of applying reason to the scriptures as to everything else, and their quest for moral order and perfection. A deep belief in rational education as a prerequisite for all[,] if they were to obtain true morality and religion[,] underpinned their huge commitment to educational ventures and social reform, including greater equality for women than was the norm.[4]

Unitarianism was essentially a religion of liberal religious reforms, and the chief reform was to begin with a just and correct notion of God—a reform of which Jefferson made purchase. Prominent minister William Ellery Channing writes of Unitarianism at the ordination of Rev. Jared Sparks: "We believe in the doctrine of God's UNITY, or that there is one God, and one only. . . . The proposition, that there is one God, seems to us exceedingly plain. We understand by it, that there is one being, one mind, one person, one intelligent agent, and one only, to whom underived and infinite perfection and dominion belong." Unitarians believe, he adds, that "God is infinitely good, kind, benevolent, in the proper sense of these words; good in disposition, as well as in act; good, not to a few, but to all; good to every individual, as well as to the general system." They do not believe Jesus was both human and the son of God, and they assert that he is "distinct from, and inferior to, God."[5]

Unitarians were not merely focused on the oneness of God. They aimed at a just, rational notion of God. Consider what Jefferson writes to

---

[4] Ruth Watts, "Unitarianism," *Oxford Bibliographies*, accessed February 6, 2019, www .oxfordbibliographies.com/view/document/obo-9780199799558/obo-9780199799558-0121 .xml.

[5] William Ellery Channing, "Unitarian Christianity," (sermon, ordination of Rev. Jared Sparks, First Independent Church of Baltimore, MD, May 5, 1819), accessed June 29, 2017, http://people.bu.edu/dklepper/RN212/unitarian.html.

Welshman Dr. Richard Price (26 Oct. 1788): "Plutarch, it is well known, has observd very justly that it is better not to believe in a God than to believe him to be a capricious and malevolent being. These reflexions have Struck me very forcibly.[6] . . . They shew how incumbent it is on all who wish the happiness of the world to endeavour to propagate just notions of the Deity and of religion. I can reflect with Some Satisfaction that this has been one of the Studies and labours of my life." This notion harkens back to the argument posited in Chapter One. Failure to grasp whatever we can of Jefferson's deity and of his cosmos places us in a sorry position to grasp his religious views. If we begin with wrongheaded notions of God, then we misconstrue divine and cosmic purposiveness, and anthropocentric views of deity, like those expressed in the Old Testament, color the sort of sectarian religion we craft and the metaphysical claims we embrace. For Jefferson, true religion begins with a just notion of God.

Price, with whom Jefferson exchanged mostly political letters in the late 1780s, was a prominent Unitarian minister, ethician, and mathematician. He was pastor of London's Newington Green Unitarian Church and shared many of Rev. Joseph Priestley's views. Like Priestley, he rejected the notions of the Trinity, original sin, and a retributive deity. Like Priestley, he also believed that Christ was a cynosure and great moral reformist—"God who sent Christ into the world and who is his, no less than he is our God and father"[7]—and that humans were capable of much moral improvement. Yet, pace Priestley, he believed in the immateriality of the soul and that the immaterial soul had human free will.

Observations on the Importance of the American Revolution (1785), which Price sent to Jefferson and which Jefferson read,[8] shows Price's Unitarianism was especially democratic:

---

[6] The context concerns Jefferson's thoughts on reading a book by Jacques Necker, *On the Importance of Religious Opinions* (London: J. Johnson, 1788).
[7] Richard Price, "Observations on the Importance of the American Revolution," Constitution.org, accessed 4 June 2017, www.constitution.org/price/price_6.htm.
[8] TJ to Richard Price, 1 Feb. 1785.

It is indeed only a rational and liberal religion, a religion
founded on just notions of the Deity as a being who regards
equally every sincere worshipper, and by whom all are alike
favoured as far as they act up to the light they enjoy, a religion
which consists in the imitation of the moral perfections of an
almighty but benevolent governor of nature, who directs for
the best all events, in confidence in the care of his providence,
in resignation to his will, and in the faithful discharge of every
duty of piety and morality from a regard to his authority and the
apprehension of a future righteous retribution.[9]

True religion—and this view is the result, for Price, of years of research
on the history of Christianity—begins with a correct notion of the one
God: almighty, all-good, all-benevolent, and all-just. Knowing God's goodness, humans, with the promise of a future "righteous retribution," ought
to live as much as they can in imitation of God. Human moral duties, then,
consist in love of God and loving all other persons with an equal love.
"Christianity teaches us that there is none good but one, that is, God, that
he willeth all men to be saved, and will punish nothing but wickedness,
that he desires mercy and not sacrifice (benevolence rather than rituals),
that loving him with all our hearts, and loving our neighbour as ourselves,
is the whole of our duty, and that in every nation he that feareth him and
worketh righteousness is accepted of him." Our kingdom, we must understand, "is not of this world, and requires us to elevate our minds above
temporal emoluments and to look forwards to a state beyond the grave
where a government of perfect virtue will be erected under that Messiah
who has *tasted death for every man.*"[10]

Having more than his share of the optimism of Enlightenment times,
especially as it relates to the promise of representative democracy taking
root and flourishing across the Atlantic, Price writes of America as "the seat
of liberty, science and virtue." Once seated, "there is reason to hope these

---

[9] Price, "Observations on the Importance of the American Revolution."
[10] Price, "Observations on the Importance of the American Revolution."

sacred blessings will spread till they become universal"—that kings and priests will no longer oppress and slavery will be exterminated. "The world has hitherto been gradually improving. Light and knowledge have been gaining ground, and human life at present, compared with what it once was, is much the same that a youth approaching to manhood is compared with an infant." There is "the hand of Providence in the late war working for the general good."[11] In *The Evidence for a Future Period of Improvement in the State of Mankind* (1787), he says, "There is a progressive improvement in human affairs which will terminate in greater degrees of light and virtue and happiness than have been yet known appears to me highly probable and my present business will be to represent to you the nature, the grounds, and the uses of this expectation."[12] Price's gradualism—the notion of human progress through gradual eradication of human ignorance—is one that Jefferson and numerous other Enlightenment thinkers openly embraced.

Another prominent Unitarian minister, Dr. Joseph Priestley—a true polyhistor who wrote on religion, metaphysics, political philosophy, science, epistemology, grammar, literary criticism, and history—was one of the early movers of religion in England and America. With Theophilus Lindsey, he founded the Unitarian church in London and established in Boston America's first Unitarian church, attended by Vice President John Adams. As illustrated in Chapter Three, his books—*History of the Corruptions of Christianity* (1782), *An History of Early Opinions concerning Jesus Christ Compiled from Original Writers, Proving That the Christian Church Was at First Unitarian* (1786), and *Socrates and Jesus Compared* (1803)—had a hefty influence on Jefferson's religious thinking, especially concerning the significance of Christ as a great moralist and cynosure.

More than Price, Priestley was a radical Unitarian, as he had radical religious views, aligned with his materialist philosophy, which followed two procedural rules of Isaac Newton: to "admit no more causes of things

---

[11] Price, "Observations on the Importance of the American Revolution."

[12] Richard Price, "The Evidence for a Future Period of Improvement in the State of Mankind," Constitution.org, accessed June 4, 2017, www.constitution.org/price/price_7.htm.

than are sufficient to explain appearances" and "to the same effects we must, as far as possible, assign the same causes."[13] In *Disquisitions Relating to Matter and Spirit* (1777), Priestley claimed that matter was capable of thought, once we reject the notion that solidity is the essential property of matter;[14] that the soul is material;[15] that God is material;[16] and that all things are necessitated by God—and hence there was no room for free human agency. "Even a sparrow falls not to the ground without the will, the knowledge, and design of our heavenly father, and . . . the very hairs of our heads are numbered."[17] His necessitarianism had its roots in natural law, which was God-created and God-directed, and that necessitarianism was fueled by scientists' and scholars' enthusiastic embrace of Newtonian dynamical physics. In Newton's physical universe, humans were mere material bodies, comprising atoms, just like other bodies. As such, they were subject to the same dynamical laws to which all other material bodies were subject. So complete was the triumph of Newtonian dynamical physics over the flimsy teleological physics built on false Aristotelian principles that Pierre-Simon Laplace boldly asserted of God, "Je n'avais pas besoin do cette hypothèse-là."[18]

Priestley's materialist metaphysical views were weaved into his Unitarianism. He believed God was one; that eternal punishment was inconsistent with divine goodness; that Jesus was mortal but endowed by God to perform superhuman deeds; that Jesus lived to be an example of the perfectibility of men; that Jesus rose from his grave for the sake of the reformation of sinners, not a divine sacrifice; that men were born with original sin; that Jesus ought not be worshipped; that Jesus would again come to earth; that humans were to be judged by deeds, not faith, a doctrine inconsistent with Calvinist predestination; that there was no soul,

---

[13] Isaac Newton, "Rules of Reasoning in Philosophy," in *Principia Mathematica*, vol. 2, trans. Andrew Motte (Berkeley: University of California Press, [1934] 1962), 398. Joseph Priestley, *Disquisitions Relating to Matter and Spirit* (London: J. Johnson, 1777), 2.

[14] Priestley, *Disquisitions Relating to Matter and Spirit*, xxxviii and 24ff.

[15] Priestley, *Disquisitions Relating to Matter and Spirit*, 33ff.

[16] Priestley, *Disquisitions Relating to Matter and Spirit*, 153.

[17] Priestley, *Disquisitions Relating to Matter and Spirit*, 152.

[18] "I have no need of that hypothesis."

separable from the body; and that life after death was possible, insofar as death was merely a bodily decomposition, and thus, in some future state, there could be a bodily recomposition. His Unitarianism was a spirited attempt to reconcile Christianity with reason and the scientific advances of his time. With the advances of reason and science, he believed that God planned for continued intellectual and moral improvement in man.

In his short work *Unitarianism Explained and Defended*, he sums his position: "I only preach *Jesus and the resurrection*; this, rightly explained, having ever been the sum and substance of all my preaching."[19] Here he later affirms his belief in a hereafter but cautions that "the doctrine of *eternal torments* is altogether indefensible on any principle of justice or equity; for all the crimes of finite creatures, being of course finite, cannot in equity deserve infinite punishment."[20]

Priestley's radical views on Unitarianism were captured in a provocative sermon on November 5, 1785:

Unitarian principles are gaining ground every day. We are, as it were, laying gunpowder, grain by grain, under the old building of error and superstition, which a single spark may hereafter inflame, so as to produce an instantaneous explosion; in consequence of which that edifice, the erection of which has been the work of ages, may be overturned in a moment, and so effectually as that the same foundation can never be built upon again.[21]

As the sermon illustrates, Priestley was no stranger to incendiary language. His Unitarianism, as his 1785 sermon exemplifies, might be grasped as a religion befitting the revolutionary times.

As the differences between Priestley and Price show—with Priestley being a full-fledged materialist and determinist, and Price embracing immaterialism and freedom of human will—there were sometimes

[19] Joseph Priestley, *Unitarianism Explained and Defended* (Philadelphia: J. Johnson, 1796), 17.

[20] Priestley, *Unitarianism Explained and Defended*, 40.

[21] John Monohan, *They Called Me Mad: Genius, Madness, and the Scientists Who Pushed the Outer Limits of Knowledge* (New York: Berkley Books, 2010).

considerable differences among early Unitarians, especially on the nature of Christ. Jefferson, though no expert on Unitarianism, was abundantly aware of those differences. Many of these conflicts arose as a consequence of Unitarian's Christology. Socian-based Unitarians, so named after early Unitarian Faustus Socinus (1539–1604), maintained that Christ had no existence prior to his birth. That view had been articulated prior to Socinus, but Socinus is the person who cemented it. Arian-based Unitarians thought that Christ, prior to his incarnation, had some sort of existence prior to his incarnate birth—as a demigod or *Logos*—though not on an equal footing with God. While all denied that Christ was a god, some proposed that Christ had a status that was nearly divine.

For a fine illustration of the radical differences among Unitarians, consider a letter by a Unitarian preacher and refugee of the failed Dutch Revolution, Francis Adrian Van der Kemp, to Jefferson. Jefferson wished to see Van der Kemp undertake the fleshing out of his "Syllabus" in the form of a book. Van der Kemp consented to do so. And so, he sent a letter to Jefferson (1 Nov. 1816) detailing a précis of what he proposed to write. The précis articulated a focus on revelation and not reason, and accounts of Jesus's virgin birth, of Jesus being both a real human and part of the godhead, of Jesus's resurrection, of the reality of miracles, of "unquestionable proof" of a future state, and of Jesus dying on the cross for the sins of the human race. One can only imagine that Jefferson must have been rankled upon reading the précis, as in all such things; Van der Kemp was offering a depiction of Jesus almost identical to the account in the New Testament, not Jefferson's own eventual deterged account, *The Life and Morals of Jesus of Nazareth*, in 1820. Van der Kemp, who considered himself and was considered by others to be Unitarian, did not seem to be offering an account of Jesus that was unconventional. It is fair to say that Unitarianism, if it could be considered in some measure to be a religious sect, was more of a movement toward a liberal religious sect than it was an established religious sect.

Thus there were Unitarians and Unitarian churches in Jefferson's day, but no established unified doctrine. Yet all Unitarians were committed to just and proper, nonpejorative notions of God and to monotheism, which implied that Christ was not a member of the godhead. All were committed to liberalizing Christianity along Enlightenment lines to allow for a politically small-beer notion of Christianity—small-beer in that it would refrain from intrusion on political matters. Yet it is clear that Unitarians did not think political matters were indifferent to religious ones. Price and Priestley, for instance, sought out a précised notion of Christianity that would allow for a religion in partnership with representative democratic governing, in which rights were championed and liberty was a government's top priority. As we shall see, Jefferson agreed.

A letter from John Adams to Jefferson (25 June 1813) shows that even Unitarianism could get out of hand. Adams limns the Unitarians Lindsay, Disnay, Farmer Price, Priestley, Kippis, Jebb, Vaughans, Bridgen, Brand Hollis, and Belsham: "All were learned, Scientific, and moral, Lindsay was an heroic Christian Philosopher. All, professed Friendship for America, and these were almost all, who pretended to any Such Thing." Adams then adds: "I wish you could live a year in Boston, hear their Divines; read their publications, especially the Repository. you would See how Spiritual Tyranny, and ecclesiastical Domination are beginning in our Country: at least Struggling for birth." The letter shows clearly that Unitarianism at the time was more of a movement than a sectarian religion. The liberalism undergirding that movement perhaps made it unsuited for morphing into a sectarian religion.

"The Remote Remedy to This Fever of Fanaticism"
Jefferson's Interest in Unitarianism

Though much has been written on Jefferson's religious views, there is surprisingly little written on his views of and commitment to Unitarianism. Jefferson claims to have a commitment to Unitarians, and scholars merely take him at his word, without critical analysis of any sort. To what was Jefferson committing? What did he mean by "Unitarianism"? Did he use the term ambiguously?

In the lengthy biography *Thomas Jefferson and the New Nation*, Merrill Peterson notes that Jefferson had a keen interest in the Unitarian controversy in New England and that Jefferson even predicted that every young man in America would die a Unitarian. He writes, "In Unitarianism he saw the possibilities of a unifying religion of humanity, and this new accent counterpointed the earlier individualism of Jefferson's religious creed." Still, he adds that Jefferson "was not a Unitarian," as he "belonged to no church." Peterson sums, "He was a sect to himself so far as he knew. He continued, as in his younger days, to aid churches of different denominations in his neighborhood and often attended their services; but he belonged to no church."[22] The sentiment seems to be that Jefferson considered Unitarianism to be a distinct religious sect and the best hope to be a religion of humanity, but he could not pledge complete allegiance to it because he could not pledge complete allegiance to any religious sect.

In his book on Jefferson and religion, Edwin Gaustad has much to say on Jefferson and Unitarianism. Unitarians were his closest contacts vis-à-vis religion. Among those correspondents, there were—other than Price, Priestley, and Van der Kemp—Jared Sparks, minister of the First Independent Church in Baltimore; James Smith, a Methodist who converted to Unitarianism; John Davis, a professor at the University of Virginia; George Thatcher, a statesman and lawyer from Massachusetts; and Dr. Benjamin Waterhouse, a physicist and physician. Moreover, Gaustad adds that Jefferson often attended Unitarian services while in Philadelphia.[23] Spotting Jefferson at such services prompted Joseph Priestley to comment, "He cannot be far from us. He now attends public worship very regularly, and his moral conduct was never impeached." Yet Jefferson, continues Gaustad, in agreement with Peterson, "never formally declared his affiliation in the ranks of the Unitarians."[24]

---

[22] Merrill D. Peterson, *Thomas Jefferson and the New Nation: A Bibliography* (Oxford: Oxford University Press, 1970), 960–61.

[23] To Benjamin Waterhouse (19 July 1822), Jefferson writes: "When I lived in Philadelphia there was a respectable congregation of that sect [Unitarianism], with a meeting house and regular service which I attended, and in which Dr. Priestley officiated to numerous audiences."

[24] Gaustad, *Sworn on the Altar of God*, 206.

Richard Samuelson states: "Against the 'Platonizing Christians,' Jefferson upheld what he called 'Christianism,' a rationalistic form of Unitarianism. Once the wheat was separated from the chaff, there remained 'the outlines of a system of the most sublime morality which has ever fallen from the lips of man.'" Though "Christianism" tends to be used today pejoratively, Samuelson elaborates on Jefferson's unique Christianism: God is one and perfect; there is an afterlife where one will be rewarded or punished for the sort of life he used to live; and God must be loved unconditionally and other persons must be loved, just as each loves himself.[25] Nothing in what Samuelson says indicates a preference for Unitarianism as a form of sectarian religion, yet one must be mindful of drawing conclusions from what Jefferson does not say.

Of Jefferson's interest in and enthusiasm for Unitarianism, Eugene Sheridan says: "He carefully followed the controversy between Calvinists and Unitarians in New England, which became particularly acute after 1815, and rejoiced in any progress the latter made at the expense of the former. He welcomed the Unitarian rejection of the Trinity and its emphasis on the moral precepts of Jesus over the dogmas of the churches, seeing in this the harbinger of a return to the pristine purity of primitive Christianity—a prospect in which he took great pleasure." Jefferson saw Unitarianism as a religion that embraced both God's oneness and the simplicity and purity of the morality of Jesus. Still, his "exaggerated estimate of Unitarianism's future prospects in America" was a prime motivator apropos of his own efforts to demythologize and decontaminate the New Testament. "It convinced him that his demythologized view of Christianity was rapidly gaining ground and thereby led him to persist in his quest for Jesus's genuine acts and teachings."[26] The implications seem to be that he saw Unitarianism as a distinct religious sect and that the progress of that sect

---

[25] Richard Samuelson, "Jefferson and Religion: Private Belief, Public Policy," in *The Cambridge Companion to Thomas Jefferson*, ed. Frank Shuffleton (Cambridge, UK: Cambridge University Press, 2009), 147.

[26] Eugene Sheridan, Introduction to *Jefferson's Extracts from the Gospels*, by Thomas Jefferson, ed. Dickinson W. Adams (Princeton: Princeton University Press, 1983), 36.

at the expense of Trinitarianism motivated him in his personal quest to demythologize the Bible.

In *The Religious Life of Thomas Jefferson*, Charles Sanford broaches the issue of Jefferson's Unitarianism in several places, but he never addresses the prickly issue of Unitarianism as a sect of Christianity and Jefferson's appropriation of the term. He offers a brief discussion of Jefferson's aversion to Trinitarianism, a Cerberus-like deity with one body and three heads, in his seventh chapter, but speaks only of Jefferson's uptake of the "pure Unitarianism of Jesus" and not much more. Sanford says of Jefferson: "He had read Priestley's *Corruptions of Christianity* over and over. These readings strengthened his belief in deism and Unitarianism. He took approving notes, for example, about the 'Sabellians' and 'Socinians' who were regarded as heretics by early Christians because of their Unitarian beliefs."[27]

Adrienne Koch maintains that it is only with difficulty that one can consider Jefferson a sectarian. "If one must take sides in the sectarian contest, it really seems fair to admit that Jefferson, at least toward the end of his life, was content to call himself a Unitarian." She appeals to "one very important letter," at the end of Jefferson's life, in which Jefferson writes, "I must therefore be contented to be a Unitarian by myself."[28] Yet this is not much of an admission, nor does it clear up any of the confusion concerning whether Jefferson considered Unitarianism a religious sect or merely a sort of anti-Trinitarian movement.

John Ragosta states that free rational inquiry would "foster Unitarianism consistent with his own beliefs." He adds that Jefferson's Unitarianism was a "'low' Unitarianism"—a "largely demystified Unitarianism."[29] The implication seems to be that Jefferson ambiguously used the term. In another essay, he says, "Jefferson is a theist (he believes in God). If a more precise

---

[27] Charles B. Sanford, *The Religious Life of Thomas Jefferson* (Charlottesville: University of Virginia Press, 1984), 88–89.

[28] Adrienne Koch, *The Philosophy of Thomas Jefferson* (Gloucester, MS: Peter Smith, 1957), 26–27.

[29] John Ragosta, "Thomas Jefferson's Religion and Religious Liberty," in *Religious Freedom: Jefferson's Legacy, America's Creed* (Charlottesville: University of Virginia Press, 2013), 30.

label is sought, he might be labeled a Unitarian (a theist who rejects the Trinity), although there are many variations in Unitarians (some who believe Jesus was more than human, others who do not)." Still, Jefferson "never formally joined that church."[30] Here, again, we find evidence of a commitment to Jefferson's varied uses of "Unitarianism."

In an essay on religious liberty, Cushing Strout elaborates on Jefferson's "common-sense Unitarianism." He says, "Jefferson's sense of his own religion was profoundly individualistic." He was aware that his views would seem eccentric to many Virginians and New Englanders, so he kept them to himself. Strout says John Adams had a similar take on Unitarianism, though Jefferson's "seemed much more individualistic."[31] The implication here, too, is that Jefferson used the term in a slippery manner.

In his book *Jefferson on Religion in Public Education*, Robert Healey argues that Jefferson was not only an ambassador for republicanism but also an ambassador for Unitarianism. Jefferson links Trinitarianism to Federalism and Unitarianism to Republicanism. "Religious, philosophical, and political reasonableness all went together for Jefferson. To him this meant that Trinitarians were Federalist, Tories, enemies to freedom and above all to freedom of belief; they could not be depended upon to abide by majority rule or to safeguard minority rights. Materialists, on the other hand, were strong, moral, reasonable fellows, good Republicans by temperament."[32] Moreover, Jefferson's feigned partnership with Unitarianism was more fantasmic than real. "In Boston Jefferson was denounced as soundly from Unitarian pulpits as from any other." Last, Jefferson was a Unitarian evangelist, though he never recognized that. "He devoted his life to the cause of freedom on earth, and essential to this . . . was the development of

---

[30] John Ragosta, "Jefferson's Religious Beliefs," *Thomas Jefferson Encyclopedia*, accessed February 8, 2019, www.monticello.org/site/research-and-collections/jeffersons-religious -beliefs.

[31] Cushing Strout, "Jeffersonian Religious Liberty and American Pluralism," in *The Virginia Statute for Religious Freedom*, ed. Merrill D. Peterson and Robert C. Vaughan (Cambridge: Cambridge University Press, 1988), 213.

[32] Robert M. Healey, *Jefferson on Religion in Public Education* (New Haven, CT: Yale University Press, 1962), 243.

moral men in a moral society. To develop them he encouraged the spread of Unitarianism and prophesied its complete victory."[33]

Finally, Alf Mapp turns to a brief discussion of Jefferson's Unitarianism when he refers to Jefferson's criticisms of Calvinism in his 1822 letter to Benjamin Waterhouse. Mapp, following Jefferson in the letter to Waterhouse, mentions Jefferson's disdain of "formulas of creed and confessions of faith," as well as his abandonment of "morals for mysteries, and Jesus for Plato."[34] Unitarianism, for Mapp, is merely a rejection of the unsavory principles of Calvinism.

As his correspondence shows, Jefferson was greatly influenced by the religious views of Price and Priestley, especially the latter (see Chapter Three). Consistently throughout his writings, from his *Literary Commonplace Books* to late-in-life letters, Jefferson was antipathetic to Trinitarianism and to religious creeds that vilified deity by refusing to acknowledge God's goodness and justness.

Though he was interested in the writings of religious reformists, with an eye toward liberating religion in the 1780s, it was not until late in his presidency that he began to express particular interest in Unitarianism as a religion. He writes to Thomas Dobson in 1807 (18 Nov.), requesting copies of certain essays that Dobson edited on Unitarianism. Some two years later, Jefferson replies to a letter from physician, lawyer, and newspaper editor James Fishback[35] (5 June 1809). Fishback, in his letter, says, "I have thought it not incompatible with your philosophic & philanthropic mind to solicit a reading of my little piece, & a communication of your judgment upon the conclusiveness of the reasoning." Jefferson replies (27 Sept. 1809) that all religions have in common certain core precepts: "all forbid us to murder, steal, plunder, bear false witness, &c., and these are the articles necessary for the preservation of order, justice, & happiness in society." He then

---

[33] Healey, *Jefferson on Religion in Public Education*, 243–44.

[34] Alf Mapp, *Thomas Jefferson: Passionate Pilgrim: The Presidency, the Founding of the University, and the Private Battle* (Lanham, MD: Rowman & Littlefield, 1998), 311.

[35] Fishback would become a Baptist minister in 1816. *The Papers of Thomas Jefferson*, Retirement Series, vol. 1: *4 March 1809 to 15 November 1809*, ed. J. Jefferson Looney (Princeton: Princeton University Press, 2004), 254–55.

mentions the "particular dogmas" that cause the "bitter schisms" among various sectarian religions—Nazarenes, Socinians, Arians, Trinitarians, Unitarians, Catholics, Lutherans, Calvinists, Methodists, Baptists, and Quakers. Unitarians, here, merely listed as one of eleven sects.

In 1820, Jefferson writes to Unitarian minister Jared Sparks (4 Nov.) of the "metaphisical insanities of Athanasius, of Loyola, & of Calvin," which are "mere relapses into polytheism, differing from paganism only by being more unintelligible." Jesus, in contrast, preached the "Unity of God."

To Massachusetts politician Thomas Pickering (27 Feb. 1821), Jefferson expresses his views on religious tolerance: "[I]n the present advance of truth, which we both approve, I do not know that you and I may think alike on all points. as the Creator has made no two faces alike, so no two minds, and probably no two creeds. we well know that among Unitarians themselves there are strong shades of difference, as between Doctors Price and Priestley for example." He ends, "I have little doubt that the whole of our country will soon be rallied to the Unity of the Creator, and, I hope, to the pure doctrines of Jesus also." That summary sentiment is revelatory, as it offers evidence of Jefferson's take on Unitarianism, considered merely as a doctrine that maintains the unity of God.

By 1822, Jefferson begins to take partisan interest in Unitarianism. He writes of the assault on Unitarianism at the time in Massachusetts. He writes to Thomas Whittemore (5 June 1822), "witness the present internecine rage of all other sects against the Unitarian." He then cites the Quakers as religious exemplars. The Quakers have no creed, and exhibit harmonious quiet and brotherly affections, in their "exemplary and unschismatising society of the Friends." He adds, "I hope the Unitarians will follow their happy example."

Some weeks later (26 June 1822), Jefferson writes to Unitarian and Harvard natural philosopher Benjamin Waterhouse—the letter to which Mapp refers. Jefferson enumerates the "demoralizing doctrines of the Calvinists." Calvin and Athanasius were committed to five dogmata: (1) there are three gods; (2) benevolence and beneficence are nothing; (3) faith, especially in what is unfathomable in religious matters, is everything; (4) reason is unavailing in religious matters; and (5) people are saved or damned if predestined by deity to be saved or damned, and not from our good or ill works. In contrast, Christ taught (1) belief in one omniperfect deity, (2) belief in a future state of rewards and punishments, and (3) complete love of deity and of one's neighbor as one loves oneself. Thus Jefferson's Christ rejected each of Calvin's tenets.

Jefferson again cites the example of the Quakers, who "schismatise about no mysteries, and keeping within the pale of Common sense, suffer no speculative differences of opinion, any more than of feature, to impair the love of their brethren." He adds, "be this the wisdom of Unitarians; this the holy mantle, which shall cover within it's charitable circumference all who believe in one God, and who love their neighbor." Here, too, he implicitly endorses Unitarianism. "I trust that there is not a *young man* now living in the United States who will not die an Unitarian."

A letter to Dr. Thomas Cooper (2 Nov. 1822) later in the same year deserves special attention, both because of the respect Jefferson had for Cooper as a man of uncommon intellect and liberal religiosity and because of his great affection for Cooper. Cooper, an able, if not brilliant, political philosopher, was appointed by Jefferson to a position at the newly forming University of Virginia, beginning in 1820. The appointment was postponed by the university's board till 1821, because of strong opposition to the appointment. With the postponement, there was an offer for him to resign, with a pledge of $1,500 for breach of contract. Cooper would not resign, but fortunately was offered and accepted a position at the University of South Carolina, and the controversy of his appointment at the University of Virginia was settled with Cooper receiving his breach-of-contract money.

What was the controversy? Why was there such strong opposition to his appointment?

Cooper, an unabashed Unitarian, was ultimately rejected due to grave opposition by Presbyterians—especially John H. Rice, who published two essays against Cooper's appointment in *Virginia Evangelical and Literary Magazine*—because of his maverick Unitarian views. Among those maverick views, there were disavowals of the Trinity, of the separation of the soul from the body at death, of free will, of future punishment, and of transubstantiation, which Cooper expressed in a contribution to *Memoirs of Dr. Joseph Priestley* (1806), formally published two years after his death.[36] The episode is revelatory and sheds light on Jefferson's reticency concerning the publication of his own views, which were sufficiently similar.

In the letter to Cooper, Jefferson speaks in a laudatory manner of the example of Boston, where "unitarianism has advanced to so great strength as now to humble this haughtiest of all religious sects." In Boston, Unitarians "condescend to interchange with them and the other sects the civilities of preaching freely & frequently in each other's meeting houses." The consequence was an upsurge in Bostonian Unitarians. Jefferson here seems to have forgotten the "Spiritual Tyranny" and "ecclesiastical Domination" Adams mentioned in an 1813 letter to Jefferson (as referenced earlier in this chapter).

Jefferson then contrasts the religiosity of Richmond with that of Charlottesville. In Richmond, there is great fanaticism—especially among women, for whom worship takes the form of sexual ecstasy. At night meetings and praying parties with priests, "they pour forth the effusions of their love to Jesus in terms as amatory and carnal as their modesty would permit them to use to a more earthly lover." In Charlottesville, there is much religion and little fanaticism. "[T]he Court house is the common temple, one Sunday in the month to each. here episcopalian and presbyterian, methodist and baptist meet together, join in hymning their maker, listen with attention and devotion to each others [sic] preachers, and all mix in society with perfect harmony."

Yet where "presbyterianism prevails undividedly," that harmony is not to be found. He continues to Cooper, "[T]heir ambition and tyranny would tolerate no rival if they had power. systematical in grasping at an ascendancy over all other sects, they aim at engrossing the education of the country, are hostile to every institution which they do not direct, and jealous at seeing others begin to attend at all to that object." What is

---

[36] Dumas Malone, *The Sage of Monticello* (Charlottesville: University of Virginia Press, 1981), 376–78.

the remedy for the empleomania of Presbyterianism? "The diffusion of instruction . . . will be the remote remedy to this fever of fanaticism, while the more proximate one will be the progress of Unitarianism, that this will ere long be the religion of the majority from North to South."

In December 1822, Jefferson writes Ohioan and Unitarian James Smith (Dec. 8) to thank him for having sent him certain pamphlets on Unitarianism and for Smith's "efforts for the revival of primitive Christianity in your quarter." "[N]o historical fact is better established than that of the doctrine of one god," he writes, "pure and uncompounded was that of the early ages of Christianity." He attacks Trinitarianism for creating a "hocus-pocus phantasm of a god, like another Cerberus, with one body and three heads." He adds, "[T]he pure and simple unity of the creator of the universe is now all but ascendant in the Eastern states; it is dawning in the West, and advancing towards the South; and I confidently expect that the present generation will see Unitarianism become the general religion of the United States. the Eastern presses are giving us many excellent pieces on the subject, and Priestley's learned writings on it are, or should be in every hand." The focus here is exclusively on Unitarianism as a doctrine of one God.

To Yale lawyer and Unitarian John Davis (18 Jan. 1824), Jefferson again begins with thanks for having received Unitarian sermons from Rev. Bancroft.[37] "I have read them with great satisfaction, and always rejoice in efforts to restore us to primitive Christianity, in all the simplicity in which it came from the lips of Jesus. had it never been sophisticated by the subtleties of Commentators, nor paraphrased into meanings totally foreign to it's character, it would at this day have been the religion of the whole civilized world." He then rails against the "metaphysical abstractions of Athanasius, and the maniac ravings of Calvin, tinctured plentifully with the foggy dreams of Plato."

Finally, just beyond a year before his death (8 Jan. 1825), Jefferson responds to a request of Waterhouse to use Rev. Bertrum as a teacher in

---

[37] For more, see William Sprague, *Annals of the American Pulpit*, vol. 8 (New York: Robert Carter and Brothers, 1865), 134.

Charlottesville. "I wish we could do it as a Preacher. I am anxious to see the doctrine of one god commenced in our state." Yet the Charlottesville population "is too slender, and is too much divided into other sects to maintain any one Preacher well." He concludes, "I must therefore be contented to be an Unitarian by myself."

"Preaching Freely & Frequently in Each Other's Meeting Houses"
Jefferson's Unitarianism

What are we to make of Jefferson's writings on and references to Unitarianism? Does Jefferson have a particular take on Unitarianism? How does Jefferson's Unitarianism differ from the Unitarianism of Price or of Priestley?

Jefferson's letter to Pickering shows that he acknowledges differences, sometimes radical, among Unitarians. Yet he nowise objects to them and adds that the country will surmount those differences and rally to the cause of Unitarianism, which amounts to belief in one God and purchase of the intemerate and simple (meaning demythologized) teachings of Jesus.

In his letters to Whittemore and Waterhouse, Jefferson expresses his hopes that Unitarians will follow the lead of the Quakers and exist without a creed. The notion, cleanly expressed, is that Unitarianism is a specific religious sect that can go in the direction of metaphysical overabundancy or it can trim all metaphysical fat. The essence of religion is love of God (who is one) and love of other persons.

To James Smith, as in his 1825 letter to Waterhouse, Jefferson proposes that the essence of Unitarianism is a belief in one God. In his letter to John Davis, Jefferson writes of a desire to return to "primitive Christianity," which comprises the teachings of Jesus, uncontaminated by schizmatizers.

Finally, in his letter to good friend Thomas Cooper, Jefferson writes of Unitarianism as a religion tolerant of sectarian differences of religious opinion. Unitarians interchange with other sects "the civilities of preaching freely & frequently in each other's meeting houses." The focus here is on Unitarianism as a liberal religion, friendly to the sort of republicanism espoused by Jefferson.

If we follow the lead of those letters, then we find that there is nothing else to Jeffersonian Unitarianism beyond a belief in certain axial "dogmata," such as monotheism and a commitment to primitive Christianity (i.e., duties to God and duties to man, as Jefferson says, for instance, in the letters to Law, Whittemore, and Waterhouse).

Yet here I am loathe to speak of *Jeffersonian* Unitarianism, for the axial principles of Jeffersonian Unitarianism are, for him, just those principles to which all true Unitarians or true Christians adhere. Nonetheless, they are also principles, Jefferson believes, that no religionist of any legitimate sect would reject—those principles of naturalized religion (see Chapter Two). The nodus is that sectarian religionists adopt other "metaphysical insanities" as axial, or at least indispensible, and those adoptions lead to political squabbles, often with long-term sanguinary implications. As Jefferson says to Matthew Carey (11 Nov. 1816), "On the dogmas of religion, as distinguished from moral principles, all mankind, from the beginning of the world to this day, have been quarreling, fighting, burning, and torturing one another, for abstractions unintelligible to themselves and to all others, and absolutely beyond the comprehension of the human mind." In contrast, Unitarians merely agree to disagree on metaphysical differences, considered ancillary to the axial principles.

We have only to consider the published exchange of letters between Priestley and Price, who despite their metaphysical differences remained good friends, committed to the spread of Unitarianism. Priestley writes thus in 1787 to Price as a preliminary to a proposed exchange of letters: "Dear Friend, Without any view to engaging you in a controversy with you have expressed a fixed resolution to decline, but merely from the satisfaction I feel in addressing myself to a person for whom I entertain the highest degree of esteem, and even veneration, and whose candour exceeds that of almost every other man, I choose to throw a few remarks upon your late *Sermons* into the form of *Letters to yourself.*"[38]

---

[38] Joseph Priestley, *The Theological and Miscellaneous Works of Joseph Priestley*, vol. 18 (London: G. Smallfield, 1817–32), 370.

It is easy to see now why Jefferson accepted Unitarianism and considered himself, late in life, to be a Unitarian. The Unitarianism that Jefferson openly advocated was a meta-religion—something beyond religious sectarianism because it was at the core of all legitimate religions, thus overpassing their nugatory metaphysical debates. That meta-religion was simply naturalized religion, which we have seen was equivalent to the "principles of morality," impressed in the heart of every person and sensually utilizable in everyday life—even in complex circumstances. Historian John Boles, writing about Jefferson's exuberance concerning the many gains of Unitarianism, agrees with this sentiment: "Since evangelicalism was in ascendance in the South, Jefferson perhaps did not mean the literal triumph of the Unitarian Church but rather the success of a vastly simplified theology that resulted in more of a folk religion than a hierarchal and rigid system of belief and practice."[39] Jefferson's personal physician late in life, the young Dr. Robley Dunglinson, says much the same: "His religious belief harmonized more closely with that of the Unitarians than of any other denomination, but it was liberal and untrammeled by sectarian feelings and prejudices."[40]

Yet as a meta-religion, Unitarianism was perfectly suited to be a "religion" appropriable for Jeffersonian republicanism. Peter Onuf writes, "From Jefferson's perspective, Unitarianism did not represent an elite reaction to the evangelical surge, but rather the precocious fulfillment of its ultimate theological tendencies," which were democratic reforms of church hierarchies.[41] Those reforms were intended to provide the simple moral undergirding—love of and duties to God, who is one, and love of and duties to man—of progressive, liberal republicanism: government of and for the people through elected representatives who would pledge foremost to protect the rights of the citizenry and to serve their interests.

[39] John B. Boles, *Jefferson: Architect of American History* (New York: Basic Books, 2017), 500.

[40] Henry S. Randall, *The Life of Thomas Jefferson*, vol. 3 (Philadelphia: J. B. Lippincott, 1871), 549.

[41] Peter Onuf, *The Mind of Thomas Jefferson* (Charlottesville: University of Virginia Press, 2007), 157–59, and also 151.

In such things, Jefferson differed little from numerous others of his day—such as Dr. Benjamin Rush and James Madison, as well as the Frenchmen Condorcet and Louis-Sébastien Mercier.

Yet even if Jefferson was not sectarian, he might have had a sectarian attitude or a sectarian zeal, as Robert Healey argues, and so his Unitarianism was not so free of the biases of religious sectarianism. "Jefferson may fairly be charged with being as sectarian as the Trinitarians whom he opposed." First, Jefferson's own religious views were "fired by a missionary zeal," as if he saw himself as a prophet. Second, Jefferson refused to consider seriously views that he outright rejected (i.e., Trinitarianism). "He set his rule concerning what all men believe, and rode roughshod over evidence to the contrary." Last, Jefferson, too, "had his excess metaphysical baggage in the form of a doctrine of materialism." Healey concludes, "Jefferson could thus be said to be guilty of exactly what he accused the early Christians of doing: adulterating and sophisticating his doctrine with artificial constructions."[42] He sums Jefferson's Tartuffery later in his discussion. Jefferson claimed to be "of a sect by [himself]." Yet he also believed that those principles common to all religions were the principles of true religion. In doing so, Jefferson was essaying to "bring everyone over to his own religious point of view," that is, "opinions which they disbelieved and abhorred."[43]

In chapter 9 of his book, Healey argues that Jefferson's overall approach to religion was biased and thus sectarian. "Like other *philosophes*, he was trying to establish religion on a rationally, morally, and empirically valid basis. . . . Yet he was tripped up here by his distaste for personal controversy, his belief that arguments never changed anyone's opinion, and his conviction that there was no hope of reasoning with anyone subscribing to a creed. These attitudes, incidentally, are those of a sectarian: whoever holds them prevents free discussion by closing his ears."[44]

Just how damning are Healey's objections? The first objection is difficult to take seriously, given Jefferson's missionary zeal was a matter of

---

[42] Healey, *Jefferson on Religion in Public Education*, 114–15.
[43] Healey, *Jefferson on Religion in Public Education*, 225–26.
[44] Healey, *Jefferson on Religion in Public Education*, 177.

"proselytizing" repeatedly that religion is a personal and not a political affair. Upon his death, even his own family did not know his religious views. Healey's second objection is also insignificant, as Jefferson never told others what to believe, but only to put all seemingly reasonable beliefs to the test of reason. Jefferson objected to stones sweating blood or calves speaking, because such wonders have never been observed and confirmed by others. If we reject Jefferson's plausible test of reason, then anything goes and absurdities must be taken seriously as rationally argued inferences. Third, the doctrine of materialism, in the days of Newton, was accepted by all scientifically minded persons. It might be considered a sort of metaphysics, but one not wholly ungrounded in experience—at least, it might be construed as a metaphysical inference to the best explanation of the rest and motion of physical bodies. Finally, Healey's summary argument of Jefferson's Tartuffery likewise is unpersuasive, for if Jefferson embraced as the principles of true religion just those principles that all religions embraced, then how can those principles be "disbelieved and abhorred" if they are principles that all religionists accept?

It also seems unfair to label Jefferson as sectarian because, in effect, he believed that persons subscribing to a creed would be unmoved by argument. Jefferson's empiricism disinclines him to think much of metaphysics. Moreover, his claim that those strongly wedded to religious sectarianism will not be moved by reason is certainly backed by much experience. Jefferson never closed his ears to religion, and he never prevented the free discussion of religion. If he can be accused of anything, it would be his championing of this free discussion with the passage of his Bill for Religious Freedom, the subject of the final chapter.

Concluding Thoughts

Jefferson's attitude toward Unitarianism was plainly ambiguous. On one hand, he recognized, as many scholars have noted, that Unitarianism was the name of a particular religious sect—perhaps better grasped as a religious movement. Jefferson much respected that movement, as it was a movement, in another sense of the word, away from what he considered metaphysical nimiety—a sort of unnatural, and unhealthful, gibbosity on the body of natural religion.

On the other hand, he used the term *Unitarianism* to connote his belief in love of God, as one, as well as love of one's fellow man. It was this second sense of the term that Jefferson sometimes appropriated for his own religious views, which, once fully grasped, were just not as radical as scholars sometimes make them out to be. They often seem to be radical because of contextomy: scholars are wont to study Jefferson's religiosity independently of his moral views and his views on God and the cosmos God crafted. Yet Jefferson's personal religious views were naturalized and were identical to his core moral views. Those core moral views—duties to God and duties to man—were derived from Jefferson's perceived proper view of God as derived from Bolingbroke. Jefferson's god was just, unfathomably powerful, and worth loving, without a promise of reward in an afterlife.

"Building a Wall of Separation"

A Large Legacy of Freedom of Religion

"Politics and the pulpit are terms that have little agreement. No sound ought to be heard in the church but the voice of healing charity. The cause of civil liberty and civil government gains as little as that of religion by this confusion of duties. . . . Surely the church is a place where one day's truce ought to be allowed to the dissentions and animosities of mankind."

—Edmund Burke

CHAPTER SIX

Jefferson's religious beliefs have been the subject of much attention in the secondary literature of both his day and ours. Many scholars appeal to Jefferson's alleged religious hypocrisy. He was highly secretive about his personal religious views, as articulated in selected letters and in his bible, and published liberal religious views in his *Notes on Virginia* that led to accusations of antireligiosity, anticlericalism, and even atheism. Nonetheless, he attended religious services, gave generous donations to parishes, befriended certain ministers, and even recommended the published works of favorite sermonizers. I hope to have shown that the charge of religious hypocrisy leveled against Jefferson cannot be sustained. He was consistently antisectarian.

Yet the primary reason for scholarly interest Jefferson's religious views is his stubborn commitment over the years to freedom of religious expression. "There was, in this view," writes Stuart Gerry Brown, "neither liberty nor equality in a system which assumed any body of mean to possess a monopoly on truth with an attendant right to be supported by public money, no matter how tolerant they might be."[1] Jefferson not only spoke on behalf of religious freedom—a heretical stance in the eyes of most people, given the centuries of entrenchment of the partnership of government and religion—with the indispensable aid of James Madison, he also acted successfully on behalf of religious freedom. In doing so, he set a template for the rest of the liberal, progress-wedded globe to follow. Jefferson is remembered for that legacy almost as much as he is recognized for having produced the Declaration of Independence.

Jefferson's work on freedom of religion is often judged by Jeffersonian yea-sayers to be on account of his respect for and embrace of all religions. Yet, as I have tried to show throughout, that is incorrect. Jefferson was generally hostile toward sectarian religions chiefly because of their treadmill religious squabbling (consider the animadversions he suffered while running for president), which often had sanguinary political implications (consider the Crusades). In short, Jefferson was interested in freedom of religion chiefly to nullify the toxic effects of governmental sanction of any particular sect. He had no great expectation that affording freedom to all religious sects would prove to advance some significant societal boon. Thus, freedom of religion was needed for the sake of peace. Freedom of religion was also needed because God had so crafted humans, even the most gifted of mind (e.g., Priestley and Price), to have significant religious disagreements, and so deity must have had a reason for that. Such disagreements might be cause for respectful dialogue or debate—again, consider the relatively polite exchange of ideas between Priestley and Price—but they were not cause for enmity and violence, and they were not to enter into the political arena.

In this final chapter, I set the stage, as it were, for an analysis of Jefferson's views on religious freedom by examining the influence of

---

[1] Stuart Gerry Brown, "The Mind of Thomas Jefferson," *Ethics* 63, no. 2 (1963): 87.

four significant utopian works on Jefferson's religious thinking—especially as they relate to freedom of religion. I then turn to Jefferson's Bill for Religious Freedom. Next, I analyze Jefferson's sustained discussion of the need for religious freedom in Query XVII of his *Notes on Virginia*. Finally, I examine his letter to the Danbury Baptists. I end with some thoughts on religious education.

"Never More to Write on the Topic"
Religion in Jefferson's Utopian Literature

In a previous publication on Jefferson's political philosophy, I emphasized the significance of his purchase of utopian literature.[2] He owned and enjoyed, for instance, future-looking books such as Thomas More's *Utopia*, Louis-Sébastien Mercier's *L'An 2440*, Constantin François de Volney's *Les ruines,* and Condorcet's *Progress of the Human Mind*. All such works are remarkable in that the views on religion expressed in each utopian frame are extraordinarily Jeffersonian—that is, all such works were in large agreement with Jefferson's own views on religious expression and politics. The influence of such works must have been profound for Jefferson, if only because they reinforced the views he already entertained on political philosophy and the role of religion in a thriving society.

More's *Utopia* (literally, "No Place") is about the travels of a wayward seafarer, Ralph Hythloday, who chances on an unknown island, Utopia. He is astonished at the islanders' virtue, health, and happiness. The island is so partitioned and governed to promote concern for others and discourage slothfulness, and to promote simple agrarian living and discourage extravagance.

Religion is a significant part of Utopia. There are many religions, not one. The first ruler, Utopus, noticed that there were "great quarrels concerning Religion," and so he legislated that "every Man might be of what Religion he pleased, and might endeavor to draw others to it by the force of Argument, and by amicable and modest ways, but without bitterness

---

[2]M. Andrew Holowchak, *Jefferson's Political Philosophy and the Metaphysics of Utopia* (London: Brill, 2017).

against those of other Opinions." In short, he noted that the tolerance of religious differences was necessary for maintaining social tranquility. It is, as we saw with Jefferson, not so much the great benefit to be derived by allowed free religious expression, but more that a disallowance of free religious expression is a gargantuan obstacle to social justice.

Though religions in Utopia are numerous, all agree there is one "*Father of all.*" Adds More, "They think there is one supream Being that made and governs the World."[3]

Mercier's *L'an 2440*—set in Paris, a model city in the year 2440—is the utopian work that most shaped Jefferson's philosophical thinking on an ordered, thriving society. A Parisian of Jefferson's day falls asleep after an engaging conversation with an Englishman and finds himself in Paris in the year 2440. When he wakes, he relates a description of the city, now much perfected. Paris, 2440, has a lean government, promotes the natural equality of all men, judges men by deeds and not by status, has natural-law justice, embraces simple moral laws and moral progress, is self-sufficient, disdains monopolies, has lenity of government, has abolished slavery, has mild taxes, has increased leisure through the elimination of unneeded goods, eschews war, has few criminals and humane treatment of them, uses public utility as a measure of moral and political improvement, has a focus on praxis and not principles in medicine, embraces prophylaxis in health and usefulness of education, has governmental patronage of the useful sciences, teaches history for its moral lessons and that true religion is a personal and not a preceptorial matter, acknowledges the indispensability of free presses and the centrality of simple agrarian living, loves industry and disdains indolence, and knows of the significance of neology in language. All such ideals were embraced by Jefferson, and it is difficult to find areas of disagreement between Jefferson and Mercier.

Theology, a detestable discipline in the eighteenth century, has become in 2440 a "sublime science" because metaphysical speculation is abandoned. There are no "ponderous folios" written about what is inscrutable.

---

[3] Thomas More, *Utopia*, trans. Gilbert Burnet (London: Ralph Chiswell, 1684), 177.

"We have determined never more to write on that topic." Religion is personal, as the soul communicates directly with God; there is no need of futile attempts at scrutability.[4] The ministers are few but are men of broad vision, of toleration and of exemplary virtue. The most virtuous men are not solitudinarians, who "make a merit of fasting, of chanting bad Latin, or of remaining dumb and stupid," but men who have the world in sight and who engage in "good and charitable works."[5] The moral laws are few and simple. "It is with religion as with laws; the most simple are the best. Adore God, love thy neighbor; hearken to that conscience, that judge which continually attends thee; never stifle that secret and celestial voice; all the rest is imposture, fraud, falshood."[6] True religion involves benefaction, and that begins with rationality.[7] "Morality is the only religion necessary to man; when he is rational, then he is religious; when he is useful, then he is virtuous."[8] Jefferson's views are incredibly similar, so much so that it is difficult to believe that he did not read and reread the book throughout his life—especially during his years of political engagement.

Les ruins of Constantin-François de Chasseboeuf, Comte de Volney, was published in French in 1791, during the French Revolution. Visiting the United States from 1795 to 1798, Volney met with then Vice President Jefferson, who agreed to translate Volney's book into English, so long as he, upon translating, would remain anonymous. Jefferson is thought to have translated the Invocation and the first twenty chapters, after which Joel Barlow translated the rest.

The book is a fictive account of certain musings of Volney while he travels through Egypt and Syria and inspects the ruins he sees there. The experience is overwhelming and leads to a weighty "religious pensiveness." A phantom appears and bids Volney not to be demoralized. Those great

---

[4] Louis-Sébastien Mercier, *Memoirs of the Year 2500* (Philadelphia: Thomas Dobson, 1795; repr., Clifton, NJ: A. M. Kelley, 1973), 65.

[5] Mercier, *Memoirs of the Year 2500*, 93–94.

[6] Mercier, *Memoirs of the Year 2500*, 104.

[7] Mercier, *Memoirs of the Year 2500*, 92–95.

[8] Mercier, *Memoirs of the Year 2500*, 122.

cultures have fallen due to the excesses of the people. They were responsible for their fall.[9]

Yet the voice of the tombs, says the phantom, bespeaks the rights of the people, who will soon rise up against their leaders and demand equal and exact justice. They will overthrow their leaders and choose their representatives—a bid for representative, republican governing.[10]

A global religious congress will form—under the banners of nature, reason, justice, and union—to "banish all tyranny and all discord." Each religious faction will argue in open discussion for the truth of its doctrines, yet the congress will prove bootless, says the phantom, as each religious faction will argue in its own interest.[11]

At that point, "men from various standards" will come forth to examine the "origin and filiation of religious ideas." They will disclose eight systems of religious filiation. Yet the religions of the day will have shown themselves to have lost all notions of their "filiation of ideas," and so religion will prove itself to have become nothing more than a "political engine to conduct the credulous vulgar."[12] The phantom sums:

> The whole history of the spirit of religion is only the history of
> errors of the human mind, which, placed in a world that it does
> not comprehend, endeavors nevertheless to solve the enigma;
> and which, beholding with astonishment this mysterious and
> visible prodigy, imagines causes, supposes reasons, builds sys-
> tems; then, finding the one defective, destroys it for another not
> less so; hates the error that it abandons, misconceives the one
> that it embraces, rejects the truth that it is seeking, composes
> chimeras of discordant beings; and thus, while always dreaming

---

[9] Constantin François de Volney, *The Ruins, or Meditations on the Revolutions of Empires* (Teddington, UK: Echo Library, 2010), 21–28.

[10] de Volney, *The Ruins*, 63–72.

[11] de Volney, *The Ruins*, 79–109.

[12] de Volney, *The Ruins*, 141.

of wisdom and happiness, wanders blindly in a labyrinth of illusion and doubt.[13]

The problem with religions arises with metaphysics. When people argue about matters of sensation, the arguing ceases by appeal to sensation. When matters are beyond the reach of the senses, no appeal to sensation can stop the arguing.[14] Moreover, much of religious belief has no bearing on human action. "What is believing, if believing influences no action?"[15] The solution, notes the phantom, is natural-law morality, following "the constant and regular order of events, by which God governs the universe; an order which his wisdom presents to the senses and reason of men, as an equal and common rule for their actions, to guide them, without distinction of country or sect, towards perfection and happiness."[16] Through the law of nature, men can become virtuous.[17] The account is in keeping with the later philosophical movement of Positivism.

Finally, in *Progress of the Human Mind*, Jean-Antoine Nicolas de Caritat, better known as Condorcet, writes of ten epochs in the history of humanity. Each epoch roughly marks human progress. With the sixth epoch, there is retrogradation, as Christianity takes root in Europe through the bloody Crusades. "The triumph of Christianity was thus the signal of the entire decline both of the science and of philosophy." With "expiring liberty," moral science could not be refined.[18]

With the decline of learning, "theological reveries, superstitious delusion, are become the sole genius of man, religious intolerance his only morality." Europe wallows in "sacerdotal tyranny" and "military despotism." Religion intrudes upon and is intermixed with all transactions of daily living. Kings and warriors serve the church. Christian armies lay waste

---

[13] de Volney, *The Ruins*, 152.
[14] de Volney, *The Ruins*, 162.
[15] de Volney, *The Ruins*, 154.
[16] de Volney, *The Ruins*, 165–171.
[17] de Volney, *The Ruins*, 165–87.
[18] Jean-Antoine Nicolas de Caritat, *Outlines of an Historical View of the Progress of the Human Mind: Being a Posthumous Work of the Late M. de Condorcet* (London: J. Johnson, 1795), 96–136.

to the provinces. "A tribunal of monks is established, with powers of condemning to the stake whoever should be suspected of making use of his reason." Claims are substantiated not by observation but supernaturally, and truth or untruth is decided by superstitious experiment or combat. Western nations conquer Eastern territories and claim "places rendered holy" by the miracles and death of Christ. Ancient authorities supplant reason. "The morality of this period, which it was the province of the priests alone to inculcate, comprehended those universal principles which no sect has overlooked; but it gave birth to a multitude of duties purely religious, and of imaginary sins."[19]

The revivification of science occurs in the seventh epoch. There is a gradual turning away from religion and continued progress through the embrace of science.

The tenth epoch, which is yet to come, concerns the limits of knowledge and human perfection. "The absolute perfection of the human species" is the true limit of human knowledge. In keeping with the virtue-ethics thinking of Greek and Roman antiquity, Condorcet says that when reason walks with science, humans will know, in a sentiment earlier proposed by Aristotle, that their duty is not to propagate beings but to propagate good beings. "[They] will have for their object, the general welfare of the human species; of the society in which they live; of the family to which they are attached; and not the puerile idea of encumbering the earth with useless and wretched mortals."[20]

Humans must become aware of their moral sentiments. "Is not the practice of reflecting upon our conduct; of trying it by the touchstone of reason and conscience; of exercising those humane sentiments which blend our happiness with that of others, the necessary consequence of the well-directed study of morality, and of a greater equality in the conditions of the social compact?" Like other sciences, the "moral goodness of man"

---

[19] de Caritat, *Progress of the Human Mind*, 137–58.
[20] de Caritat, *Progress of the Human Mind*, 362.

is "susceptible of an indefinite improvement."[21] Religion, adds Condorcet, is now obsolete.[22]

One cannot say that such works—and numerous others could be added here—shaped Jefferson's thinking on religion, for I have argued that his religious views were mostly in place in his youth, when he read and assimilated Bolingbroke. Still, there is no question that such works at least largely reinforced Jefferson's religious beliefs and his notion of the need for religious freedom.

"It Could Only Be Done by Degrees"
Bill 82 of 126 Bills

Jefferson's most significant writing apropos of freedom of religion is his Bill for Religious Freedom, Bill 82 of the 126 bills proposed by him, Wythe, and Pendleton, for the revisal of Virginia's code of laws in 1776.

Dumas Malone states, "Belief in the freedom of religion—which to him meant freedom of the mind—lay at the heart of his philosophy and he was always proud to be identified with it."[23] Merrill Peterson adds: "More than a statute, it was an eloquent manifesto of the sanctity of the human mind and spirit. It gave mature expression to convictions that, though they might have been reached wholly along the untroubled path of reason, were, in fact, tempered and formed in the crucible of religious controversy in Virginia. In denouncing the establishment and in advocating the fullest freedom in religious concerns, Jefferson drew on his experience as well as his philosophy."[24]

Malone and Peterson correctly note that the bill is substratally philosophical, not political. Jefferson begins in Section I with a complex and

---

[21] de Caritat, *Progress of the Human Mind*, 337–62.

[22] It is ironic that Condorcet, an optimistic man and perhaps a bit of a shandy, was sent to prison in 1794 and died shortly thereafter. It is believed that he, greatly loved by the French citizenry, was poisoned or killed while in prison so that he would not suffer the indignity of the guillotine.

[23] Dumas Malone, *Jefferson and the Rights of Man* (Boston: Little, Brown and Company, 1951), 110.

[24] Merrill D. Peterson, *Thomas Jefferson and the New Nation: A Biography* (Oxford: Oxford University Press, 1970), 134.

broad statement of the philosophy undergirding his politics. He starts with a statement of human rationality, turns to a statement of the freedom of the human mind, and follows with a statement of the futility of coercion concerning freedom of the human mind. It is plain "that Almighty God hath created the mind free, and manifested his supreme will that free it shall remain by making it altogether insusceptible of restraint; that all attempts to influence it by temporal punishments, or burthens, or by civil incapacitations, tend only to beget habits of hypocrisy and meanness."

Jefferson then turns to several other claims—some of which are political implications of his undergirding philosophy. First, ecclesiastical and civil rulers who have established their own opinions concerning religion as law have "established and maintained false religions over the greatest part of the world and through all time." Second, compelling anyone "to furnish contributions of money for the propagation of opinions which he disbelieves and abhors, is sinful and tyrannical." Third, forcing anyone to support a particular pastor of his own religion that is not of his own choosing is wrongful. Fourth, "our civil rights have no dependance on our religious opinions, any more than our opinions in physics or geometry." Fifth, prohibiting anyone from public office because of his religious convictions is wrongful, and so is allowing a person to hold public office only on condition of disavowing nonsanctioned religious opinions. Sixth, it is not the object of civil government to tell men how to think. "Truth is great and will prevail if left to herself," Jefferson sums. "She is the proper and sufficient antagonist to error, and has nothing to fear from the conflict unless by human interposition disarmed of her natural weapons, free argument and debate; errors ceasing to be dangerous when it is permitted freely to contradict them."

In Section II, Jefferson summarizes the political implications as a proposed code of law:

> We the General Assembly of Virginia do enact that no man
> shall be compelled to frequent or support any religious worship,
> place, or ministry whatsoever, nor shall be enforced, restrained,

molested, or burthened in his body or goods, or shall otherwise suffer, on account of his religious opinions or belief; but that all men shall be free to profess, and by argument to maintain, their opinions in matters of religion, and that the same shall in no wise diminish, enlarge, or affect their civil capacities.

The final statement of Section III grounds religious freedom in natural rights. "We are free to declare, and do declare, that the rights hereby asserted are of the natural rights of mankind, and that if any act shall be hereafter passed to repeal the present or to narrow its operations, such act will be an infringement of natural right." As natural, God-given rights, one can ignore them, but no act can nullify them, just as one can fail to recognize Robert Boyle's law concerning the inverse relationship of pressure and volume of a specific mass of an ideal gas at a constant temperature ($P \approx 1/V$), but failure to recognize it does not mean that the law ceases to obtain.

Bill 82 was, Jefferson recognized, one of his greatest services to humankind—one of three services to humankind listed on his obelisk at the cemetery behind Monticello. About that bill, he writes the following in his "Summary of Public Service," composed sometime in or around 1800:

I proposed the demolition of the church establishment, and the freedom of religion. It could only be done by degrees; to wit, the Act of 1776, c. 2, exempted dissenters from contributions to the church, and left the church clergy to be supported by voluntary contributions of their own sect; was continued from year to year, and made perpetual 1779, c. 36. I prepared the act for religious freedom in 1777, as part of the revisal, which was not reported to the Assembly till 1779, and that particular law not passed till 1785, and then by the efforts of Mr. Madison.[25]

---

[25] Thomas Jefferson, *The Papers of Thomas Jefferson*, vol. 32: *1 June 1800–16 February 1801*, ed. Barbara B. Oberg (Princeton: Princeton University Press, 2005), 122–25.

When the bill passed in 1785, it made Jefferson, who was already famous for his Summary View of the Rights of British America (1774) and Declaration of Independence (1776), an even larger celebrity. He had put into law, with much help from James Madison, what visionaries like Mercier and Condorcet had merely envisaged. Jefferson, while in France, writes to Madison (16 Dec. 1786) of the bill's reception abroad: "The Virginia act for religious freedom has been received with infinite approbation in Europe & propagated with enthusiasm." He continues, "It is comfortable to see the standard of reason at length erected, after so many ages during which the human mind has been held in vassalage by kings, priests & nobles: and it is honorable for us to have produced the first legislature who had the courage to declare that the reason of man may be trusted with the formation of his own opinions."[26]

"Introduce the Bed of Procrustes"
Query XVII of Jefferson's Notes on the State of Virginia

In Query XVII of Notes on Virginia, Jefferson writes succinctly of metaphysical religious squabbling: "The way to silence religious disputes, is to take no notice of them."[27] The sentiment here is that if all religions are allowed expression and none is given political patronage, religious disputes will produce at best parochial turbulences, which will, like numerous small storms over a large ocean, go unnoticed catholically.

Jefferson also writes of the commonly accepted notion of Christ coming to reform sinful humans: "If the almighty had begotten a thousand sons, instead of one, they would not have sufficed for this task. If all the sovereigns of Europe were to set themselves to work to emancipate the minds of their subjects from their present ignorance and prejudices, and that as zealously as they now endeavor the contrary, a thousand years would not place them on that high ground on which our common people are now setting out." Want of religious freedom and religious taint of

---

[26] See also TJ to George Wythe, 13 Aug. 1786.

[27] Thomas Jefferson, Notes on the State of Virginia, ed. William Peden (Chapel Hill: University of North Carolina Press, 1954), 161.

politics are responsible for ignorance, superstition, poverty, and oppression. Jeffersonian republicanism demands religious freedom.

Query XVII also offers an expressive defense of religious toleration. Jefferson begins with an account of how the various religions of Virginia came into the state. Many fled England to avoid religious persecution but found similar intolerance in Virginia, as Anglicanism was the dominant, state-sanctioned religion for some one hundred years. An act of assembly ratified in 1705 exemplified the insularity and bigotry:

> If a person brought up in the Christian religion denies the being
> of a God, or the Trinity, or asserts there are more Gods than one,
> or denies the Christian religion to be true, or the scriptures to
> be of divine authority, he is punishable on the first offense by
> incapacity to hold any office or employment ecclesiastical, civil,
> or military; on the second by disability to sue, to take any gift or
> legacy, to be guardian, executor, or administrator, and by three
> years imprisonment, without bail.[28]

Soon, other religions "began then to creep in" until Anglicans were not in the majority. A convention in 1776 declared that free exercise of religion was "a truth, and a natural right."

Jefferson then turns squarely to the topic of religious freedom. Rulers have authority over the natural rights of citizens only insofar as citizens grant to them such authority. No citizen has or even could ever submit "rights of conscience." He continues in an oft-quoted, somewhat infamous passage: "The legitimate powers of government extend to such acts only as are injurious to others. It does me no injury for my neighbor to say there are twenty gods, or no god. It neither picks my pocket nor breaks my leg." Constraint might lead to a conformity of actions, but it does not lead to truth. For truth, there must be reason and free inquiry. "Give a loose to them, they will support the true religion, by bringing every false one to their tribunal, to the test of their investigation."[29]

---

[28] Jefferson, *Notes on the State of Virginia*, 158–59.
[29] Jefferson, *Notes on the State of Virginia*, 159.

It is easy to take this passage (as do many scholars) as evidence of open-mindedness vis-à-vis rational debate between religious sects. Jefferson seems to be acknowledging that there might be a true religion and that the only way to get at it is for there to be rational debate that weeds out the false ones, leaving the true one unscathed. Yet we must take notice of the indirect method of arriving at truth: eliminative reasoning. Rational exposure to religions will show the pretenders as pretenders, with the passing of time. If any one cannot be shown to be a pretender, it will over time have its claim to being the true religion. That is not *evidence*, however, that it is the true religion, but it will have escaped refutation, and escaping refutation through exposure to rational criticism is a condition sine qua non of the true religion.

We must also take notice of eliminative reasoning, in large part, as just the method Jefferson advocates in constructing his versions of the life and teachings of Jesus in his bible. He puts the passages of the Gospels to the test of reason and is left with Jesus, preaching love of and duties to God, who is one; love of and duties to others; and belief in an afterlife. Of those, as we gave seen, Jefferson bases his own religious or moral views on the first two and rejects the last. Thus, when all religions are put to the test of reason, one true religion will be left, but this does not involve any of the sectarian religions. The true religion is, instead, a universalized Christianity or meta-religion, thus named because what, for Jefferson, survives the test of reason and is common to all reasonable religious sects are merely our twin duties: duties to God and duties to man.

Jefferson then gives several other arguments for religious freedom concerning religious truth. First, only error needs governmental succor; "truth can stand by itself." Yet, for centuries, governments have imposed religious uniformity in religious matters. Such imposition, thus, is a sign of sanction of falsehoods.[30] Second, political coercion in religious matters occurs for the sake of uniformity. Yet uniformity in religious inquiry is no more desirable than uniformity of face and stature. "Introduce the bed of Procrustes then, and as there is danger that the large men may beat the small, make us

[30] Jefferson, *Notes on the State of Virginia*, 160.

all of a size, by lopping the former and stretching the latter."[31] Third, uniformity through coercion is impossible. The reasons are twofold. On the one hand, uniformity through coercion has been practiced for centuries, and it has not worked. "Millions of innocent men, women, and children, since the introduction of Christianity, have been burnt, tortured, fined, imprisoned; yet we have not advanced one inch towards uniformity. . . . What has been the effect of coercion? To make one half the world fools, and the other half hypocrites. To support roguery and error all over the earth." On the other hand, uniformity through coercion cannot work. Assume, says Jefferson, that the globe has on it some one billion people, that the number of religions is one thousand, and that one of those religions is the correct one. To effect uniformity through coercion, members of the one correct religion would have to coerce the numerous members of the 999 different sects, which if it is not impossible, is a Gordian task. Only through reason and free inquiry is religious truth possible.[32]

Jefferson ends with the fair experiment in Pennsylvania and New York. Both states "have long subsisted without any establishment at all," and "they flourish infinitely." We can best silence religious disputes, he adds, by ignoring them.[33] Jefferson supported religious freedom more because of his wish to bring an end to the toxicity of religious coercion than because of anticipation of some great social gain to be had.

"A Matter Which Lies Solely between Man & His God"
Letter to the Danbury Baptists

Jefferson also argues for religious freedom in a letter, as president, to the Danbury Baptist Association, a group of twenty-three western Connecticut and three eastern New York Baptist churches. On October

---

[31] Jefferson, *Notes on the State of Virginia*, 160. Cf. Jefferson's notes on uniformity in "Jefferson's Outline of Argument in Support of His Resolutions, 11 October–9 December 1776," in Thomas Jefferson, *The Papers of Thomas Jefferson*, vol. 1: *1760–1776*, ed. Julian P. Boyd (Princeton: Princeton University Press, 1950), 535–39.

[32] Jefferson, *Notes on the State of Virginia*, 160. Similar to an argument by Shaftesbury that Jefferson relates this in certain notes in 1776. Jefferson, "Notes on Locke and Shaftesbury."

[33] Jefferson, *Notes on the State of Virginia*, 161.

7, 1801, members of the association—Nehh Dodge, Ephram Robbins, and Stephen S. Nelson—drafted a letter to the newly elected President Jefferson, presented here in full:

> Our Sentiments are uniformly on the side of Religious Liberty—
> That Religion is at all times and places a matter between God
> and individuals—That no man ought to suffer in name, person,
> or effects on account of his religious Opinions—That the
> legitimate Power of civil government extends no further than
> to punish the man who works *ill to his neighbor*: But Sir our
> constitution of government is not specific. Our ancient char-
> ter together with the Laws made coincident therewith, were
> adopted on the Basis of our government, at the time of our rev-
> olution; and such had been our Laws & usages, and such still
> are; that Religion is considered as the first object of Legislation;
> and therefore what religious privileges we enjoy (as a minor
> part of the State) we enjoy as favors granted, and not as inalien-
> able rights: and these favors we receive at the expense of such
> degrading acknowledgements, as are inconsistent with the rights
> of freemen. It is not to be wondered at therefore; if those, who
> seek after power & gain under the pretense of *government &*
> *Religion* should reproach their fellow men—should reproach
> their chief Magistrate, as an enemy of religion Law & good order
> because he will not, dare not assume the prerogatives of Jehovah
> and make Laws to govern the Kingdom of Christ.
>
> Sir, we are sensible that the President of the United States,
> is not the national legislator, and also sensible that the national
> government cannot destroy the Laws of each State; but our
> hopes are strong that the sentiments of our beloved President,
> which have had such genial affect already, like the radiant beams
> of the Sun, will shine and prevail through all these States and
> all the world till Hierarchy and Tyranny be destroyed from the
> Earth. Sir, when we reflect on your past services, and see a glow

of philanthropy and good will shining forth in a course of more than thirty years we have reason to believe that America's God has raised you up to fill the chair of State out of that good will which he bears to the Millions which you preside over. May God strengthen you for the arduous task which providence & the voice of the people have cald [*sic*] you to sustain and support you in your Administration against all the predetermined opposition of those who wish to rise to wealth & importance on the poverty and subjection of the people.

The letter is drafted in recognition that each state is responsible for the condition of religious affairs in it—"the national government cannot destroy the Laws of each State," a sentiment Jefferson iterates in his Second Inaugural Address[34]—but there is nonetheless an appeal to Jefferson by the Danbury Baptists, if only to reply with words of encouragement to sanction their cause. "Our hopes are strong that the sentiments of our beloved President . . . will shine and prevail through all these States and all the world till Hierarchy and Tyranny be destroyed from the Earth."

On January 1, 1802,[35] Jefferson drafts a brief reply to the concerns of the Danbury Baptists—a coruscant testimony of the power of words. The letter contains his now-famous wall-of-separation metaphor—the subject of considerable debate in the secondary literature today. Acknowledging receipt of the letter of the Baptists, Jefferson writes of his duty as president to recognize and represent the interest of the citizenry. "My duties dictate a faithful and zealous pursuit of the interests of my constituents, & in proportion as they are persuaded of my fidelity to those duties, the discharge of them becomes more and more pleasing." He then proceeds to a brief, yet

---

[34] "In matters of religion, I have considered that its free exercise is placed by the constitution independent of the powers of the general government." Thomas Jefferson, "Second Inaugural Address," in *Jefferson: Writings*, ed. Merrill D. Peterson (New York: Library of America, 1984), 519–20.

[35] The day prior, a "mammoth cheese," weighing more than 1,200 pounds, arrived as a gift for Jefferson from a group of farmers of Berkshire County, Massachusetts. John Leland was among the delegates when the cheese was formally presented.

eloquent, expression of the freedom of religious practice, which introduces the famous metaphor of a wall of separation:

> Believing with you that religion is a matter which lies solely between Man & his God, that he owes account to none other for his faith or his worship, that the legitimate powers of government reach actions only, & not opinions, I contemplate with sovereign reverence that act of the whole American people which declared that their legislature should "make no law respecting an establishment of religion, or prohibiting the free exercise thereof," thus building a wall of separation between Church & State.[36]

What was Jefferson's intention in this carefully crafted letter, which was given to members of his cabinet for suggestions prior to being mailed? James Hutson argues that Jefferson's primary intention was political. The FBI's reconstruction of Jefferson's original letter—some seven of twenty-five lines were circled for possible deletion and many words were inked out after some cautionary advice from Attorney General Levi Lincoln—shows Jefferson's "principal reason for writing the Danbury Baptist letter" to be a chance to say, in Jefferson's own words in his letter to Lincoln (1 Jan. 1802), "why I do not proclaim fastings & thanksgivings" as did Washington and Adams. The occasion was the Treaty of Amiens (25 Mar. 1802), which put an end, at least temporarily, to the hostilities between France and Britain, and thereby relieved the United States at that time of potential involvement with one of the nations against the other. Jefferson knew that Federalists, as a result of the treaty, would ask him for a day of thanksgiving, which would likely be pronounced "unconstitutional" by Jefferson, thereby proving his

---

[36] He quotes John Locke in certain notes on religion in 1776. "[A church] is 'a *voluntary* society of men, joining [themselves] together of their own accord, in order to the [publick] worshipping of god in such a manner as they judge [accept]able to him & effectual to the salvation of their souls. [It is] *voluntary* because no man is *by nature* bound to any church. the hopes of salvation is the cause of his entering into it. if he find any thing wrong in it, he [sh]ould be as free to go out as he was to come in." Jefferson, "Notes on Locke and Shaftesbury."

godlessness. By smartly drafting his reply to the Danbury Baptists, Hutson says, Jefferson could "strike back, using the most serviceable weapon at hand," deliver "a partisan counterpunch, aimed by Jefferson below the belt," and "mount a political counterattack against his Federalist enemies"—thereby proving false his infidelity and showing himself to be a "friend of religion."[37]

Hutson's thesis has been roundly refuted by Isaac Kramnick and R. Laurence Moore. Hutson's argument, they say, is strange because it is based solely on what Jefferson ultimately decided to omit. "No effort is ever made to indicate how that deletion/omission in any way affects the meaning or purpose of what Jefferson left in." They continue, "We are asked to understand and evaluate a document by what is left out and ignore what is left in."[38] To their sockdolager, I merely add two remarks of my own. First, were Jefferson's principal reason for writing the letter to be a "political counterattack against his Federalist enemies," then it is strange that he would soften the draft, as he writes in keeping with Levi Lincoln's advice in one of the marginalia, to placate "republican friends in the eastern states," where thanksgivings are customary. Second, an attempt to parry or avoid perceived Federalists' animadversions is nowise a "political counterattack," a strike with a "serviceable weapon," or even a "partisan counterpunch."

Let us now turn to what Jefferson left in the letter. There is and continues to be considerable scholarly disagreement on such content. Here I offer a merely representative sample.

Jefferson's phrase, "the whole American people which declared that their legislature should 'make no law respecting an establishment of religion, or prohibiting the free exercise thereof,'" suggests to some that

---

[37] James Hutson, "'A Wall of Separation': FBI Helps Restore Jefferson's Obliterated Draft," *Library of Congress Information Bulletin* 57, no. 6 (1998), accessed May 22, 2015, www.loc.gov/loc/lcib/9806/index.html; and James Hutson, "Thomas Jefferson's Letter to the Danbury Baptists: A Controversy Rejoined," *William and Mary Quarterly* 56, no. 4 (1999): 776.

[38] Isaac Kramnick and R. Laurence Moore, "The Baptists, the Bureau, and the Case of the Missing Lines," *William and Mary Quarterly* 56, no. 4 (1999): 820.

Jefferson's intendment was a prohibition of government intervention in matters of religion.

Derek Davis writes: "A fair examination of Thomas Jefferson's 1802 letter to the Danbury Baptist Association clearly shows that Jefferson understood the religion clauses to militate against religious institutions being government's guiding force or the beneficiaries of government benefits. His 'wall of separation between church and state' would be a permanent barrier to such practices." Consistent with the abolition of entails and primogeniture and his Bill for Religious Freedom, Jefferson was attempting, once again, to redress the issue of an artificial aristocracy—the centuries-old notion that Jefferson articulates in a letter to John Adams (28 Oct. 1813) that birth or wealth qualify one for public office. Nonetheless, he argues that the wall of separation is not unidirectional. It is meant to prohibit religious encroachment in political affairs as well as political encroachment in each person's religiosity.[39]

That is also the sentiment of R. Freeman Butts. "The clause 'establishment of religion' included all the desires to prohibit a single established church, but it also applied to plural support to many or all religions. . . . It prohibited any financial support, directly through tax funds, or indirectly through land for any one or more churches, or for religion in general."[40] He sums: "A careful study of Jefferson's entire career and his views on education from 1779 to 1825 will show that Jefferson was one of the earliest advocates of a public education divorced from all sectarian religious influences. He saw clearly that the principle of separation of church and state for which he worked so long must mean a secular educational system."[41] In consequence, Jefferson's notion of separation of church and state was

---

[39] Derek H. Davis, "Thomas Jefferson's Letter to the Danbury Baptist Association: The Meaning of the Famous 'Wall of Separation' Metaphor," in *Thomas Jefferson and Philosophy: Essays on the Philosophical Cast of Jefferson's Writings*, ed. M. Andrew Holowchak (Lanham, MD: Lexington Books, 2013), chap. 5.

[40] R. Freeman Butts, *The American Tradition in Religion and Education* (Boston: Beacon Press, 1950), 91.

[41] Butts, *The American Tradition in Religion and Education*, 119.

thorough and complete, and his views on education, qua secular practice, were rooted in his thinking on religious freedom.

J. M. O'Neill argues otherwise. He maintains that Jefferson's views of religion were always friendly. If we follow the pattern of Jefferson's life, we find a commitment to three fundamental principles: democratic governing, freedom of and equality in religion, and a states'-rights approach to decisions on religion and education. "Jefferson's total record is consistent proof. In fact he never did or said anything at any time to indicate that he thought the states could not do whatever they thought wise in regard to government provision of religion or religious education so long as they treated all religions alike and preserved religious freedom."[42]

Robert Cord is in fundamental agreement. Appealing to several of Jefferson's actions as a politician as well as Bills 84 and 85 of the *Revisal of the Laws of Virginia*—which he assumes were in the hand of Jefferson—Cord argues that Jefferson was not averse at times to using sectarian institutions for secular ends, so long as in doing so he was not privileging any one religion to the detriment of others. Thus, the "wall of separation" metaphor employed by Jefferson in the Danbury-Baptist letter is "nonabsolutist": particular religions can never use government to advance their aims, while government can sometimes use particular religions to advance secular aims.[43]

Anson Phelps Stokes goes further. He argues that religious instruction was needed for democracy to thrive. Jefferson, himself a devout religionist, argued for the separation of church and state for the sake of the state—that is, a healthy nation. Concerning Jefferson's University of Virginia, he writes, "even in the establishing a quasi-state university on broad lines, the greatest liberal who took part in founding our government felt that instruction

---

[42] J. M. O'Neill, *Religion and Education under the Constitution* (New York: Harper, 1949), 205–6, 248.

[43] Robert L. Cord, "Mr. Jefferson's 'Nonabsolute' Wall of Separation between Church and State," *Religion and Political Culture in Jefferson's Virginia*, ed. Garrett Ward Sheldon and Daniel L. Dreisbach (Lanham, MD: Rowman & Littlefield, 2000), 167–88.

in the fundamental of Christian theism and Christian worship were both important and proper."[44]

Daniel Dreisbach, in keeping with Cord's thesis, argues that Jefferson's Bill 82 should not be taken independently of the four other companion bills—Bills 83 through 86, of which "Jefferson was the chief architect, if not the actual draftsman," even though "a couple of them were revisions of provisions that had long been on the statute books of Virginia." Those bills allow for "limited state cooperation with religious institutions . . . if it advanced freedom of religious belief and expression" or if they advanced "the legitimate secular goals of the civil state." The wall-of-separation metaphor, then, was meant to apply strictly to the federal government and religious institutions or practices.[45]

Johann Neem says Jefferson had in mind something more fundamental than a wall that protected church from state or state from church. Its implications went beyond political and religious concerns. Jefferson's intendment was free inquiry. "The wall of separation was not intended to banish religion from the public sphere of civil society. Instead, it was intended to prohibit an alliance between ministers and politicians that would limit free inquiry. Free inquiry would allow persons to question centuries of fabricated mysticism invented by ministers."[46]

With all these points in mind, what are we to conclude?

Davis is correct to note that freedom of religion was both for freedom from governmental intrusion in citizens' personal affairs—that is, matters of conscience—and for freedom from religious intrusion in governmental affairs, which historically have been contaminated by religious prelates. Moreover, the conclusions of Cord and Dreisbach must not be given short

---

[44] Anson Phelps Stokes, *Church and State in the United States*, vol. 1 (New York: Harper, 1950), 515–16.

[45] Daniel L. Dreisbach, "Religion and Legal Reforms in Revolutionary Virginia," in *Religion and Political Culture in Jefferson's Virginia*, ed. Garrett Ward Sheldon and Daniel L. Dreisbach (Lanham, MD: Rowman & Littlefield, 2000), 194, 206.

[46] Johann Neem, "Beyond the Wall: Reinterpreting Jefferson's Danbury Address," *Journal of the Early Republic* 27, no. 1 (2007): 142.

shrift, if it is the case that Jefferson fully endorsed the proposals of Bills 83 through 86. Finally, Stokes's view, with some modification, is relevant.

However, I shall follow up on the suggestion of Neem that Jefferson's real intent in setting up a wall of separation between church and state was free inquiry. That claim has, I believe, much in its favor.

Yet Neem does not go far enough, as, for Jefferson, free inquiry was not an end but a means. As always, Jefferson's true aim was continued human advance (i.e., human thriving or happiness). For that to happen, the natural, not the artificial, aristocrats needed to govern, and the natural aristocrats, for Jefferson, comprised those persons preeminent in genius and virtue.[47] Religiosity was irrelevant. Thus, there needed to be a wall of separation between church and state so that political affairs, at least at the federal level, were not decided by religious partialities of sectarian religions. Thus the wall was meant to work both ways: to prohibit religious intrusion in governmental matters, especially at the federal level, and to prohibit governmental intrusion in religious matters. Yet, as implied by the passage in Jefferson's *Notes on Virginia* about silencing religious disputes by ignoring them, his real aim was preventing religious intrusion in political matters—religious empleomania. The prohibition of governmental intrusion in religious practices was, in some sense, throwing a bone to a dog. Jefferson wished to concede something to religious clerics and willingly did so because he recognized that the concession, given prohibition of religious intrusion in governmental affairs, would be effete. Rigorous debate on whether God is three or one or on whether Jesus could walk on water would be just so much ignis fatuus.

"Lay Aside All Prejudice on Both Sides"
Religious Education

Jefferson provides numerous other articulations of his views on religious freedom or religious toleration; here we explore but a few. Jefferson drafts a proposed constitution for Virginia in 1776. In it, he states, "All persons shall

---

[47] See TJ to John Adams, 28 Oct. 1813.

have full and free liberty of religious opinion; nor shall any be compelled to frequent or maintain any religious institution."[48] In a memorandum titled by Merrill Peterson "Services to My Country" (ca. 1800), Jefferson states, "All persons shall have full and free liberty of religious opinion; nor shall any be compelled to frequent or maintain any religious institution." Jefferson lists "freedom of religion" and "demolition of the church establishment" as two elements of one of his services—eleven are listed in total—and thereafter writes briefly of his efforts to write up and pass Bill 82.[49] In a 1781 proclamation, Jefferson invites British mercenaries to desert, and one of the reasons given for the desertion is "the free exercise of their respective religions."[50] In Article 11 of a proposed treaty between the United States and Denmark and Norway, Jefferson says, "The most perfect freedom of conscience and of worship is granted to the citizens or subjects of either party within the jurisdiction of the other without being liable to molestation in that respect for any cause other than an insult on the religion of others."[51] It is fair to say that freedom of religion was a subject that was always dear to his heart, even if partly motivated by the persecution in the press that he continually suffered on suspicion of his nonconformist religious views.

Given that there was nothing worth salvaging from the dogmata of religious sects, Jefferson was skeptical about the worth of religious education, because it would always be sectarian, and he was especially guarded apropos of early exposure to the tenets of formal religions, which would corrupt young minds that were not fully rational.

---

[48] Thomas Jefferson, "Draft Constitution for the State of Virginia," in *The Papers of Thomas Jefferson*, vol. 1, ed. Julian P. Boyd (Princeton: Princeton University Press, 1950), 337–47.

[49] Thomas Jefferson, *Thomas Jefferson: Writings*, ed. Merrill D. Peterson (New York: Library of America, 1984), 702.

[50] Thomas Jefferson, "Proclamation Inviting Mercenary Troops in the British Service to Desert, [2 February 1781]," *The Papers of Thomas Jefferson*, vol. 4, ed. Julian P. Boyd (Princeton: Princeton University Press, 1951), 505–6.

[51] Thomas Jefferson, "IV. Draft of a Model Treaty, 1784," *The Papers of Thomas Jefferson*, vol. 7, ed. Julian P. Boyd (Princeton: Princeton University Press, 1953), 479–90.

Jefferson writes in Query XIV of *Notes on Virginia* that in the first stages of education in the ward schools, "wherein the great mass of the people will receive their instruction," children should not be studying "the Bible and Testament," for their "judgments are not sufficiently matured for religious inquiries." Thus, according to Jefferson, utmost care must be used in early education. Instead of studying religion, young minds can be exposed to "the most useful facts from Grecian, Roman, European and American history," through which "the first elements of morality . . . may be instilled into their minds."[52]

Jefferson's concerns here are principally twofold. First, ward-school education is critical, as it "lays the principal foundations of future order." Thus, such subjects need to be taught what will allow for future order—useful facts from history and the first elements of morality (and the two, for Jefferson, are not exclusive). The first elements of morality are not moral precepts to be internalized—each has an innate sensory faculty that discerns right from wrong—but merely factual and fictive stories to be read to reinforce each person's moral–sense faculty.

Second, cognizant that human rationality takes years to develop and mature, Jefferson insists that youths should not be exposed prematurely to subjects that require critical reflection. Religion is listed as the only example here, and that speaks volumes. The two concerns are related. Premature exposure to religion can impede an underdeveloped rational faculty by disallowing its capacity for critical engagement with religious issues in later life, thereby making one a slave for life to its precepts, most of which, metempirical, are incapable of verification. Such uncritical acceptance of religious precepts, due to premature exposure to them, is not a voluntary acceptance of them and, hence, it is not an avowal of them. In contrast, useful facts from history that are not directly related to morality complement the first lessons of morality without taxing the burgeoning rational faculty. That is merely a matter of reinforcing what we already naturally sense to be morally true: love of God and love of others. Eschewing religion

---

[52] Jefferson, *Notes on the State of Virginia*, 147.

and bolstered by the lessons of history, each person develops a strong sense of independency and learns that being happy is not a matter of things outside one's control but the result of "good conscience, good health, occupation, and freedom in all just pursuits."[53]

Jefferson also investigates the topic of the proper timing for religious study in a significant letter to Peter Carr (19 Aug. 1787). Carr, born in 1770, is sufficiently mature at the time to undertake critical reflection on the subject of religion. Jefferson proffers fatherly counsel, as he was, for all intents and purposes, Peter's father. Peter's biological father and Jefferson's brother-in-law and close friend, Dabney Carr, died in 1773,[54] and Carr's wife and six children were cared for by Jefferson at Monticello.

The letter between Jefferson and Carr, which factors prominently in understanding how Jefferson constructed his bibles, provides a step-by-step recipe for how to study religion. Jefferson begins with mental preparation. First, he tells Carr to approach the subject with "novelty and singularity of opinion," not bias. Second, Carr is to broach the subject with courage, not "fears and servile prejudices." Third, Carr is to allow reason full jurisdiction. "Question with boldness even the existence of a god; because, if there be one, he must more approve the homage of reason, than that of blindfolded fear." Fourth, Carr must entertain and carefully weigh every relevant fact and opinion.

Jefferson then turns to critical engagement with the Bible. It is to be read just as one would read a text of Livy or Tacitus—the latter being Jefferson's favorite historian. "The facts which are within the ordinary course of nature you will believe on the authority of the writer, as you do those of the same kind in Livy and Tacitus. The testimony of the writer weighs in their favor in one scale, and their not being against the laws of nature does not weigh against them." Yet "facts" contradicting the laws of nature must be handled with extreme mental caution. For Jefferson, it is the same with the Bible. It is not a privileged book.

---

[53] Jefferson, *Notes on Virginia*, 147.
[54] So close was his friendship to Jefferson that Carr was buried in the Monticello cemetery.

What of commonly accepted miracles—events in clear contravention with the laws of nature? Jefferson, in keeping with his empiricism, falls upon probabilistic assessment. "Here you must recur to the pretensions of the writer to inspiration from god. Examine upon what evidence his pretensions are founded, and whether that evidence is so strong as that it's falsehood would be more improbable than a change of the laws of nature in the case he relates."[55]

Jefferson illustrates this, first, with an example from Joshua 10:12–13, in which the sun is said to have stood still for numerous hours to allow the Israelites more time to engage in battle with and defeat the Amorites—a passage made famous by Galileo in his "Letter to the Grand Duchess Christina."[56] Following Galileo, Jefferson argues in *reductio ad absurdam* manner. He notes that the sudden stoppage of a body such as Earth, which turns on its axis,[57] would prostrate animals, trees, and buildings, and the same would occur on resumption of Earth's rotation. Yet the writer of Joshua was said to be inspired by God, and millions believe that the account is true, in spite of the tale's supernaturalism.

Jefferson next illustrates contemporary accounts of Jesus, drawn from the New Testament. Some say that "he was begotten by god, born of a virgin, suspended and reversed the laws of nature at will, and ascended bodily into heaven." Others say that "he was a man, of illegitimate birth, of a benevolent heart, enthusiastic mind, who set out without pretensions to divinity, ended in believing them, and was punished capitally for sedition by being gibbeted according to the Roman law which punished the first commission of that offence by whipping, and the second by exile or death *in furcâ*." Carr is invited to examine all accounts of the life of Jesus,

---

[55] Cf. Hume, who argues similarly in his largely read essay titled "On Miracles." David Hume, "On Miracles," in *Dialogues Concerning Natural Religion*, ed. Richard H. Popkin (Indianapolis: Hackett, 1998).

[56] Galileo Galilei, *Discoveries and Opinions of Galileo* (New York: Anchor Books, 1957), 211–15.

[57] And does so at roughly one thousand miles per hour at the equator.

so long as he allows reason free expression. Jefferson does not share his own beliefs with his nephew.

Jefferson bids Carr to avoid being frightened by the perceived consequences of putting Jesus's life and the existence of a deity to the test of reason. If disbelief in God follows, "you will find incitements to virtue in the comfort and pleasantness you feel in it's exercise, and the love of others which it will procure you." If belief in God follows, "a consciousness that you are acting under his eye, and that he approves you, will be a vast additional incitement." Moreover, inquiry might also bring about belief in a future state, thereby increasing "the appetite to deserve it" by promoting good deeds. Finally, inquiry might also bring about belief that Jesus was God, thereby offering the believer added comfort. It is noteworthy here that Jefferson is asking Carr to consider all conceptual space on the issue, not imposing his own beliefs on his nephew. That says much about Jefferson's purchase of the view that religion is a private matter. It also says much about Jefferson's respect of each person's private space.

Jefferson sums: "In fine, I repeat that you must lay aside all prejudice on both sides, and neither believe nor reject any thing because any other person, or description of persons have rejected or believed it. Your own reason is the only oracle given you by heaven, and you are answerable not for the rightness but uprightness of the decision." The final sentiment is critical. Should there be an afterlife with a judgment, Jefferson suggests, Carr will be judged more severely for having abandoned his God-given reason in search of religious veridicality more than for sincerely using it and coming to a wrong conclusion. More important is the uprightness of the decision—the gravity, solemnity, and sincerity of the undertaking and the intentions behind it—than the correctness of one's decision. Obtaining the right answer through sloppy or hasty reasoning or without reasoning is, for Jefferson, an unpardonable crime; obtaining the wrong answer through a right-intended, thorough, and unbiased process is not only pardonable but also praiseworthy.

In short, Jefferson thinks it is presumptuous and perhaps morally wrong for him to impose his religious views on another, even an intimate, yet he also thinks it is important to encourage the use of God-given reason in religious inquiry. This is consistent with the empiricism he lifelong embraced. That empiricism would allow for the probability of truth, not truth, and so Jefferson's reticency is graspable. He cannot know, or know infallibly, that his own religious views are correct—that true religion is merely reducible to duties to God and to man—so he has no business in proselytizing to others. That is precisely the definition of an above-board empiricist.

This sentiment is corroborated in Henry Randall's biography of Jefferson. Grandson Thomas Jefferson Randolph wrote thus to Randall concerning his grandfather's views on religion: "It was a subject each was bound to study assiduously for himself, unbiased by the opinions of others—it was a matter solely of conscience; after thorough investigation, they were responsible for the righteousness, but not the rightfulness of their opinions; that the expression of his opinion might influences theirs, and he would not give it!"[58] Thus it is both astonishing and perplexing that scholars tend to make so little of Jefferson's refusal to proselytize on religious matters.

Concluding Thoughts

In keeping with the views of Condorcet, sectarian religions were deemed by Jefferson to be inconsistent with healthy and progressive republicanism. Thus, Jefferson's view of separation of church and state was not so much that he wished for citizens to enjoy full expression of their religious views without the intrusion of government, but more that he recognized through his study of history the insuperable difficulties created by state auspices of a particular religious sect.

For Jefferson, freedom of religion was a consequence of buying into freedom of thinking. No one had a right to tell another how to think, what to think about, or even what path to take in life. Such things were guaranteed to all citizens in a rightly functioning republican government

---

[58] Henry S. Randall, *The Life of Thomas Jefferson*, vol. 3 (New York, 1858), 672.

and concretized by Jefferson's own Declaration of Independence. These axial liberties had religious implications. Each individual should be free to choose to believe in God, and to worship that deity in a manner of his choosing, or to believe in no God.

Jefferson's unique contribution in arguing for the separation of church and state was a recognition that there did not need to be any relationship between one's religious beliefs and one's political orientation or political practices. The key to a thriving republic was a recognition that true freedom entailed a toleration of diversity of thought and action.

Yet Jefferson recognized that all persons were capable of grasping that there were commonalities to all religions, right intended: belief in the oneness of God and commitments to duties to God and to our fellow humans. When a person—whether Catholic, Protestant, or Quaker—fulfilled his duties to God and others, he was acting religiously, in the natural and fullest sense of the term. The metaphysical excrescences of sectarian religions were thus hindrances to natural religion and obstacles for good governing. Jefferson's real legacy concerning the separation of church and state was the discovery that by giving free rein to all religions, the potential for any particular religion to cause political harm would be neutralized, if not nullified. None of this shows that Jefferson did not believe in any partnership of government and religion. He did. Yet the sort of minimalist religion that government ought to take up comprised the demythologized religious, and ethical, views of Christ, minus a belief in an afterlife, which, like Dr. Thomas Cooper, Jefferson found superfluous.

Concluding Thoughts

As an author, often the last thing I settle on is the title of the book I have written. This was certainly the case with this book. I fiddled with a few titles that I thought got at the gist of the book, but eventually I became dissatisfied with them. It was only during the process of polishing a draft of the manuscript that the title *Secular Messiah: The Surprisingly Simple Religious Views of Thomas Jefferson* hit me and stuck with me, till my friend and fellow Jeffersonian scholar Art Scherr proposed that "American" might be preferable to "Secular." I went with his proposal. The title implies what I think is manifest to most persons—Jefferson, especially because of the passing of his Bill for Religious Freedom in 1785 and because of its influence parochially and globally, was a large religious reformist. The secondary title gets at the gist of this book, and was created by the publishers—Jefferson's religious views, similar to those of Jesus, were remarkably simple—and yet there still is remarkable confusion concerning them.

That there should be so much scholarly confusion is not all that surprising. When it came to his religious views, Jefferson preferred a noiseless path. His reasons were chiefly twofold. First, Jefferson recognized that there existed myriad differences between people on religion. Given that, the prospect of achieving uniformity of view through political sanction of any one view was nil, and the differences that persons had concerning religion nowise disqualified them from the attainment of political office. Second, had Jefferson's "Unitarian" religious views become known (e.g., his rejection of the divinity of Christ and his capacity to perform miracles), he would have suffered as much politically as he did personally. Consider the fate of his good friend Dr. Thomas Cooper—"one of the ablest men in America, & that in several branches of science"[1]—who was kept from tenureship at the fledgling University of Virginia because he was outspoken about his unconventional Unitarian views.

Because of his noiseless path, there was always public suspicion that Jefferson was a religious radical or, even, like some of the *philosophes* he enjoyed reading, an atheist. Consequently, many of Jefferson's proreligious public displays had at least the secondary aim of quieting suspicions of his irreligiosity. At times, he worshipped in churches of different denominations, he donated handsomely to churches, and he befriended certain ministers.

Yet he chiefly did such things because he found them to be rewarding. There were clerics in his day—his beloved Laurence Sterne is a prime illustration—who were exceptional sermonizers and fine men. Having spent numerous hours writing a sermon and preaching it with verve, those sermonizers found their sermons much in demand, and it was not uncommon for them to have their sermons published for public erudition. Jefferson enjoyed hearing or reading a good, morally moving sermon, and he was sufficiently rationally mature "to strip it of it's meretricious trappings, and to see it in all it's native simplicity and purity."[2] In an 1814 letter to John Minor (Aug. 30), Jefferson recommends an extensive reading list for a promising lawyer. Under "Religion, sectarian," he lists "the Sermons of [Revs.] Sterne, Massillon & Bourdaloue." It is significant to note that

---

[1] TJ to Joseph C. Cabell, 27 June 1810.
[2] TJ to John Davis, 18 Jan. 1824.

Jefferson found moral inspiration wherever he could find it—in history, poetry, novels, moral essays, and sermons. That said, Jefferson's view was largely anticlerical, because the large majority of religious clerics were more politically moved than morally moved.[3]

For Jefferson, what was worth salvaging from all such works was their moral content, which could be reduced to our duties to God and to others. We fulfill our duties to God not through prayer, worship, or sacrifices—for Jefferson's God, I have argued, was oblivious to such empty gestures—but through fulfilling our naturally assigned role in the cosmos by the study of the cosmos and by behavior such as humans are naturally crafted to behave, following the example of the mortal moralist Jesus, as benevolent social creatures. When we accept our role as benevolent social creatures and act appropriately, we fulfill our duties to others.

Jeffersonian republicanism demanded, in a Lockean manner, political liberty for each citizen to determine his own course to happiness, but it also demanded, in a Platonic manner, the fullest political participation of each citizen, insofar as his time and talents allowed.

Jefferson recognized that, through his talent with his pen, he had a larger role in deity's cosmic plan, and so he wrote, and wrote abundantly, and he also acted politically, with an eye to progressive political reforms that served a moral agenda, comprising human liberty and human happiness. Through such writings as Summary View on the Rights of British America, the Declaration of Independence, Draft Constitution for Virginia, Bill for the General Diffusion of Knowledge, Bill for Religious Freedom, Report on the Western Territories, The Kentucky Resolutions, *Notes on the State of Virginia*, and even such seemingly immaterial works as his Observations on Whale-Fishery and Plan for Establishing Uniformity in Coinage, Weights, and Measures, and through such actions as the repeal of entail and primogeniture, his work for the eradication of slavery, and numerous other deeds in and outside of his nearly forty years of public service, Jefferson labored

---

[3] That anticlericalism could readily have been formed, or at least reinforced, during his days at William & Mary College, through interaction with his good friends Dr. William Small; George Wythe, Esq.; and Governor Fauquier.

to improve Virginia, the United States, and even the world, through better global relations between nations. That was Jefferson's role, a noiseless but significant role, as a secular American messiah.

Jefferson foresaw a time in the distant future when all nations would be Jeffersonian republics—when all nations, liberty embracing, would be relatively independent of, though amicably disposed toward, each other. For that to occur, there needed to be moral progress through religious reforms to restore the true teachings of Jesus and partnerships of politics and science.

Like many others of his day (e.g., Weishaupt and Rush), Jefferson saw Jesus's precepts as the basis of a universal or meta-religion and a perfect religious/moral platform for his own republicanism, grounded in the moral sense that God had given to each human. Thus, while his respect for, and love of, Jesus and Jesus's uncorrupted teachings was unconditioned, there were happily certain political benefits to be derived from them.

Why Thomas Jefferson Was Really No Friend of Religious Freedom

Because of the passage of his Bill for the Establishment of Religious Freedom, Thomas Jefferson is customarily viewed by scholars as a paladin of religious freedom. Yet there is reason to question that view. To show why that is so, a distinction between "advocacy of religious freedom" and "advocacy of religious tolerance" is needed.

> *Advocacy of religious freedom* is a commitment both to sectarian religiosity being a good thing and to the freedom to choose one's own religion being a decided social gain.

> *Advocacy of religious tolerance* is a commitment both to sectarian religiosity not being a good thing and to lack of freedom to choose one's own religion being a decided social ill.

Nothing material rides on a commitment to religious freedom or religious tolerance, but settling the issue will tell us much about the mind of Jefferson, and that is a gain. An advocate of religious freedom focuses on the pluses of religious freedom. An advocate of religious toleration focuses on the social ills of not having religious freedom.

In Query XVII of *Notes on Virginia*, Jefferson writes succinctly but unfavorably of metaphysical religious squabbling: "The way to silence religious disputes, is to take no notice of them." If all religions are allowed expression and none is given political succor, their disputes will produce at best parochial turbulences that will be swamped out catholically.

For Jefferson, religion is a personal matter, while established sectarian religions are politicized. The rituals attending on politicized religions are put into place for the sake of political and moral oppression. Want of religious freedom and religious taint of politics are responsible for ignorance, superstition, poverty, and oppression. Republicanism demands religious freedom.

For Jefferson, religion, correctly apprehended, is equivalent to morality. Religion is only legitimate when it acts in the service of morality and justice—that is to say, subtly, when it works quietly. However, for Jefferson, formal religious systems—political in nature and inveigling people through mysteries of miracles, such as a dead man coming back to life and water mysteriously and immediately being converted to wine, and other matters at odds with common sense, such as one god being three—are anything but quiet, and thus are mostly metaphysical nonsense for the sake of establishing empleomaniacal priestly intermediaries between humans and God.

People, essentially social beings for Jefferson, are adequately equipped with a moral sense to guide them in social situations, as a benevolent deity would not make humans social beings and also create them to be morally deficient. In short, humans have an innate and naturally sensual understanding of their moral duties, which are, thinks Jefferson, both other-directed and god-directed.

People fulfill duties to fellow humans through recognizing correct moral action in circumstances in their daily interactions with others. There is no need for moral instruction, as a sense of morally correct action is innate—hence, Jefferson's disadvises to nephew Peter Carr (10 Aug.

1787) concerning attending lectures on morality, as our moral conduct is not "a matter of science"[1]—but there is need for goading and honing morality to incite persons to act when circumstances call for action.

Humans fulfill duties to God through study and care of the cosmos in which they were placed. That largely explains Jefferson's appreciation for, and love of, science. The truths disclosed by science allow humans to get a glimpse of the mind of God. That is why Jefferson, in his tour of the French villages, speaks disparagingly of the mass of French peasants, who, having no farm houses, huddle in villages and "keep the Creator in good humor with his own works" by mumbling "a mass every day." Consider also what Jefferson writes about Maria Cosway, living at the time in a convent, to Angelica Church: "I knew that to much goodness of heart she joined enthusiasm and religion; but I thought that very enthusiasm would have prevented her from shutting up her adoration of the God of the universe within the walls of a cloister."[2]

True, natural religion is natural moraltiy. There is no need of priests as intermediaries between people and God, as natural religion is generic, exoteric, and simple. Jefferson writes to James Fishback of sectarian religions: "every religion consists of moral precepts, & of dogmas. in the first they all agree. all forbid us to murder, steal, plunder, bear false witness &c. and these are the articles necessary for the preservation of order, justice, & happiness in society."[3] Yet most of the doctrines of a sectarian religion are esoteric; they are not crafted for the sake of honest or benevolent living. Clerics use indecipherable metaphysical claims to their political advantage. They also engage in fatuous disputes. Jefferson continues:

> in their particular dogmas all differ; no two professing the
> same. these respect vestments, ceremonies, physical opinions,
> & metaphysical speculations, totally unconnected with moral-
> ity, & unimportant to the legitimate objects of society. yet these

---

[1] TJ to Peter Carr, 10 Aug. 1787.
[2] TJ to Angelica Church, 27 Nov 1793.
[3] TJ to James Fishback, 27 Sept. 1809.

are the questions on which have hung the bitter schisms of
Nazarenes, Socinians, Arians, Athanasians in former times, &
now of Trinitarians, Unitarians, Catholics, Lutherans, Calvinists,
Methodists, Baptists, Quakers &c. among the Mahometans we
are told that thousands fell victims to the dispute whether the
first or second toe of Mahomet was longest; & what blood, how
many human lives have the words "this do in remembrance of
me" cost the Christian world![4]

Sectarian religions do not follow, but rather deviate from, nature.

Outside of certain core beliefs that all genuinely religious persons
share, there are considerable differences in personal religious convictions.
Yet none of those differences have any bearing on a citizen's capacity to
govern, or to be governed. To ingeminate a sentiment from *Notes on
Virginia*: "It does me no injury for my neighbor to say there are twenty
gods, or no god. It neither picks my pocket nor breaks my leg." Religious
conviction is a personal matter. "The care of every man's soul belongs
to himself," writes Thomas Jefferson in his *Notes on Religion*, written in
1776. "Laws provide against injury from others; but not from ourselves."
Four decades later, Jefferson writes similarly to Mrs. Harrison Smith: "I
have ever thought religion a concern purely between our God and our
consciences, for which we are accountable to Him, and not to the priests.
God himself will not save men against their wills."[5]

Since it is a personal matter, religion cannot be politicized. When
clergy, driven by empleomania, engraft themselves into the "machine
of government," he tells Jeremiah Moor, they become a "very formidable engine against the civil and religious rights of man."[6] That shows
Jefferson's distrust of the politically ambitious religious clerics of his day
and of prior days.

---

[4] TJ to James Fishback, 27 Sept. 1809.
[5] TJ to Mrs. Harrison Smith, 6 Aug. 1816.
[6] TJ to Jeremiah Moor, 14 Aug. 1800.

For Jefferson, government functions best when it is silent, and it is most silent when its laws are few. Those governing must be like machines insofar as they grasp and actuate the will of the majority. Jefferson says to Dr. Benjamin Rush about his role as president, "I am but a machine erected by the constitution for the performance of certain acts according to laws of action laid down for me, one of which is that I must anatomise the living man as the Surgeon does his dead subject, view him also as a machine & employ him for what he is fit for, unblinded by the mist of friendship."[7] When government is stentorian and its intrusions are many, its loudness and intrusions are sure signs that the rights of its citizens— choice of religion being one—are being suffocated.

Jefferson says to Miles King that deity has so authorized matters that each tree must be judged by its fruit. The suggestion here is not that each action is to be judged moral or immoral when it has a fruitful or fruitless outcome. Jefferson, like Aristotle, is referring to actions over the course of a lifetime. He adds that religion is "substantially good which produces an honest life," and for that, each is accountable solely to deity. "There is not a Quaker or a Baptist, a Presbyterian or an Episcopalian, a Catholic or a Protestant in heaven; . . . on entering that gate, we leave those badges of schism behind."[8] The suggestion, if not implication, is that religious clerics are otiose. Allen Jayne states, "Jefferson eliminated all interme-diate authorities between God and man as the source of religious truth, such as exclusive revelation or scripture, church or tradition, and most of all, the clergy."[9]

In sum, careful analysis of Jefferson's advocacy of freedom of religion shows little consideration in large respect for sectarian religions, but instead demonstrates worry that lack of freedom of religious expres-sion and, especially, partnership of any one religion with government will be prohibitive of republican government, which has as its primary function protection of the liberties and rights of the citizenry. In sum,

---

[7] TJ to Benjamin Rush, 13 June 1805.
[8] TJ to Miles King, 26 Sept. 1814.
[9] Jayne, *Thomas Jefferson's Declaration of Independence*, 151.

republican government demands freedom of religion, and for Jefferson, whose views on sectarian religions are far from reverential, that amounts to advocacy of religious toleration, not religious freedom. If all religions are allowed free expression and none are given political sanction, then the empleomania of religious clerics will be reduced to provincial metaphysical squabbles, which will be drowned out at the levels of state and federal government.